IT STARTED WITH MALAGA

A Memoir of Spanish Travels

Blue Jacket Travels
Book 1

KAREN O'CONNOR

Copyright © 2024 Karen O'Connor

Formatted and produced by Ant Press - www.antpress.org

Published by Blue Jacket Press

All rights reserved.

Please note that this book is the original creation of the author. The author wrote and compiled it entirely without the use of any artificial intelligence.

USE OF THIS BOOK FOR AI TRAINING:

Without in any way limiting the author's and publisher's exclusive rights under copyright, any use of this publication to "train" generative artificial intelligence (AI) technologies to generate text is expressly prohibited. The author reserves all rights to license uses of this work for generative AI training and development of machine learning language models.

No part of this book may be reproduced in any form or by any electronic or mechanical means, including information storage and retrieval systems, without written permission from the author, except for the use of brief quotations in a book review.

For my son Johnny, because you asked me to go,
For my hubby James, because you encouraged me to go,
For my entire family, for putting up with my new "eS" Word!

Contents

Prologue	1
1. Opportunity Knocks	5
2. Countdown: Six Weeks to Departure	11
3. Countdown: Five Weeks to Departure	19
4. Countdown: Four Weeks to Departure	27
5. Countdown: Three Weeks to Departure	35
6. Countdown: The Last Two Weeks	41
7. The Adventure Begins	51
8. Welcome to Malaga	61
9. Exploring Home Base	65
10. Waking Up in Malaga	73
11. Paco's Keys to the City	81
12. Port Business and a Coincidence	91
13. We Meet Lori	103
14. Kindness Rises Like Cream	111
15. Victoria's Secret Meeting Place	119
16. A Visit to a Pretty Vineyard	129
17. Friendships in the Moment	137
18. Juan Diego Tells a Story or Two	147
19. Echoes of Malaga's Dead	157
20. An Evening of Flamenco	165
21. Lost … and Found!	173
22. A Perfect Paella	183
23. The German Bridge	193
24. Wet Wash and Dry Run	203
25. Race to an Orange Umbrella	215
26. Ears, Eyes, and Feet, No Hands	225
27. History's Unstoppable Echo	233
28. One More Important Stop	241
29. Sangria with a View	249
30. Our Last Day	253
31. The Dublin Dash	263
32. First, Beer …	271
33. …Then Whiskey	279

34. Homeward Bound	285
Epilogue	293
Afterword	299

RECIPES

SEAFOOD PAELLA	302
TRADITIONAL SANGRÍA	304
GAZPACHO	305
A Request	306
What happened next?	307
About the Author	311
Contacts and Links	312
Acknowledgments	313

Prologue

*D*o you ever look back on the synchronicity of certain events that appear unrelated in the moment, but on reflection seem as if two versions of your life have converged, with barely a catch in your breathing?

It is the morning of Thursday, February 29, 2024 – a Leap Year Day that will change everything. Just a few hours ahead of the monumental life change that is to come, in an impulsive grasp at creativity, I find myself doodling on my iPad using an app I had never even realized was there. Using my finger to draw crudely on the device, I sketch myself stretched out on my bed in my favorite blue tie-dye Macy's PJs, golden rays emanating from my flat-screen TV on the opposite wall. It's 6:30 am and, as I'm doodling, I'm also following the stock market on my computer, listening to the talking heads on TV, and absorbing the morning market news.

It is my first effort at using the iPastels drawing app – and my last. This one rude attempt to capture the moment reveals my state of mind in that moment, more than I could ever have envisaged. You can see my clumsy drawing and photos that accompany this memoir at *www.bluejacketpress.com*. The odd-looking red object in my drawing is a wicker rocking chair. The rest speaks for itself.

A few short hours later, the biggest event of my retirement life begins to unfold. My creativity will be satiated in ways I could not have anticipated …

Within days, I find myself distressingly short of people to talk to about it. There are several reasons for this. I can't talk with this person because it isn't them going and it might sound like bragging; I can't talk with that person because they're too busy and don't have time; I can't talk with yet another person because they're already tired of hearing about it!

It's frustrating because I'm super-excited and I want to share my unfolding plans – but the pieces of my story that do make it to another human ear are politely, if impatiently, squeezed into the ditches of their day, a bit like runoff they didn't really want to process. I imagine they either wish they, too, were going, or they are doubtful about the whole plan, perhaps even secretly thinking I am losing my mind, and feeling they should caution me against potential dangers.

In my fourth year of an unexpected – though ultimately not unwelcome – retirement, after a lifetime of trying too hard to prove myself, being over-committed to my career and overly volunteered at my professional organization, I find myself in a somewhat uninspired state where I am trying to find meaning in not having to do much of anything at all.

This new life is vastly different from my working life, when the job would spill over into my leisure hours, and weekends would be barely distinguishable from any other day of the week. In retirement, I give myself permission to spend the better part of a day engrossed in yet another Kindle Unlimited book; the ticker says I have read 116 weeks in a row. Other highlights are putting together a challenging jigsaw puzzle – especially now that my whole family has indulged my newest passion by providing me with puzzles for birthdays and Christmas. In the evenings, I multi-task, doing brain puzzles on my iPad while binge listening to (rather than binge watching) old-fave TV series like Cheers, Frasier or Bluebloods with my husband.

During Covid, I am certain we watch every British crime drama ever produced, one rerun on demand at a time.

I try to keep a healthy balance by working in the yard in summer, but in winter I find myself differentiating one day from the other by cycling through three pairs of PJs that double as a tracksuit should the need arise to answer the door. This particular year, where the story begins, the dreary, dark and at times exceptionally cold (then exceptionally warm) Eastern Washington winter seems to go on forever.

Until … quietly and unexpectedly, the most welcome yet unforeseen opportunity drops into my lap and I am suddenly alive with nearly obsessive focus. Is it any wonder? We are, after all, on the heels of a worldwide pandemic, bad enough to live through without the added traumatic experience of being cut off from family in Canada when international borders closed – just when we had moved 1,200 miles closer so we could see them more often.

I'd never been more ready to embrace such a startlingly fresh step out into the world. And I want to share. I simply cannot pass up the opportunity to tell the world about this part of my life story that, if history repeats itself, would never be written. I'm retired now, after all. I no longer have the excuse of lack of time or resources. I can put the puzzles away for another day.

Nevertheless, my story is written not so much with the reader in mind – though I'll certainly be exceedingly happy if it piques your interest. I suspect that at heart the reason I want to tell the tale is to capture for myself and for all time the journey that brought me to these days of exploration, surprise and outright lust for travel. A wanderlust that the shadow of Covid cast over what I have concluded is my least favorite season – winter – almost tricked me into believing had been forever dimmed.

So, dear reader, please turn the page, read on and come along with me on the most unexpected and transformative adventure of my life.

1

Opportunity Knocks

A few days ago, I had never even heard of the city in Spain that is Malaga. Not even in an 'I used to know and forgot' way that seems to be happening all too often these days. Not even in one of the hundreds of historical novels I'd read over the years – if you don't count a fuzzy recollection of Queen Isabella and the inquisition.

Quite naturally I *had* heard of Switzerland, and when my youngest son Johnny texts in response to my "What's up?" that he is going to Switzerland soon with his new job, I grab the too-rare-these-days opportunity to connect and text him back straight away.

"Can I come along?" I beg, in a 'please take me in your suitcase' sort of way.

There ensues a short pause, and I assume he is already back to doing whatever he'd been doing when I interrupted him. I also assume that he won't take me seriously, anyway.

"No, Ma. I would like to fly with you sometime, but not this trip." Pretty much as I expected.

The Toronto Maple Leafs vs. Coyotes hockey game my husband James and I are watching on TV goes to intermission.

The bit I do *not* expect comes about five minutes later, though it seems more like thirty.

At 8:15 pm on Thursday February 29, Johnny replies, "Do you want to meet me in Spain for the weekend of April 20 and 21st?"

So he did take me seriously! "Spain would be fun," I text back, trying to quell my excitement. "For how long?" I am stunned. Spain?

"Well, I have a sales kick-off I'm working on from the Monday through to the Thursday night, but I could arrive a few days before or depart a few days after."

Heart thumping, I reply, "I'll check it out. Tell me more."

"Of course, you could come for as long as you want, but I'm gonna be busy all day on those days with the event."

"Understood." If we are negotiating here, he holds all the cards. I'll do whatever it takes.

"But it seems I am free on the Friday, and then it's the weekend, and my new company has unlimited vacation days ... though it would be bad for my quota if I use too many so soon."

Heart racing, "It *is* something to think about," I text back. SOMETHING TO THINK ABOUT? Oh, my gosh! I stare at the texts on my device, not quite believing my eyes.

My thoughts flip at record speed. The tantalizing thought of taking my son up on the invite contrasts wildly with sudden doubts about the whole idea.

I grab the remote control and pause the game. The hockey can wait, and the Leafs are in the lead now, anyway.

"Johnny just asked me if I want to go to Spain with him."

My husband doesn't even look up from his iPad where he is checking out a new song to play on his guitar. Dressed in his fuzzy plaid PJ pants with his T-shirt from the Eric Clapton and Steve Winwood concert we saw in Las Vegas seventeen years ago, he says convincingly, "Oh, ya? Sounds fun. I think you should go."

It Started with Malaga

The bookkeeper, organizer, spring garden yet-to-plant Karen argues internally with the momma Karen. Is this even possible? In an indulgent micro-second, I decide it is. Then I decide it is not. I can't believe I am even considering Spain! My brain is telling me it is not possible, and my heart is telling me to ask more questions; maybe my brain is wrong.

We text back and forth about tentative details, and then decide to pause the chat until morning. In a matter of forty-five minutes, it looks like the concept of Spain is at least open for further discussion.

"Oh, btw, where in Spain are you going?" My thoughts are coming down to earth, and I realize this might be important.

"Well, I'm going to Marbella, which is right next to Malaga. That's where the airport is."

Somewhere in the next thirty-minute span, I manage to search out Malaga on a map. I can still remember *precisely* that moment when all I knew about Malaga equaled the total sum of zero, as I gazed for the first time at the city's location in the Mediterranean not far from Gibraltar.

Little did I know that from that point on, my retirement life was never going to be the same!

The hockey game is over and the Leafs have won. Several members of my family will be happy, and now it is late. Thoughts are bouncing like practice pucks against the warmup goalie inside my head. I know that what I need to do is sleep, so I PJ up and crawl into bed. But sleep is not going to happen. My mind is spinning with the possibilities – or impossibilities – of the idea. I make a cup of lemon-ginger tea to calm myself.

To slow down my racing thoughts, I start a new note on my iPad titled 'SPAIN. YES OR NO'.

Under 'YES', I list:

- It's an opportunity that won't come along every day – to spend time with my son and see a new country.
- Spain is a reasonably safe place in the world to visit. (I've checked the state department website for travel alerts.)
- It's a good time of the year to visit. Weather in mid- or upper-60s°F and not much chance of steady rain.

Under 'NO', I list:

- What is a realistic budget, and can I afford it?
- What are the risks of being alone in a foreign country?
- Would I have language difficulties?

I type: 'Notes to Self' and then think, *Aren't they all notes to self?* I shake my head at myself and rearrange my pillow. *I might be a little unglued*, I reflect. Under 'Notes to Self' I enter:

- Prefer to travel with Johnny at least one way.
- Marbella is about thirty miles from Malaga. Which location would be better to stay in?
- Is there a Marriott?

Determinations to be made:

- How fast can I learn Castilian Spanish?
- Where is the best place to stay? Hotel or apartment?
- Which airline is best and what is a reasonable time frame for a flight?

It Started with Malaga

Finally, I sleep, the key considerations temporarily offloaded and locked-in on my list.

During the night, my brain wrestles with the thrilling notion of it all.

When I wake in the morning, it takes only one split second before I remember the enticing dilemma of the night before. Spain: YES or NO? In my heart, I am leaning toward 'YES', as the 'NO' list doesn't present anything insurmountable except perhaps for one thing – affordability.

I get out my iPad and log onto the Marriott website. Being a platinum life member with scads of points earned from my conference-organizing days, it makes sense that this is my first choice. I check out Costa del Sol hotels and am aghast at the prices – easily US$300-500 a night with tax. I check out where Johnny is staying with his company – not that I want to intrude on him while he is working, just out of curiosity – but his hotel is even harder on the pocketbook. I look for places near where he is going to be staying in Marbella and then widen my search to Malaga.

I Google to find out more and see that Malaga has plenty to keep me exploring and entertained – a cathedral; an ancient fortress and castle overlooking the ruins of a Roman theater; plus, it's the birthplace of Picasso. I read about flamenco dancing, see that there are dozens of interesting-looking museums, a delightful marketplace, a port promenade – and that Malaga is a hub for Spain's high-speed train network. Local websites list more tours than I could ever hope to fit in in a month, never mind a week.

I decide I should definitely stay in Malaga.

I find the link to a site called Marriott Homes and Villas. I discover that I can rent a one- or two-bedroom apartment for a week, without using all my points, simply by topping up with a reasonable amount of cash. As I pore through all the stylish rentals on offer, I realize this really might be possible.

But what about flights? A quick Google search results in several options at what seem like decent prices.

By the time James is up and having his first cup of coffee, I am using the 'IF' word quite a lot.

"If I can get an apartment for a decent price … If the flights work out for both of us … If I go … this will be amazing."

From the other end of the breakfast-nook table he replies, "Why do you keep saying IF? Just GO if you want to go. I'm not going to stop you. You know you wanna go. Have you seen my earbuds?"

"Where did you last use them? Do you really think so?"

"Heck ya, I do. I already told you. This kind of opportunity doesn't come along every day. You and Johnny will have a great time. I think you should go."

So, I ban the IF word from my vocabulary and let the idea of YES sink in!

2

Countdown: Six Weeks to Departure

Now that the 'I'm really going to do this' summit has been breached, I need to remove the last obstacles and see if the cost of the trip is going to break the bank. At first glance, the airfares look reasonable, and the Marriott Homes and Villas options are affordable. I don't require a room that is priced as an 'all-inclusive' from which the guest need never depart. My goal is to see the sights, not bounce around inside the boundaries of a beachy hotel. It would be different, perhaps, if I was going with my hubby, but I really want to explore Malaga.

After doing this initial research I give Johnny a call.

"Hey kiddo, do you have time to chat about plans?"

"Sure Ma, but let me call you back in five, okay? I need to help middle boy pump up his soccer ball." I can hear the kids in the background, and what sounds like a ruckus with the dog. "Hey, Finnigan's water spilled. Wipe that up and get him some more, please. Take that shoe away from him! I gotta go, but I'll call you back, okay?"

"I'll see what I can find online about flights. And then let's talk about how many days you can take off, okay?"

"Well, I have to check out the company portal. I need to get my ticket there unless it's cheaper somewhere else." I'm thinking, I just hope it works out that we can travel together both ways.

"We can check all of that out. Talk soon, bye." Johnny is not one for long goodbyes, so I don't drag it out.

The five minutes stretches to fifteen, as it always does when the kids are involved. But this gives me time to do more research. Google Flights reveals that my preferred airline, Alaska, is the most reasonable option. The Alaska-Aer Lingus partnered flight has a convenient departure and arrival time and a layover in Dublin both ways, although the layover for the return flight is thirteen-and-a-half hours. While I'm exploring, a web ad pops up with enticing information on how to spend four hours, six to eight hours, and up to 24 hours in Dublin on a layover. Certainly, a dash around Dublin would be a bonus.

I did a DNA test ten years ago and then set up the rest of the family to do the same. It turns out I am 70% Irish with some English thrown in, much of which Johnny has inherited. So why not explore some of our roots on the way home?

My phone screen lights up with an image of my youngest son's smiling face, framed in a helmet, that someone, probably his wife Jane, took one winter's day when they were out skiing.

"Hi kiddo, I found a potential flight and it's in a comparatively good price range – under $1,100 each for a round trip. The flight goes from here to Seattle, then to Dublin …"

"Dublin. That's cool. Do we get a layover?" I can hear the wheels turning.

"And then to Malaga. Well, I wanted to talk with you about that," I reply. "On the way over, the layover is too short to do anything, but on the way home, we could choose the one that stops in Dublin for thirteen-and-a-half hours. There's a website that shows how easy it is to get into Dublin and back in as little as a four-hour window – although I wouldn't want to risk it that short when we're flying international."

"That sounds great. Let's do it. Let's go have breakfast in the Temple Bar area."

"Right, it's a deal," I answer excitedly. "I know you said your event is Monday through Thursday, and of course we lose time getting over there, so I found a flight that leaves Friday and gets us to Malaga on Saturday night, which means we have Sunday together. Then Monday you can go to your hotel in Marbella."

"That is doable. I can take the day off on the Friday, no problem."

"Great, then after your event finishes you can come back to the apartment and we can have the Friday together and part of Saturday. We gain nine hours coming back, so we'd be home Sunday night. This one is with Alaska and Aer Lingus. Does that sound like it would work?"

"Okay, what are the flight numbers? I'll check my company website." I give him the flight numbers, and the price I had found is hundreds of dollars less than the company site can offer. We book our flights in tandem because he needs his own receipt. Within minutes, confirmation arrives by email and our flights are in the bag.

"We arrive in Dublin at 2:00 am on the return trip, so I'll book a hotel right at the airport. We can catch a handful of hours' sleep and then take a bus or cab to downtown Dublin in the morning. With only thirteen-and-a-half hours – and much of that at night – we won't have a ton of time, but we'd have plenty of time for breakfast. I wonder if it's too early to have a Guinness?"

"Hey Ma, it's Ireland. It's never too early for a Guinness! I have to go, but if you use your points to get that apartment in Malaga, I'll pay the cash part, okay?"

"That sounds great to me. I already found a couple of options that are super-cute."

By 11:00 am I have chosen my home for a week. 'Modern Apartment in the Heart of the City' is a two-bedroom, two-bathroom, nicely renovated apartment, complete with a sewing machine, apparently. This seems significant somehow, because I love to sew. It must be a sign I am on the right track.

Plus, it is just across the street from Picasso's birthplace and the Plaza de la Merced in historic central Malaga. From this location, I can walk to everything, so I won't need to hire a cab every five minutes. Before my research, I didn't even realize Picasso had been born in Malaga, or even in Spain for that matter. I decide that if I get the chance to walk in his footsteps in the place where he was born, I am not going to miss it. I feel happy that I have chosen a terrific location from which I can easily stroll to many sights.

Later that morning I freeze a frame of a 'Top 12 Places to See' YouTube video and spot my apartment building.

"James, come and look at this." I cast the footage to our flatscreen TV on the wall. "Look how close this place is to everything I want to do and see. Isn't it perfect? This building with the red shape on the side is my apartment building."

"That looks great, lovie. Have you seen the supplies list I made on that yellow paper?"

"Is it on your nightstand? Do you want to see this video of things to see in Malaga?"

"I'd rather not right now. I need to run to Barneys to pick up some stuff."

Barneys is our favorite everything store, where we can buy hardware, groceries, a great cut of meat and liquor, and it's just a mile away.

James has been gearing up to get started on this year's project for the warmer months. We've talked about how nice it would be to have a stairway leading from the house down the steep hillside to his workshop. This would be a huge project, and not one that is straightforward. But the workshop is pivotal in our lives, both for drinking tequila while reminiscing about our lives together by the glow of chili-pepper lights, as well as for multiple practical purposes, be it woodworking, welding or anything mechanical.

Last summer we renovated our kitchen. I have to admit I say 'we' in the royal 'we' way, as I can take credit more by association than by actual work. I do okay at elbow-grease tasks like sanding cupboards before they are painted, but my talented husband is the builder, designer and, ultimately, the vision-maker of these projects. I am better described as the loyal helper, painter, tool-fetcher and sidekick who is sometimes there and sometimes not, although usually within a shout away for assistance.

This means there is always something we need at Barneys. When James is in project mode, far be it from me to slow him down.

"Never mind, I can show you later. Can you please pick me up a bottle of Deep Eddy Lemon Vodka while you're there? I checked and we are out at JO's too." JO's Place is our self-built pool room, lounge and bar in our basement, so named in memory of James's daughter Amanda, who sadly passed away in 2015 and who, when she was little, instead of calling him Dad called him JO from reading his initials on his toolbox. During Covid, we used to go 'out' to JO's for a change of scenery and it really did feel like we were at some other place.

"Okay, but don't give me a big list. I just want to get in and out and get back." He is out the door in a jiffy, before I can remember I need milk or a cucumber. When he goes to the store, he has laser focus and just gets what he needs at the time. When I go to the store, I browse all the aisles and try to get what I need for the next two weeks (or maybe to be prepared for a zombie apocalypse?) so I don't need to go back right away. He still thinks it's funny I can't go into a store and come out with one thing. I always shake my head. What's the point of that?

Suddenly an email pings through from the property management company, and I check it out right away.

I have chosen a niche Calle Victoria location, drenched in Malaga's historical significance – but it turns out it is in the middle of a lot of ongoing construction. The property manager has sent me a photo of my balcony view. You can see the Alcazaba, Malaga's very own fortress, but the vista also includes significant construction activity. They offer me a 20% discount or free cancelation. Cancel? No way, I just made that reservation. I accept the 20% discount. I am not planning to spend a lot of time in the room during the hours when construction would be taking place, anyway.

Johnny texts and asks a favor. "Hi, can you please try and get good seats for the trans-Atlantic flight? It's over nine hours."

"I'm on it," I reply. This task requires the patience of a saint to track down a human to talk with, but I have nothing but time and the reward will be great, so I suck it up.

Online, Alaska says to book seats with Aer Lingus, the Irish airline, while Aer Lingus says to book with Alaska. 'Call for Help', it says. After a frustrating button-pushing exercise, there is finally a human voice on the Aer Lingus Helpline. For $100 each covering both ways on the long flights, I select two seats next to each other, near the front of the plane instead of in the tail. Johnny gets a window and there is just an aisle on my side.

I breathe a sigh of relief to have some of the major decisions settled and paid for. I review my budget:

- Flights: $1,250 including upgrades
- Accommodation: $0 for me because of points – Johnny's portion, $250
- Food estimate: $500

- Tours estimate: $300
- Transportation: $200
- Miscellaneous: $250

Budget estimate: $ 2,500

After this flurry of activity, I pause from the mechanics of the trip planning and ponder the situation.

It has all happened so fast. *Is this real?* I ask myself. One day my biggest challenges are completing a 1000-piece jigsaw puzzle and manipulating the garbage and the recycling bin the quarter-mile round trip down to the road. The very next day I have signed up for a world adventure!

Normally at this time of the year I am outside raking pine needles, which are shed all along the driveway by our small forest of pines or cleaning up my greenhouse to make room for planting 'starts' to later transplant into my garden.

Not this year. Now that the flights are booked and the accommodation is reserved, I am evaluating the plan to see where it might need fine tuning. Which tours should I book? What clothes should I take? I need to learn some Spanish. I'm crafting my week in Malaga as if I'm building a quilt, stitching all the pieces together, one by one. I like how it is turning out.

For my Spanish lessons I choose an online learning tool, Pimsleur, on a 7-day free trial, and begin with Lesson One. With Pimsleur, the focus is primarily on what an adult might need conversationally for travel or business, so this seems perfect. I plan to complete a lesson a day.

It eventuates that during the 7-day free trial, I am more ambitious than I am focused. The date feels so far off, and I convince myself I have plenty of time to learn. In spite of my good intentions, I end up completing only one lesson during the free trial, so I sign on to pay by the month.

Meanwhile, in the midst of all my excitement – and perhaps because of it – there is a nagging sense of disbelief, and a tiny seed of guilt begins to grow. This sense of guilt becomes so pervasive that I need to talk it out with hubby.

3

Countdown: Five Weeks to Departure

The breakfast room is often our default place to connect with each other about our plans for the day. As any married couple knows, this is so important. The longer we are married, the more often we 'think' we have told each other what's on our minds, when the reality often is that we have not, so I regularly insist on making time to talk. James is not so eager, though he doesn't fight me on it.

I make us both a mug of coffee and set them down on the big table he made for us, perfectly sized for our window-lined, half-octagon-shaped nook and always covered with a bright, seasonal tablecloth and a protective plastic cover. The 2 x 4 legs are painted black. Nobody ever notices it is just a piece of plywood.

"I can hardly begin to describe how excited I am. I can't believe I'm going to Spain!" The words sound odd coming out of my mouth.

He smiles from the other end of the table as he sucks on a piece of candied ginger, barely having taken his first sip of coffee for the morning. He is wearing his telecaster Fender shirt and his cozy red plaid PJ bottoms.

He doesn't respond right away. "You know I'm barely awake."

"Sorry, lovie. It's just that I feel like I'm buzzing inside. It's like I'm tuned in to some sort of grand purpose and the closer I get, the stronger the buzzing gets. Isn't it crazy? After Covid I thought I would never travel again."

From the other end of the table comes, "Okay?" It's not exactly a grunt, but I can tell his mind is elsewhere. "I am so happy for you. You deserve this. Have you seen my iPad?"

It's a big house, and there are lots of places for us to lose things.

"Where were you when you last used it?" His face goes blank for a moment while he tries to remember when he might have last used his iPad. As the years go by, we both do a lot more of this kind of reflection. Things just don't come to mind as quickly as they used to.

When James isn't in the shop, he loves to play one of his favorite guitars. Actually, they are all his favorite guitars. Our formal living room has morphed into a music room; it's lined with all our instruments, and when I am around but not playing, he can play silently with the sound from his guitar redirected to his headset. When I play too, all the hanging instruments vibrate along with us as if we are one big band. He is always forgetting he left his iPad in the music room.

"Is it in the music room?"

"Ah, ya. That's probably where I left it." The soles of his feet make papery sounds as he shuffles off across the luxury vinyl tile floor he installed in the nook a couple of years ago. He tends to shuffle when he isn't quite awake. Before he gets back to the table, I top up his coffee so it is hot again. And then he is back in his chair at the west end, and I'm in mine in the east. From these perches, we have spent countless hours gazing at our piece of forest and the family of squirrels that run among the trees.

"You know how I always say that I love our place, and I'm

so blessed that I don't need to leave the property to have a great retirement?" I begin. "I can play my bass and keyboard. I have a great kitchen, and I love cooking in it. We have room for the whole family to visit and stay. I have my sewing room upstairs, and my office with the nice desk you built for me. I'm so glad we didn't leave it in California like we thought we might need to. I can't believe we never even got to meet the people who bought our house. It would have sucked to leave them my desk. Here, we can even go downstairs to JO's Place, and the outdoors is like we live in our own state park. I feel guilty. How come I get to do this thing, too?"

"Did you put sweetener in this?" He gets up to get a spoon.

I take a breath. There's no one else I can talk with about this. And sometimes you just need to talk it through.

"Is it weird I'm so excited to go even though I'll be by myself most of the time? My apartment has two bedrooms and a pull-out couch. There are even two full bathrooms. Maybe I should be inviting someone else to go along with me?"

"Why? If you are by yourself, you can do what you want and not worry about other people's problems. No *#!*#! (*expletive*) way you should be feeling guilty. You deserve this."

There was a reason for his vehemence.

I had just been getting started with summer trips to Europe with my professional colleagues when James and I suddenly retired. In fact, I had been about to leave on a trip for Italy and Greece back in 2019, when my husband was diagnosed with cancer.

That was two weeks after a 7.3 earthquake hit our desert town. The epicenter was just 10 miles from our home. All but one bottle of tequila from the display shelves over our flatscreen TV was destroyed.

The college where we had both taught, each chair of our departments, was walking distance from our home – but we lived at least 70 miles from the nearest available cancer treatment center. We would have had to make the drive there and back five days a week for at least twelve weeks.

The final straw was when my youngest son, Johnny, his wife, and three of my grandchildren coincidentally decided to relocate from their home near us to a town just inside the Washington/Idaho border. Their new place would be 1,200 miles away from our nice house with the palm-tree-lined pool that their eldest girl and middle boy had learned to swim in.

But Johnny was done with a yard that could never grow grass, and the long drive to LA dodging crazy traffic just to get to the nearest airport when he had to fly out for work. They had gone for a vacation and decided to take the plunge. The area was just a couple of hours south from where we had lived before moving to California, so we knew what we were in for – snow and plows and the whole nine yards. Our decision had been made within 24 hours. And in answer to our prayers, nearby Spokane Valley had a world-class treatment center. Talk about synchronicity. By the time James was ready for treatment, we lived just four miles away.

Admittedly I had not been prepared to leave my career so soon. I had to be hit by a 2 x 4 to see it was time. I cried for three months every time I tried to talk about it. I don't cry about it anymore. What a goof. And now … Spain.

"Just go and have a good time," James insists "How long are you going to be gone? Are the kids still coming down on spring break?"

"I think so. They might be here next week. The plan is for them to spend a couple of days helping you get the stairs project started."

"Do you really want me to build the stairs to the shop?"

"Do you think it can be done? It would be so cool if it can. Let's go for it."

The royal 'let's' is a partner to the royal 'we'. Ultimately, James's work.

I know before I ask that James is not interested. But I ask, anyway.

"Are you sure you don't want to come with me?"

Of course, he would always say he *loved* Spain, and that it was his favorite place from his Navy days. In our music room is a beautiful dancing flamenco doll, bent over backward and dressed in swirling red lace, that he sent to his mother in 1967 from Madrid. But he no longer has any desire to go abroad. That is not his idea of adventure.

He has seen enough of the Mediterranean Sea to last a lifetime after spending two years of his life there aboard the aircraft carrier, 'America', in the sixties, straight out of high school. He did go to Malta with me for two weeks over Christmas 2018 (that's another untold story!), but only because I had caught him in a rare moment of acquiescence and booked the tickets the same day.

"Are we ever going to ride on the Goldwing again?" he protests now, referring to our beautiful merlot-colored motorcycle and matching trailer he designed and built, now sitting dormant in the garage. "That's the only travel I want to do. If it's just going to sit there, we might as well give it to Joe now and let him pay the insurance."

Oops, we're going down that road again. The 50,000-plus miles we did in the early years around the American west is my Mediterranean. I've already seen all the parks and I have grown nervous in traffic. I might just have scraped the last insect off my beautiful helmet.

Joe, my middle son, is a mechanic and a firm believer that vehicles have souls. He lives in Canada, not far from where my eldest son Jay and his wife Faye live, with two more of my beautiful grandkids, a girl, the older of the two, and a boy. They really ARE beautiful – and not just because they're *my* grandkids. They're both smart, too. Like all the rest.

Seven of the grandkids come from my offspring, and an

eighth, Hunter, is a gift from James's late daughter Amanda. It's a sad and tragic story.

One calm day, an ancient tree fell from a cliff onto her car while she was driving by at 60 miles an hour on the way home from her colleague and nurse friend's funeral. She was only two miles from home and her baby, who was just two at the time, and her loving husband, who is still the best dad ever.

Saying it like that it's like I've ripped off a Band-Aid. Forever missing Amanda reminds us like a sledgehammer that there are no guarantees in life. If we didn't know it before, we know now that we need to act when we get the opportunity.

In the words of the Canadian band, The Tragically Hip, 'life ain't no dress rehearsal'.

When James and I found each other, we already had teenage children. Twenty-nine years later my sons, each in their own way, have benefitted from having James as a dad in their life, and I marvel at how much they have learned from him. We are all so blessed.

When James returned from active duty in late 1968, the world he came home to was radically different from the one he had left. Stations that had echoed 'Red Rubber Ball' now vibrated with 'Purple Haze'. Walking through Chicago's O'Hare airport, long-haired protesters spat at him and called him 'baby killer'.

Adjusting to this new environment, and drawing on his childhood love of motorcycles, he took up racing, eventually becoming a professional motocross racer. Connecting the dots from those days to when we met in Canada will require another memoir someday, but the side of him that loves motorcycles makes him most like my son Joe. The Goldwing is really Joe's. We just haven't physically given it to him yet.

"I'm not saying we'll never go for a ride. You know Joe doesn't have room to store it." I defend the space the bike takes up in our garage. Joe's yard is filled to the last inch with vehicles he flips after making them roadworthy when others have given up. Most of the family's cars have been blessed by Joe's hands at one point or another.

I steer the subject away from the bike and back to the stairs.

"Can we really build those steps? If we're going to do it, we might as well start this year. That way, we'll have more years to enjoy it. Jay can help you get the first part started when they come down."

Inwardly, my thoughts drift back to Malaga. It is one thing to *know* I shouldn't feel guilty. But in my heart, I cannot quell a nagging sense that I am quite selfish if I do not invite someone else to share this experience.

4

Countdown: Four Weeks to Departure

I know that Johnny will be working on four of the days that we won't be spending together, and if history is any guide he might well be preparing for his rendezvous at the new job while we fly and fill layover time at airports. I'm aware that sitting side by side with my son does not necessarily equate to having quality time with him. Still, compared to a few texts here and there and the rowdy holiday dinners we spend spread out along our long dining room table, parts of these nine days are going to be a lot of fun.

As a mother of three sons, I understand the adage, 'A son is a son till he takes him a wife' better than I would like to admit: I have been lucky, and I have a great relationship with all three of mine, but I am still greedy for time with them. It makes this coming trip and a shared discovery of Malaga and Spain even more precious.

I have also been fortunate to work alongside Johnny in the past. In fact, a one-sentence email to him in 2006 brought him home to us from the war in Afghanistan. He had been stationed in Kandahar with the Canadian Army Reserves for nearly a year when, one summer day in 2006, a network tech job opened up at my college in the desert. The week prior, one of his platoon members had been injured in the heart by incoming shrapnel. I popped off an email to him forwarding the potential job, with the words that are now famous in our family history: *This is way within your skill set, kiddo.*

That night he called me from the base telephone. I asked him if he had seen my email. What transpired is another unwritten story, but the result was that he flew home for the job interview on the first plane out in August, instead of the last as had been scheduled. He told me later he had been considering re-upping. He did not want to come home and just sit around. But the tech job, even though it would move him out of Canada and sadly mark the end of his active allegiance to the Queen, lit a fire under him.

We hired an immigration lawyer and got him a visa, something to do with the need for technology workers to work in the USA. I am an American citizen, but my sons were all born in Canada and, because I was younger than 16 when my USA citizen parents moved me to Canada, my kids don't inherit my citizenship. Go figure. Don't get me started.

In my heart, Joe had come from one of the most dangerous places in the world to one of the safest places, his office situated just behind mine in the same building.

But *this*, tagging along with Johnny for a work trip? I am ecstatic.

So why the nagging guilt? I feel so lucky and special to be included in this trip. Spain is over the top. I imagine a few people are jealous. I certainly would be! And then there is the matter of my beautiful apartment, which has room for up to six. And Johnny will be there for just three of the nights.

Here is where my imagination is not necessarily my friend.

Johnny's wife Jane can't go, or she would have been in at the start and there might never have been a question of mom/grandma going. This one is easy to dismiss. All three kids are still in school and, yes, there is Finnigan the dog, whom I swear is more work than the kids all put together. These kids can honestly say the dog ate their homework, and the carpet, the baseboards and the corner of the dining room table. So, Jane can't get away although I am certain she would have loved to. Of course, if I were a really good grandma, I might have offered to stay with the kids, so she could go. *Spark of guilt.*

The other grandma, Juanita, known as Nana to the kids, would probably jump at the chance, as she was born in Spain and has never been back. But I am eager for my time with Johnny and not sure if I want to share such a short trip. Plus, three is such an awkward number. The seats are set by two and it is a pain to change all of that. Anyway, isn't she having some medical issues right now? But, of course, I don't actually ask. *Spark of guilt.*

Jay and Faye both teach middle school. Inviting them would be such a tease, and I would feel bad for suggesting it, because it's simply not feasible for teachers to take time off during the school year. There is the irretrievable loss of time with the students, making a week and a bit away simply not worth the effort, even without financial considerations. Plus, they have their own two teenagers to take care of.

But ... I muse, they have had Spain on their radar ever since teaching in the Harrow district in London for 18 months at the start of their careers. *Spark of guilt.*

I don't even realize I have been ... let's say, 'adjusting' to the idea of spending at least four days 'yo solo' in a foreign country. If I *am* worried about it, I don't admit it even to myself, but there's a niggly feeling that won't rest when I go to sleep at night. Maybe it's the sparks of guilt.

I'll be fine, I remind myself again and again. After all, three decades ago I went to Hong Kong for a week, completely by myself, and I didn't even bother to make a reservation ahead of time for a place to stay. I read *Fodor's Hong Kong* before I went and when I got there I found a place for US$15 a night, even when the going rate for an average hotel room was over $100.

As I buzzed along in the cab to the potential room in Kowloon with a stranger who said his parents ran a B&B, I hoped that if I went missing, someone might eventually find the camera currently strapped around my neck and be able to determine my last steps. It would have been a story.

It seems crazy looking back at it, but my instincts were heightened during that week and I followed my gut, which kept me safe. It was exhilarating. Not just exploring Hong Kong alone. I even got a visa and visited the city of Shenzhen in China by myself for one day.

Clutching my camera, I took light rail, bus and train, past the barbed wire rolls for fences and through long lines of people who did not look or sound like me at immigration. I emerged into a square. A young man approached me, offering to show me around for 100 Chinese dollars. I hesitated. I saw something in his eyes when he lowered the price to 80, and it convinced me he was sincere; he just needed to earn some money. I accepted the offer but paid the original price, which was equivalent to $20 Canadian in 1995. He said it was worth half a month's pay in China.

As part of the impromptu tour, I ended up aboard a bus that looked like something off the set of M.A.S.H. Having second thoughts about getting so far away from the border that I'd lose my sense of direction, I felt the urge to tell my guide I wanted to get off. I figured if there was any darker purpose to getting me into a vehicle, the sooner I found out and could yell for help the better.

The bus stopped immediately when my guide gave the instruction to the driver. We were the only occupants, anyway. At the end of the tour, I bought him a huge meal, which he greedily devoured like it was his first meal in a week. I just drank a Chinese beer before buying some tea on my way out. It tickled my fancy to be able to lay claim to my own small stash of Chinese tea, actually *in* China, instead of it being delivered via a container ship.

Someday I'll get the video I took converted to play on modern devices so I can see when I filmed a live cobra at the food market.

Hmmm ... maybe I shouldn't be let out on my own! And that was half a lifetime ago.

So, you see, I have many stories that *history never saw written*. The whole year I spent teaching in Japan as part of an agreement between my own college – Selkirk College – and its sister college in Konan City should have already been a book. But sadly, all those writings are in a closet on 3.5-inch floppy drives. I'm too afraid to boot them up, as I don't want confirmation that the content is long gone.

And so, I vow to myself: My Malaga story is simply NOT going to get away from me.

🍇 🍇 🍇

A few days pass ...

I am on a video call with Jay. I dare to bring up the topic of Spain!

I know by now that people are a bit tired of hearing the 'S' word. It's *my* Malaga story, after all. Everyone else is busy digging their daily ditches. It is what we all do in those decades before retirement. Right?

My son Jay shares the imaginative side of my nature and loves to plan and make things happen. He and Faye have a long association with Europe, from the years they taught in London. They did a lot of travelling around Europe in those days, and still consider Seville as their favorite Spanish city. Twenty years on, in addition to their teaching jobs, they have the commitment of raising two teenage hockey-playing Canadian boys.

Now, keen to talk about my recent travel developments, and at the risk of stirring up long held but always denied rivalry between the eldest and his younger brother, Johnny, I mention that I have some solid plans for my visit and am working daily on learning Castilian Spanish.

I'm certain Jay is thinking, "Oh, here she goes again," and I notice his lips purse just a little on-screen.

After a moment of silence, he blurts out, "Peter could go! He's taking Spanish at school. Mum! A trip to Spain would be amazing and he could use what he has been learning. You guys could have so much fun. It would be great!"

Peter in the background: "YES!"

I am thrilled that my seventeen-year-old grandson would even *want* to go on a trip with his grandma. And I remember what an eye-opener the class trip with my high school choir was for me at the same age. I can still smell the chocolate that was stored in my closet, from when we spent months selling candy to raise the funds for the trip.

My imagination takes off. The logistics involved in making it possible for Peter to accompany me begin to slide like blocks in a spectacular visual from the temple passage scene from *Raiders of the Lost Ark*: arranging time off school, meeting up with him, booking another flight, getting the seats organized, paying for his trip ...

I am quite sure I shriek, "YES, that would be awesome!"

I hear Faye gasp in the background. I can almost "hear", rather than read, her mind and it is shouting that this is not something Jay has yet discussed with her.

I speak to the person I cannot quite see hovering at the edge of the screen. "Well, Faye, maybe you could come, too?

A moment of silence. I know she would love to, but a week

It Started with Malaga

off during the school year is not a matter easily negotiated, even when presented with an incredibly special opportunity.

Second grandson, William, age fourteen, appears behind his dad and smiles expectantly at Grandma, who is hit by a new stab of guilt for being so ready to take off with just one of them. Oops, what kind of complicated brotherly dynamics is this going to cause? But I didn't ignite this idea. Did I?

I am already thinking of how cool it would be – after all, kids grow up so fast – to have this kind of adventure with them, with any of my grandkids, in fact, before they are all out on their own as adults. It would be so great to witness the boys' eyes opened by this opportunity to see and experience a different world. But in that instant, I know neither Jay nor I have really thought it through. Not for this trip, anyway.

Suffice to say that over the next week or so, a lot of 'what ifs' are explored. What if Peter *and* William come? What if Peter *and* William *and* Mom come? What about school? Is a week too long to miss? The boys have sports, too, lacrosse and rugby. It is going to be expensive, and the family is already planning an all-together trip that might be compromised if some of them tag along for this one. Their family 'Yes/No' list is more complicated than mine ever was.

Nevertheless, for a week or so I start thinking *there is going to be a third party*.

And then there is not.

For one single day, I stop buzzing and mourn the loss of my companion that never was. I realize I do want to travel more, with any of my kids and their families, and certainly any of my grandkids. Could this be the start of a new era in my life? 'Grandma As Travel Companion?' My imagination cycles though every grandkid as a possible candidate, and the associated logistics. But they are too young. After each name I mentally tick: 'Not Yet'.

I check in again with James.

"Are you absolutely sure you wouldn't like to go with me?"

"Not going to happen, Vernette." He uses his nickname for me. Today he is wearing his black T-shirt with white block text that reads 'Sorry' across his chest. It is my least favorite of his T-shirts, so he wears it when he has a messy job to do. At least, that's what he says.

James accepts that I am Spain-bound. I accept that he is not.

There has been a lot of fantasizing about possibilities, but it has not all been for naught. I'd gone into the discussion with a feeling of guilt that I was the lucky one, to be able to go. By the time all the discussions and plotting are over, it has come full circle back to Johnny and me. I am thoroughly over feeling the least bit of guilt for my good fortune.

It is my Malaga story – and I am ready to own it.

And yes, the buzzing is back. I know things are unfolding as they should. I learn to take deep breaths and dream visions of travel as I calm myself to sleep each night.

Countdown: Three Weeks to Departure

With only three weeks to go, I need to start thinking about reserving some special tours. To help me make the best choices, I have been learning all I can about the history of Malaga and Spain. I hope this will give me a solid foundation for what I should explore in my short week, and to understand what I see.

Johnny and I will be arriving on the Saturday, close to sundown, and will have Sunday together. It makes sense, therefore, that we do something together to get oriented to the area, and to visit the top 'must sees' before he ducks off to work. So, Sunday is the key day. I find a tour using Trip Advisor, which I'd used to book tours for my 2019 Italy and Greece trip. I get busy over the next few days and choose this:

Tour #1: Ultimate Malaga History & Tapas

It's an 'All Included Full Experience', beginning at 10:30 am.

'Wander the streets of Malaga like a local and let your guide show you the best hidden gems all over the city. Explore historic buildings and discover important monuments and stop off on the way for some tapas and local wine in Malaga's most popular bars. Avoid the queues at the Alcazaba and the Cathedral – this tour allows you to queue jump.

'This tour is operated by 'We Love Malaga'. Included is Tapas Lunch or Dinner in 2 Local Bars, Wine Tasting, Professional Guide, Entry/Admission to Malaga Cathedral, Teatro Romano, and the Alcazaba.'

These are three of Malaga's top places to visit and food is included. This is the perfect tour for our Sunday together.

• Tour budget logs US$105.

By Monday, Johnny will be off to his work event, so I book a Malaga Hop-On-Hop Off city-sightseeing bus tour for myself. The ticket is good for a year from the date it was booked, valid for 24 hours and includes admission to two museums. I will definitely use this ticket for one of the days I'm on my own. The benefit of the Hop-On-Hop Off bus versus a regular bus is that there is a guide, and I can easily preview the stops and ... well, hop on and hop off.

• Tour budget logs US$27.50.

For Monday evening, I sign up for 'The Genuine Malaga Wine and Tapas Tour', which is run by the Spain Food Sherpas. This one starts at the foot of the famous Calle Marqués de Larios, and conveniently for me, ends at Plaza de la Merced, adjacent to my apartment. It includes five wines, dinner, food tasting, and the guide. I can be out on the town comfortably with this group, although not too late, because I have a tour planned for Tuesday morning.

• Tour budget logs US$81.

Since wine is such a historical part of Malaga history, I decide it is tempting to take in a visit to a local winery and a wine tasting. The 'Guided Visit to a Pretty Vineyard and Cellar' tour will mean less walking than the previous tours and will get me out of the city for some fresher air. Included are tapas, six wine tastings, and an air-conditioned vehicle with Wi-Fi to get there. I'll meet the guide at the Plaza de la Marina. The tour is operated by White House Tours and begins at 10:00 am. It should last around four hours.

- Tour budget logs US$99.

After this tour on Tuesday, I am free to wander around, and hopefully by then I will have a good sense of direction.

For Wednesday morning, I plan a Civil War walking tour. This is made through a different connection: info@voilamalaga.com. My guide sends me this:

Hello Karen, I have availability that day. The itinerary of the tour is a bit different from the one on the website, but the explanations are the same. We start in Paseo Reding (and in my email there is a map). If you can, I can meet you there April 17th at 9.30h. Payment would be done by cash at the beginning of the tour. Best regards, Juan Diego

- Tour budget logs: US$120 for a private tour.

This tour sounds amazing and, after the little I have read, I think it is going to be very interesting.*

Thursday morning is now the only morning left where I can take a Paella cooking class. The problem is that most cooking events require guests to sign up in pairs. Eventually, happily, the author of one of the books I read before flying out sends me a link to a place where I can sign up solo. The class I sign up for is through kulinarea.com/en/cooking-classes-malaga. It begins at 10:00 am Thursday April 17 and lasts approximately four hours, culminating in lunch when we eat the food we have

- Tour budget logs: US$83.

I organize tickets for the 'Skip the Line: Picasso's Birthplace' tour, which is right next to our plaza, for when Johnny and I are kicking around town on the Saturday, our last day. We'll also be able to take in any other top sites I've discovered during the week.

On Saturday we will check out of our room by 2:00 pm,

---

* See voilamalaga.com and tours, Civil War Tour.

leaving our luggage at the property management office. Our plane doesn't depart until 11:50 pm, so we'll have plenty of time for a last look around.

I haven't yet mentioned the Friday. I gave Johnny his choice of day trips for the one day at the end we could go somewhere together outside Malaga. He remembered the name Alhambra from a video game he used to play called *Civilizations*. The name had stuck in his head and his curiosity had been piqued, so he chose to visit the Alhambra in the real world. Neither one of us really know anything much at all about it or its history, but this will change.

Friday is going to be the big day trip to Granada for Johnny and me. We buy high-speed train tickets for the 1.25-hour trip after we get to Malaga. It's not easy getting tickets to the Alhambra, now just two over weeks off, because it is a UNESCO World Heritage site. I buy the only tickets I can find for 12:00 noon on April 19, and unfortunately these are non-refundable because within the hour I discover they do not include the Nasrid Palaces. The Nasrid Palaces are a must-see if we are going all that way. After another hour of searching, I find that I can buy tickets for our desired day at 12:30 pm, but it is the opening attraction in a 48-hour Granada City Pass, so they are accordingly expensive. Moved by the rareness of this opportunity with Johnny, I buy them anyway. Now I have two sets of tickets, though one set is inferior to the other. At least I have some backup for the day if for some unforeseen reason we don't make the first tour time. We would at least be able to see the Generalife Gardens and Palace of Charles V, with a live guide and audio.

With only three weeks to go I realize I know nothing about the Alhambra and, in fact, precious little about Spain. I still have a lot to learn and very little time to do so.

Spain is a place that has ducked in and out of my historical readings primarily when it overlapped with tales of England or France, such as in the story of Catherine of Aragon. Outside of Queen Isabella and Ferdinand's reign, I have never really studied Spain for its own sake. Now that it is smack dab in the middle of my travel radar, I desperately want to understand some of the country's history. More specifically I want to learn about Malaga's history. I quickly learn this will be a big undertaking, with hundreds of years of recorded history and just a few weeks to get a meaningful grasp. Where to start?

Since I have a vague sense of Spanish history around the time of the 'Reconquista' I delve further back and begin with Malaga's medieval period, of which I had shockingly little prior awareness. I begin mostly with historical fiction that is easy and fun to read, as well as a photography book. Here is my selection:

• Fallon, Joan: *The Al-Andalus Series* – This includes *The Shining City*, *The Eye of the Falcon* and *The Ring of Flames* (2014)

• Fallon, Joan: *The City of Dreams Omnibus Edition* – A collection of tales, including *The Prisoner*, *The Pirate*, and *The Apothecary* (2020)

• Fallon, Joan: *Spanish Lavender: Love in A Time of War* (2013)

• Murphy, D.T.: *Where the Cricket Sings* (2022)

• Sepetys, Ruta: *The Fountains of Silence* (2019)

• Fallon, Joan: *Daughters of Spain: True Stories of Life in Spain* (2014)

• Kelly, E. J.: *Street Photography in Malaga Spain – My Visual Adventure* (2024)

• *Spanish Civil War: A History from Beginning to End* (Part of the History of Spain – 3 Books series) by Hourly History (2018)

Of this last book, I manage to read up to the 39% point before I become totally confused and buried in detail that I cannot properly process. So, I stop. I begin something lighter, *The Ghosts of Malaga*, by Jefferson Bonar, which I also do not complete. I realize after only a few pages that focusing on more fiction, after all the books I've already read – even when it's based on historical events – is a luxury I cannot afford right now. I will save it for the plane, in between evolving my journal and catching up on more language lessons, which have inevitably taken a bit of a back seat while I occupied myself with these books. Time has flown as I devoured one after the other, ticking off this era and then that one, like a hungry bird flying over time at will.

Countdown: The Last Two Weeks

It is now one calendar month since the word 'Spain' entered my consciousness in such an unpredictable manner, unlike anything else in my hitherto nearly 69 years. I am reading all those books, yet I am nevertheless still overwhelmed at the history that is Spain, not least that of Malaga.

I'd been digging at it here and there, reading about one particular period of history, and then jumping hundreds of years on to another era. Historical novels are satisfying, but I am beginning to feel a sense of inefficiency in my focus of study. I decide it will serve me well if I can find a way to put all this self-education into a kind of timeline. I need something that will combine my curiosity for Spain and Malaga's history with more pragmatic needs for the approaching trip.

I search for a book that will give me some basic direction and satisfy my craving for learning at the same time. My intuition, with the help of the Amazon search engine, leads me to the perfect solution: *Malaga: A Comprehensive Guide to Spain's Most Hospitable City*, by Thomas Martin.

I cram the first sixty-two pages and find myself relieved to have discovered this fabulous collection of combined history and practical travel advice. I am so grateful that I decide to do something I have never done before. I write to the author to thank him.

3/29/2024

Hello,

I am nowhere near the end of your book, but I did not want to delay in thanking you for putting this together. A month ago, I had never heard of Malaga, and now in two weeks I will be there for a week, as my grown son has a trip to Marbella with his new company and I have the fortune of being able to accompany him. I chose to stay in Malaga, and he will be with me at the beginning and end of the trip, at my apartment which I rented through Marriott Homes and Villas.

The entire amazing and unexpected opportunity has launched me into a masterclass of my own making on the study past and present of Malaga, and a crash course in Castilian Spanish. After watching a couple of YouTube videos and reading about a dozen historical novels, all I could find on the region, I found your book on my Kindle. I'm on page 62 and just realized how comprehensive your book is, and it is so timely! I see that it was just published, in 2023, lucky me!

I have never before written to an author, but I had to jump ahead to the final pages to see if you left your contact info, as I want to thank you in advance for this special collection of information. Although reading historical novels and poring through Trip Advisor-type sites to prepare me historically and practically for my week in Malaga is useful, I can see already that in your

book I will find many answers that six weeks would not have afforded me to otherwise digest! I just wanted to say thank you. I don't have any feedback now other than this. I will turn 69 two days after my return, and I had retired just before Covid reshaped our world.
I thought my desire to travel was fading but this is not the case. No, not at all. So now, between reading your book, working through the next 22 Pimsleur language lessons, and writing my own story about this entire experience (which won't be complete until I'm home and recovered from the jet lag), I need to get packing.
Muchas gracias,
Karen O'Connor, Spokane Valley, Washington USA

I hit send and imagine that it is likely the author won't even see my email, as it will either get lost in some kind of fanmail vortex or he will be just plain too busy to respond. Within a day, I discover I am completely wrong on both counts.

3/30/2024 2:27 pm

Hi Karen (if I may),
How lovely to receive your email just now! Although I published the guide eight months ago, and it's sold reasonably well, yours is the first email I've received – so while I'll try not to make this too long, I think you deserve a 'comprehensive' response. It's so nice for an author to hear that his or her work has been useful (though the real proof of the pudding will be when you actually visit!).

I'm British, as you can no doubt tell from the spelling and style, and I love Málaga. I wrote the book in my spare time as a sort of love letter to the city. Málaga is a lovely city, but for a long time it was ignored by British travellers who holidayed at the beach resorts to the west. I wanted to write something that would be helpful to the more serious and cultured traveller. What I've ended up with is more of an encyclopaedia than a traditional travel guidebook – a book to dip into and consult, rather than to read from beginning to end. I guess that doesn't come across so well on Kindle, unless you use the search function. Websites like Trip Advisor are okay, but the algorithm prioritizes the 'top tens' – not good for finding the more interesting places, and not great for providing the background info and history.

The problem with published books, of course, is that they go out of date, hence the companion Google Map (https://bit.ly/MalagaMap) and my advice to use Google Reviews to check on opening times etc, as they tend to be more up-to-date than Trip Advisor. Incidentally, I have a short section at the end of the book on suggestions for day trips from Málaga. These entries only scratch the surface, but the section on Marbella may be of interest to your son. I'm attaching a PDF of the few pages about Marbella (from the print version of the book) in case you want to send them on – easier than trying to share on Kindle!

One section that is already out-of-date is that which recommends particular stalls in the municipal markets, as there was a lot of 'churn' following COVID and there have been lots of changes. Some stalls have closed, but others have opened, and some have moved, so it's still well worth visiting the markets! And if you're staying in an apartment, the markets are great places to pick up bread, cheese, ham, olives, cured meat, fruit, etc, for light lunches. *Check out the end of the 'Eating and Drinking' section for info about the shops selling 'comidas caseras'* (homemade dishes) – *a fantastic option when staying in an apartment – pre-prepared food, but all made on the premises, not mass-produced. The quality of the food in Málaga (and in Spain as a whole) is stunning.*

I won't make any particular recommendations as so much depends upon one's own personal tastes – some people are foodies; some love wine while others are teetotal; some like art, and others prefer just wandering through streets and parks, and so on. All I'll say is that, depending upon where your accommodation is, buying a bus pass (tarjeta transbordo) is almost certainly going to be worthwhile. It costs €4.20 ($4.50) and is good for 10 journeys.

April can sometimes be showery, but this last week (Holy Week) has seen a huge amount of rain, so perhaps April this year will be dry! The average story for April is only 4 or 5 days of rain across the entire month, so you're unlikely to face a washout. If you do have a rainy day, then that's a good day to hit the museums. Good luck with the castellano – a lot of people working in hospitality in Málaga speak some English, and the rest tend to be patient and kind. Unlike the Parisians, who are famously dismissive of foreigners' attempts to speak French, the malagueños generally love people who try to speak Spanish, even if it's just a few basic phrases.

By the way, if you try your Spanish and the other person insists on speaking English, it's not a comment on your language ability! A lot of them are just really keen to practice their English! I hope (in fact, I'm pretty sure) that you'll enjoy Málaga, and I'd love to know how you get on and hear about your impressions of the place. In the meantime, if you have any specific questions, don't hesitate to drop me a line and I'll do my best to help.

It's great to hear that post-retirement and post-COVID your wanderlust is undimmed! All the very best, and thanks again so much for getting in touch.
Thomas Martin

As it turns out, apparently I have made Thomas's day – and he more than makes mine with his response. What follows by way of back-and-forth emails over the next two weeks is an exchange of support for my travels that exceeds all expectations. The information he provides hugely benefits the organization of my travel plans and enhances my anticipation for the trip.

Thomas is the one who helps me get into the cooking class as a solo registration, connect with my Civil War Walking Tour guide, understand all sorts of logistics such as knowing where to find groceries near my apartment, and who sends me additional tips on what to see and how to go about it. I have hardly been able to take it all in. In short, Thomas has all but sent a personalized guidebook to Malaga that is completely centered on my upcoming trip. I almost feel like I have already been to Malaga after all this study!

And that's a good thing, because I am running out of time. I need to get to the last-minute details.

🌸 🌸 🌸

Since I can hardly sleep the night before departure, I get up at midnight. James has just finished watching a back episode of *Star Trek* and I tempt him with popcorn to make him stay up.

We munch on our snack and watch a video of a walking tour

of Malaga – no voiceover, just a walk around – and it was just filmed yesterday. It turns out that these very streets are near my apartment, and, in fact, we will have to walk that way to the Plaza de la Merced. The city itself looks exceptionally clean and welcoming. We can't see any garbage anywhere in the film clip – it just looks like a beautiful and hospitable city. The weather looks perfect and although it's a bit breezy there are people everywhere. I am surprised to see so many people milling around. Maybe I have subconsciously imagined I will have the place all to myself ... yeah, right. Lots of them are in shorts. I might need to go swap out one outfit.

I leave James eating popcorn and head for our room. I have a medium suitcase and a backpack, in which I've stashed air tags that will report their location. I have tags for Johnny, too. As well as providing security, these will also provide peace of mind throughout the trip. Johnny has told me he is using his oldest luggage, held secure by a strap, because Jane's luggage went missing on their trip to Madrid last year and he is worried, by association with the fact that it is Spain, that this might happen again.

We have each agreed to check one bag straight through from Spokane to Malaga. This will prove to be the wisest of all decisions and, in fact, I will later wish I had also packed my laptop in the checked bag too, as I am not planning on getting it out at any of the layovers. I will have my iPad and my phone handy, which will more than meet my needs.

It's surprising how heavy a change of clothes, a light jacket, a hairbrush, toothbrush and the collective essential electronics can become. And the backpack itself isn't the lightest. The one smart move I make here is to add a portable bag that folds out into a bigger bag. I am traveling light – for me, anyway. Nevertheless, it's 30lbs of suitcase and 19lbs of everything else, including my passport, carry-on pack, phone and other devices.

In retrospect, the suitcase should have been more like 40lbs and the pack 9lbs. This would have been a wiser traveler's plan. However, having an expandable bag is useful as it will not only allow me to split the weight, but also add snacks or small souvenirs along the way. I will then be able to put the heavier pack overhead and keep my lighter bag with items I might want during the flight under the seat in front of me.

Finally, I succeed in pushing all the excitement of the upcoming trip to my own private cloud and manage at long last to get to sleep around 2:00 am.

At 9:00 am the happy tune that is my phone alarm awakens me from my slumber. I lie, warm and sleepy in my cocoon for a few minutes before jolting properly awake as I remember what day it is. My heart is thumping wildly. Finally, after all those weeks of preparation, the departure date has arrived! I spring out of bed and head for the kitchen where James is already making coffee. I can hardly speak or even think from excitement.

I've done it – I've made it happen, I'm all packed, and I have a fabulous itinerary planned. There is just one place where all my planning has let me down. I have arrived at departure day having completed only fifteen Spanish lessons.

Although I'm becoming more familiar with the language, it has proved more challenging than I thought it would be. Strangely, from the recesses of my cobwebbed brain phrases of Japanese are emerging, learned when I taught in Japan nearly 30 years ago. Yet I can barely remember the Spain-Castilian Level 1 lesson I worked on for hours. Maybe just being in Spain and keeping my ears open will help.

As I sip my coffee, I go over all the details of the trip on my iPad. I am using TripIt to keep track of everything and the schedule looks like this:

It Started with Malaga

- Fri, Apr 12 – Arrive Seattle, 56 min layover
- Fri, Apr 13 – Arrive Dublin, 4 hr 45 min layover
- Sat, Apr 13 – Arrive Malaga
- Sat, Apr 13 – Arrive Calle Victoria Apartment
- Sun, Apr 14 – Ultimate Malaga History & Tapas – All Included Full Experience
- Mon, Apr 15 – Iconic Hop-On Hop-Off
- Mon, Apr 15 – The Genuine Malaga Wine & Tapas Tour
- Tue, Apr 16 – Guided Visit to pretty Vineyard & Cellar – 5 wines tasting & tapas
- Wed, Apr 17 – Civil War Walking Tour
- Wed, Apr 17 – Dinner and Show at Alegría Flamenco & Restaurant
- Thu, Apr 18 – Kulinarea Paella Cooking Class
- Fri, Apr 19 – Málaga María Zambrano train station → Granada
- Fri, Apr 19 – 12:00 pm Alhambra Guided Tour with Nasrid Palaces & City Pass
- Fri, Apr 19 – 12:30 pm Skip the Line Alhambra and Generalife Guided Tour
- Fri, Apr 19 – Granada → Málaga Maria Zambrano train station
- Sat, Apr 20 – Skip the Line Picasso's Birthplace Museum Entrance Ticket
- Sat, Apr 20 – Check-out Calle Victoria
- Sat, Apr 20 – Check-in Clayton Hotel Dublin Airport
- Sun, Apr 21 – Check-out Clayton Hotel Dublin Airport
- Sun, Apr 21 – Arrive Seattle
- Sun, Apr 21 – Arrive Spokane (GEG)

TripIt shows it all with times, gates, confirmation numbers and everything else we might need. Is it too much to hope that all will transpire flawlessly? Has my preparation been sufficient? For now, TripIt at least gives me confidence that all the details are together in one place. I can find the app on my phone, too, if things start to go sideways and I need to look up contact information. Armed with this arsenal, and not just blind faith, I am as ready as I will ever be. Everything looks great on paper. Now the trick is to see if we can make it all happen in the real world and be happy that we did it when all is said and done. I wonder to myself, looking back, what would I have changed if I had known then what I know now?

It must be time to go. I am starting to overthink things. It is time to find out if the reality will live up to the expectations.

The Adventure Begins

We arrive at Spokane Airport at 12:00 noon to find our flight to Seattle is delayed by around 30 minutes. That's okay, since we have a three-and-a-half-hour layover in Seattle before flying to Dublin anyway.

We will get our boarding pass for the Alaska leg to Seattle at Spokane, but even though there is a partnership between the two airlines, apparently we can't get our Aer Lingus boarding pass for Dublin until we get to the gate in Seattle, which makes it awkward, especially when you get multiple electronic reminders to check in, but you can't.

When at last we are seated for the first leg of our journey, Johnny says, "I can't believe this is finally happening."

"I'm sure your brothers are jealous," I reply. "Joe might not remember we are flying off today but I'm sure Jay is thinking about us." I would love to bring Jay and Faye and the boys to Spain one day, but we'll see.

I kick off my flat slip-ons. "Dang, I've been trying to break in these shoes, but my feet are aching already."

"Same here, I think my feet are swelling already and we aren't even to Seattle."

I think to myself, *See, Jay? Things aren't perfect for us today. Our feet are killing us already, and someday if I have anything to do with it, we will go to Spain together, too. And you could have come. It just wasn't the right time. I'm sure we will have a fantastic trip one day. Thank you for your dedication to your students.*

Our flight to Seattle is much as we expect, and we disembark at the N (north) satellite terminal. We check out the rather nice Alaska lounge when we get part-way to S (south) terminal, but it's too far from our destination gate, so we keep going. Getting from N to S requires riding all three of the underground shuttles, but it's easy and fast. All told, it takes about twenty minutes to get to S. While we wait for our flight, we check out restaurants and decide to have something to eat. We each order a spinach and salmon salad plus an order of fries to share. I enjoy nice big glass of *vino tinto*, too. At least I can remember the Spanish for red wine.

Finally, our gate opens and we are first in line to get our boarding passes for Dublin.

"Ma, what seat do you have? Mine is 20B."

"Oh crud, mine is 14A."

Argh. We have already stepped away from the busy gate counter, and now we must get back in line to get his correct seat. I cannot see the end of the line. We exclaim "Oh, no!" and gaze pleadingly at the people at the front of the queue. We are relieved and grateful when they step away to let us back in so we don't have to wait another 30 minutes from the end of the line. Phew.

Fortunately for our nine-hour flight together – and for the people behind us in line – the attendants are able to quickly fix the error, and all is well. But dang, we paid extra to sit together well ahead of time. This shouldn't have happened.

I'm feeling a little bit anxious about not being able to pick up the boarding passes for Dublin-Malaga until the last minute (and I don't even know the half of it yet!), but I console myself that being able to use and earn Alaska Air points for this long trip is a bonus that may benefit me later by way of more points for future trips.

Soon we are settled into our seats which are quite comfortable, at least at the outset. I switch the little screen on the back of the seat in front of me to show the flight progress and settle my pillow and blanket for maximum comfort. I really didn't need my own neck pillow, as the seat backs have one built in. With a roar and a rush, we are in the air.

The flight from Seattle to Dublin takes us much further north than I would have expected. The arc on the seatback screen shows we are passing over familiar territory in Penticton and Kaleden in British Columbia and I mentally wave to my family below.

Soon we will be served a meal and will then be expected to sleep, but at least for this long portion of the trip I have my son by my side. I imagine that we are relatively insulated from outside interruptions. We have hardly had a chance to talk about the plans in the weeks prior, as he has been so busy with work, so I'm thinking this might be catch-up time.

I blurt out something I believe is of immediate importance to Johnny and he ignores me. Is he asleep? I try again. Nothing.

I peer at him and realize he has his earbuds in. He is listening to a book titled *Blink – The Power of Thinking Without Thinking* by Malcolm Gladwell.

Over the course of the next few hours, I repeatedly attempt to initiate conversation and am met each time by a "What?" and the patient removal of his earbuds. Finally, the fact he has those little white things in his ears sinks in and, feeling stupid, I apologize and leave him alone. My original comment has by now lost its urgency. For me, this trip is the culmination of weeks of preparation in an otherwise relatively idle existence. For Johnny, it is squeezed into the middle of a very tight work schedule. For him, now is the time for a little rest and relaxation.

After he's had some downtime though, he takes the time to explain about the audiobook and why he is so interested.

"The book I'm listening to is fascinating. It's about the brain. The author says the human mind can and does make relatively insightful guesses with information we are not even consciously aware we are taking in at the time." He proceeds to give me some examples.

"That sounds interesting. I might read it, too. What's the name and author again?"

But it doesn't take long for me to forget all about it. At this point in time, if it doesn't have anything to do with Spain, it drops off my radar.

Eyes back to the little screen embedded on the back of the seat in front of me, I see our flight will take us far north of Edmonton, to the top of Hudson Bay, and over a decent chunk of Greenland before passing just south of Iceland (wave to friends there) and then to Dublin.

The cabin crew come around to take our order for a hot meal and we both choose the Irish Stew.

Johnny takes his earbuds out and says, "Hot meals on an airplane always make me feel so nostalgic. Remember when I was 13 and I flew to Japan when you were teaching over there? I loved the hot meals on that flight and after that I thought all flights had hot meals. I have been disappointed ever since."

"That's too bad. You guys were so young. Heck, *I* was young. That was thirty years ago right now." I hadn't thought about that for a long time. Thirty years. Wow.

"Then, when we flew over Japan, they let Joe and me go into the cockpit and said, 'See, that's Japan and your mom is down there.' Then they gave us the first-class swag, which was shaving kits. And they had *razors* in them! Golly, times have changed." He chuckled.

"Oh ya, I remember about the cockpit, but I forgot about the razors and I'm not sure that I ever knew how much you loved those hot meals. Hmmm ... you were living the rest of that year with your dad and Desiree. And the airplane food was that good compared to your normal fare?"

"No ... not like that, Ma." And back in go the earbuds. I understand.

I double-check the flightpath on the screen again. We have barely budged since the last time I looked. I want to peek out the window and see if I can see the northern lights, but I can't see much, and the attendant asks me to pull the shade down. They want everyone to get sleepy. I enjoy a small bottle of Spanish Tempranillo wine. I can't see which part of Spain it's from because the print is too small and the light is dim. The plot to get us all to sleep works and I doze off shortly after Johnny does, his earbuds no doubt on noise cancellation.

※ ※ ※

We sleep for around four or five hours under those green Aer Lingus blankets, and when we wake up we can smell breakfast. I have to admit, I like eating hot meals on a plane too, with everything you need prepared with such care, right down to the little bag to put your trash in. I do so, but when I look around, I see most people don't bother. Oh, well. Announcements are made from time to time, but the voice is very soft and has a rough brogue and I barely understand a word of it.

Johnny has his earbuds in still, so I play peek-a-boo with a happy little girl toddler sitting a row up and across the aisle. She has a pacifier in her mouth the entire trip and I never see it out once, even for the hours she conks out like a rag doll. She doesn't suck on it. It is just there, like it grew there. But she is a happy traveler. I compliment her parents, and they say last year she also flew to Japan, which I know from personal experience is a similar-length flight from Seattle, but in the opposite direction.

I marvel at this. My first flight was over fifty years ago, a school trip with North Surrey Secondary. This little girl has already experienced two major flights before she can even walk. Oh, the places she will go in her lifetime.

The rest of the trans-Atlantic flight is comfortable enough and in a different type of blink to what Johnny is reading about, it's behind us and before we know it we have landed and are in Dublin's International terminal tasting whisky, Irish cream and delicious gin – all free samples.

With four-and-a-half hours to wait before the next leg, we find a restaurant with a view of Ireland's green fields through the large plate-glass windows of the airport. It's cloudy outside, but the sun is peeking through, and we have a nice view of handprints – some too high to have been made by small children – imprinted on the glass, which articulates slightly outward. The wind is whipping through the vivid green grass between the runways, and I marvel that our landing was so smooth.

I've lost track of whether it's time for a meal, but at the airport restaurant I have a chicken Caesar salad and Johnny has a burger. I skip the wine this time and have a nice latte instead. Johnny has an Irish beer.

Finally, after sampling the last of the free whiskies, it's time to head for the plane through a warren of hallways, moving sidewalks and more steps.

As we follow along like rats in a maze to the gate, Johnny reflects, "I'm so glad we don't have to take a shuttle, like at Heathrow. At Heathrow I got stuck in the back middle seat, squished on either side by heavy-set dudes, and my head nearly went through the ceiling. It was disgusting."

Next thing, we turn a corner and enter an area with signs directing us to 'board a shuttle'. Oh well. We have to stand for the ride, but at least it's not squishy.

We go through a similar procedure to get our boarding passes as we did for the flight to Dublin, but at least they give us the correct seats on the first try this time.

It Started with Malaga

Boarding passes in hand we head outside onto the tarmac and ascend a tall set of stairs to board. I'm over 9,000 steps already. And I am very happy, all over again, not to be dragging that checked bag around in addition to my backpack, which Johnny has been carrying for me ever since we got to Dublin. By now, of course, I've unzipped my spare tote and divided my belongings including my small purse, passport, a sweater, my phone and some treats, like a couple of packages of 'Spokandy' brand mints acquired in Seattle airport for a taste of home.

At last, we are boarded for Malaga and settled in our seats.

At the window seat, Johnny puts in his earbuds and swaps out his book for *The Wheel of Time*, a fantasy series that may have been written for truckers who are hundreds of hours on the road. He is ready to unwind a little. Before we know it, we both fall asleep. We snooze through the initial water offering, but they come around again.

"Would you like something to drink?" asks the flight attendant for the zillionth time as she moves along the aisle, focusing first on Johnny because he is at the window.

"I would like the Bloody Mary mix please, but not the vodka." He says he likes the healthy side of this drink, and it still tastes like a party.

"Could I please have some water? And I'd love a cup of coffee."

"Have you tried it? It's very strong." She is sizing me up.

"Um no, I usually use cream though. Do you have regular coffee?" I am caught off guard about the coffee – not for the last time on this trip. 'Regular' coffee is not the same as 'home' coffee.

She guesses I am looking for a cappuccino instead and I accept. The seats on the Airbus 320 are three-and-three so while Johnny is on my left, as on the previous flight, instead of only having the aisle on my right I now have another gentleman seated there. He asks for a cappuccino, too.

With coffee choice in common, this opens the door for conversation, which he initiates: "I hope you like the coffee," he says to me.

I am secretly just hoping I don't spill mine, but the flight has been amazingly smooth so far.

"Me too. I'm ready, though I usually drink decaf at home. I'll take what I can get here."

"Where is home for you?"

"I live in Spokane Valley, Washington, in the Pacific Northwest of the USA. But I used to live in California, and before that I lived for forty years in Canada, and somewhere in the middle of that, one year in Japan. And you?" I always wonder if people will know that the state of Washington is on the Pacific coast.

"I am from South Africa, but I have lived in Dublin for forty years." He seems content to chat about his life in Dublin and how he came to have a home in Spain, too.

It turns out that twenty-six years ago he and his wife bought some property, an apartment near Marbella, and that when they bought it, he met a lady who has recently passed at age ninety. He is on his way to show his respects and see her family, who have become like family to him over the years.

He speaks softly and the high-pitched engine noise is making it difficult to hear. I notice that through the window the hilly Andalusian landscape is coming into view.

"I wonder what those are in the distance?"

Dublin man says: "Those are trestles for toll highways. We are almost at Malaga."

"Oh, I thought maybe they were for the high-speed trains." Later, I learn they are.

"You will love this city. It is very nice weather at this time of the year."

We chat comfortably for the remainder of the trip. As we get closer to our destination, I feel invigorated with an awakened sense of anticipation for this long-awaited adventure. I have chatted meaningfully with another human from this earth in the way one tends to when you know you will never see them again. It is a marker in time. I harbor a belief that nobody comes into our life by accident – even if the meaning *is* simply to pass time while stacked in rows inside a giant can hurtling through the air at speeds where we would not be able to breathe but for the forced air pressure inside the cabin. The thought pleases me as I ponder it. Next thing I know we have landed in Malaga. We are on Spanish soil.

True to my research, the sun is low in the sky and there is a golden glow over everything.

I stop breathing momentarily. We're here! We're finally here.

Welcome to Malaga

We walk for what seems like forever, guided by signage to the promised baggage claim. Down these stairs, along that corridor, on this moving sidewalk ... suspicious as to whether we are on the right path, as airports often make you feel. Are the people disembarking from our plane the only people in the airport? Finally, we arrive at several cordoned-off lanes designed to herd hundreds of people through immigration. There's a mob of people waiting in line, and only four or five stations open on the far side of a very large room. We still have a lot of ground to cover.

Johnny is more alert than I am. "Ma, stop ... that line is just for EU."

"Oh, thanks kiddo, I don't know how I missed that." I wonder if I am subconsciously being a little lazy because I know I have Johnny here to take the lead.

We stream through the correct 'All Passports' entry and by the time we have weaved back and forth through the empty lanes and have to stop, there are around fifty people ahead of us. We don't have to wait very long at all, though, because a smartly dressed immigration officer guides us into a newly opened slot and then, even more fortuitously, leads us back to the EU station where the queues have now been processed.

The uniformed guy is chill. He raises his bushy eyebrows at the nice lady who has steered us to the 'wrong' station but stamps our passports, anyway. Our wait has been less than two minutes.

I am impressed at the efficient handling of weary travellers and say to Johnny, "Thomas calls Malaga 'Spain's Most Hospitable City'." It seems he's correct. Malaga has scored welcoming points with us from the get-go.

But before we get out of the airport, I'm reminded that I am, after all, the new kid here. We encounter a speed bump with the luggage.

Throughout our three legs of the journey in what now adds up to 24 hours, we have been comforted by the 'reporting' of the air tags. The 'Find My' app on our phones shows both our location and that of our bags and has consistently confirmed that our checked belongings are following along behind the scenes. In fact, both are visible now as blue dots, just behind the hatch from which the luggage rides forth on the moving carousel. All the other bags tumble forward and are collected by their relieved owners who roll them to the exit and beyond the doors to their chosen modes of transport.

We wait expectantly, shifting our weary bodies from one foot to the other.

The carousel stops; our bags have not emerged. If not for the air tags, we would have kept on waiting hopefully for them to appear – but we know our bags are on the other side of that hatch.

I walk forward and slide the black rubber tabs aside and there, indeed, about ten feet beyond my reach rest the desired bags, both mine and Johnny's. His bungee strap is still doing its job. That's not a problem.

What *is* a problem is that even if I could recall enough words to put together a sentence in the native language, none of my lessons included, "Why is my luggage not coming through?" I see an attendant behind the scenes. I'm sure he is just doing his job, but to my dismay he responds to my frantic attempt at communication by rolling down the door and obliterating my view completely.

The luggage window is now closed. The door next to it has a warning sign on it but I approach it, anyway.

My son observes and with urgency advises, "Don't go in there!"

Stumped and desperate, I reply, "I'm just going to try the knob." I'm at such a loss.

"No, please, we can figure this out. You can't go in there!"

Sheepishly I agree. "Okay, okay, you're right." Six weeks of imagining our arrival in Malaga did not include the scenario of getting arrested for trespassing! A feeling of desperation washes over me. There's been a big mistake. Who can fix it?

"Maybe we can find Airport Information." I look around helplessly at the vast open spaces of baggage claim. My pack suddenly feels about ten pounds heavier. After surveying the scene and seeing no sign of anyone who can help, Johnny goes back and tries the door with the warning sign on it. But it is locked.

It takes about a half an hour to resolve the issue. Johnny and I go our separate ways to seek help. I walk what seems like a mile but never do find the Aer Lingus office that two security officers direct me to visit. 'Information' is long since closed for the evening.

I do not actually come close to crying during all of this, though my gut constricts with worry. I am so tired – and I know that somewhere outside the departure area there is a nice man waiting in vain with my name on a sign. I had been so proud of myself to have a ride to our Calle Victoria apartment all lined up. This is not how I imagined things would be.

The only thing I can think to do is leave the departures area and find our driver to let him know we still want the transfer to Calle Victoria. Fortunately, I am able to get back inside past the "No people back through this point" warning sign. You know ... the one that has a person and a big red circle with a red line across it? For the second time I'm lucky I don't get arrested, and I've only been in Spain for thirty minutes!

But all is not lost. My resourceful son, facilitated by conversations with random travelers, has managed to reclaim our air-tagged bags. He texts me to report this news, though I don't see it right away as my phone is not connecting, giving him a moment of worry. Inexplicably, the luggage had been dumped in an entirely separate room, one for luggage that arrives through Customs, even though Customs is well behind us.

Now we just need to find each other again.

I have a jolt of momentary panic because I see him, then lose him, and I'm starting to feel lost myself. Johnny has a moment of disbelief, bordering on consternation, because he looks right at me and thinks I see him, too, then I walk the other way.

I finally hear him call out my name – 'Karen!', not 'Ma', as has been his habit in public ever since we worked together. At last the bags and their humans are reunited and we head for the exit and whatever this Malaga adventure will bring.

The sky is a dark blue by the time we exit the airport, and the air is warm and humid, with a slight taste of the sea. At last, we are back in the business of meeting with our nice man with my name on a card. The transfer fee is €32, but I give him a €50 note for the long wait he has endured and motion for him to keep the change.

Breathing a sigh of relief and the fresh Malaga air, at 9:30 pm after touchdown at 8:17 pm, we are at last on our way to the apartment.

Exploring Home Base

All the map gazing I have done at home is little help as we take the freeway from the airport. Malaga is a big and unfamiliar city. I am blinded by a stream of red car lights caterpillaring nose-to-tail ahead of us and find myself thinking the city is a blurry, unexplored mystery. It looks different to what I had imagined. I hope it will all be good. But I barely stop to consider what I have gotten myself into. I am determined this week will be epic. In fact, I can feel it in my bones.

I nudge Johnny in the middle seat of our large van. "This is even better than Christmas Eve. I am so filled with anticipation."

He pulls out his earbuds. "I'm excited too. And I'm hungry, are you?"

"Sure, let's settle in and then find a place to eat. We're close to plenty of options. I saw them on YouTube. We have a famous restaurant nearby, 'El Pimpi', and lots of smaller cafes. Tapas will be perfect tonight, and I'm dying for my first glass of wine in Spain. I think we'll see the Alcazaba backlit when we get to our apartment." I'm not worried about finding dinner at this hour because I'm well informed both by reading Thomas's guidebook, and by Thomas himself.

"How much further is it?" The city seems to stretch out endlessly before us.

"Well, I think pretty soon we will be driving alongside the port, but I don't know if we'll be able to see it. After that there are lots of side streets. I'm not sure exactly."

I keep trying to recognize anything that might anchor me to something I saw on the map so I can get a grip on where we are. After about twenty minutes of following the snaking red taillights, we turn off the freeway and begin funneling into streets that change direction quickly. I imagine the route was set hundreds of years ago by vehicles with two legs, not four.

This is where my imaginary Malaga, made of Google Map colors, turns into reality. It seems like the apartment should be closer than it is. I truly believe the cab ride takes us longer than it takes to walk between the same points later on. It's just the way the streets are laid out, and when we get off the motorway, we enter streets formed hundreds of years ago in a maze to flummox an invader arriving by horse or on foot. Eventually, we navigate to Calle Victoria, and I recognize our building. The tell is that there was once a building right next to it that was demolished, and you can still see the red shape of a peaked rooftop from the side.

The driver seems immensely relieved that he has delivered us to our destination as he parks at the curb. Perhaps the narrow streets are confusing even for him if you don't know exactly where you are going. Using a combination of hand signals and broken English, he tells us that he doesn't think we will sleep because he thinks we are in a loud neighborhood, and he laughs a little as he helps us with our bags. We hope he's not correct, as it's too late to change our plans. Happily, our apartment is located at the back of the building, and we expect everything will be just fine.

We find there's not much traffic on the two-lane road in front of our apartment building. We hear voices from across the street, happy couples and families, eating and sipping wine at the outdoor tables. The air smells delicious. It is dark, but everything on the street looks as I expected from all my Google and YouTube research.

"Hang on a minute, Johnny. I have an app on my phone that I can use to get inside this door. The property management office sent it. I hope I can make it work, though. I seem to have brought up the Spanish page, rather than the English page." Why do even the smallest things seem to stretch time when you are not quite sure what you are doing?

"It's okay Ma, take your time." He is about to offer to take my phone and try it himself, but I've been to this page before, and I'm the one who's been studying Spanish.

We are both relieved when my efforts result in a buzz from the big door that separates the lobby from the street. Johnny reaches over me and grabs the bar to pull the door open. I stop to take a photo of this momentous event.

We rumble our luggage inside and look around.

"Where's the elevator? We roll our bags to the back of the lobby area and swivel our heads, looking around for something that resembles an elevator. There is a black door, but it is locked. We see only steps. But the info promised a lift!

"Do you think that's it?" Johnny nods toward a thin, odd-looking metallic door with a narrow vertical side window at the back of the lobby area. There are three buttons on the wall. Two do nothing. The third, we realize, calls the tiny car to our floor.

"Well, this is interesting. I guess this is it!" We grin at each other sheepishly. Nothing is going to stop us now. When the car reaches our floor, we can pull open the door and see ourselves in the mirror on the back wall, strategically placed to reduce claustrophobia.

The tiny lift can barely hold two people and with our luggage we only just fit. The sign says maximum four people. That would be cozy! We press another button and up we go to the fourth floor. When we exit, we have to step up a half-set of marble tile stairs to door number Four. I count eight as I lug my things up one step at a time. Johnny goes up quickly and comes back to lend a hand. The mat in front of our apartment says welcome.

I select the next box in the app on my phone and, as if by magic, the apartment door clicks, and we are able to push open the door using the knob which is dead center at waist height. We have arrived! There is a set of keys on the table just inside the door, and I am relieved I'll be able to use a physical one since my phone is old and the battery tends to die quickly.

"Ah, this is really cool. Which bedroom should I use? I like this. It's great."

"It's so nice to finally be here. Wow, what a long day."

The apartment is adorable and is what I expected from the online pictures. I claim the bedroom with the ensuite while Johnny gets the other – but he has his own bathroom, too, next to the kitchen.

"I'm so glad you came along. Wow, look at this huge closet. Look, the lights come on when I slide the doors open. This should be fun. Okay, I'm ready to eat. Do you want to take a minute to settle? Or should we head right out to explore those cafés across the street?"

"That's a great idea. Or we can just walk around until we find something. I've heard that here in Spain people don't start to eat dinner until after nine, and it's just ten, so let's go. I'm good for some exploring if you are. There's a lot to see around here. We can unpack later."

We grab the keys as we leave and turn to check that the door has locked behind us.

We decide to walk down the flights of stairs. I honestly don't know what has got into me. The marble stairs circle around the shaft that houses the lift, and I soon find that keeping up with Johnny makes me dizzy.

As we descend, I am reminded that we are not inside a fancy hotel. The hallway housing the steps is dated, the walls could use some paint, and there is a broken pane of glass here and there. But people live here, and it feels safe enough. On the second floor, I see a sign for an 'Escape Room' and, not knowing what that is, I shudder. But I have a hunch it is just some modern-day fad experience. I apologize in advance to readers who do know what this is!

Out on the street, we cross at the little crosswalk and enter the Plaza de la Merced. On the north side there is a row of enticing restaurants, all with both indoor and outdoor seating. We wander further than we need to, but Johnny thinks we should pick something that I might not find by myself. I can easily choose one of the closer ones when I'm on my own.

The walk through the historical area is refreshing and the streets are alive on a Saturday night. The shops are all still open and seem to be doing a good business. We see gaggles of bachelorette parties, the girls drunkenly balancing alcoholic drinks and walking like they are all stuck together. I've read about these parties, which are not always welcome for the trouble they sometimes cause, but there are also plenty of other folk just strolling around enjoying themselves. Nobody is too out of control, like some I witnessed in Las Vegas during our California days.

It is nearly 10:45 pm when a smiling woman approaches us with a menu as we pass by, obviously looking hungry, so we accept her invitation and head inside. We choose a table for two and sit down with a sigh. We hardly know where we are, never mind the name of the establishment – which, in spite of all my future wanderings, I never notice again.

We have settled for our first meal in Spain at the Casona Los Marangos, if my photo of the menu tells the truth. For all the advice Thomas has provided for places to eat, in the end we just land our weary bodies at the first place someone smiles at us, and in our travel-dazed state we are happy enough.

It doesn't take us long to order *una cerveza* and *una vinto tinto*, which I have learned in my Spanish lessons. By Tuesday I will know why red wine is 'tinto' – apparently all grapes start out white inside, but the skins of the reds are tinted in the fermentation process. Right now, however, I am just happy to have my first glass of Spanish wine in hand.

"Well, here we are, Johnny. Can you believe it? I just want to take it all in."

"Ya, it was a long day. What would you like to eat?" He leans expectantly over the menu, which luckily for us is written in English.

"These tapas look interesting. But Jane said you were burned out on tapas when you went to Madrid last year."

"Oh, not really. I just felt like I could never get full enough. I don't mind them at all. Which ones should we order?"

"Well, let's see." We both have adventurous appetites, so it is easy to find something we like.

We order three kinds of tapas, and then notice paella on the menu, and since it is a dish that is so iconic to Spain, we decide we should try it tonight. We ask the server.

Johnny attempts to ask: "Is this something you recommend?" Pointing at an item on the menu, in English he asks, "Do you recommend the rabbit?"

Our server stumbles with his reply, and we don't really understand, but after some confused exchanges we order the paella for two, rabbit-style, anyway. I've never eaten rabbit before, but we just want to dive right into the Spanish experience.

When our tapas are delivered, we see no sign of the paella. We try to catch the server's eye and eventually he comes back. We flounder through asking about our order. It seems it was

It Started with Malaga

never put forward to the kitchen. If we had been more alert, we might have realized that this was our 'out'. There must have been a good reason the order was not put through. If we had taken the hint, we could have simply ordered more tapas and been quite satisfied. This was not what happened. We re-ordered the paella for two and asked for our drinks to be refilled. They brought us a partly full bottle of wine and set it on the table.

Now ravenous, we dig into our tapas dishes, sipping our respective wine and beer. Johnny will remember for future reference one he particularly liked – beef empanadas. He wasn't crazy about the potato croquettes, but I didn't mind them, and the sardines were very tasty, too.

Eventually, after a suspiciously long wait, we are served our paella order. We take a couple of bites and lay down our forks. The meat is tough and tasteless. The paella itself, soggy. It's fortunate, I find myself thinking that I have a paella cooking lesson planned for Thursday, where I will hopefully learn how to make this dish correctly. By now I have had enough wine, and my appetite has up and left me, so I don't mind that the dish is not over-the-top tasty.

Later I learn that, in Spain, paella is usually made around noon and served at lunchtime. When it's all gone, that's the end of the paella for the day. Now, I might be mistaken, but based on this first experience, I'm inclined to believe this is true. If so, I can just imagine what went on in the kitchen when these two foreigners showed up and ordered paella at nearly midnight. In which case the establishment exercised as much grace as you could hope for in the circumstances. They did not argue with us about our order, although maybe they should have. I'd like to think the bottle of wine on the table was an apology in advance, and I have to admit, it helped.

We decide not to let it ruin our evening and, instead, view it as the beginning of our learning experience. Most importantly, we have had our first memorable meal in Spain and thoroughly enjoyed it. We give each other a quick 'Salud!' before we leave the table. We are sure to let the staff know we had a good time and thank them for the bottle of wine. The meal was shockingly inexpensive by our Western standards. It is hard for me to not tip, so I leave a couple of Euros under the empty wine bottle left standing on the table.

Back in the street, we wind our way through the various wedding parties that are still reveling and decide to top up with some ice cream. A vendor is still open, and the wait is short. When it is our turn, we find that she is selling frozen yoghurt, not Malaga's famous ice cream, but it's delicious, anyway.

To get back to our apartment we choose streets that lead gently uphill until eventually we find the Plaza de la Merced and cross the street to our building. There's a small Indian takeout joint next to our lobby door, and we load up on bottled water. The physical key gets us inside in a jiff.

In a youthful spur of energy, Johnny decides he will skip the lift and march up the marble stairs, instead. Not yet wanting to leave his side, and unencumbered by luggage, our clothes waiting to be neatly unpacked in the generous closets of our apartment, I follow him. WHAT WAS I THINKING? Reaching our floor, puffing and panting, I vow that will be the last time I hike *up* those steps at least.

Between us, we figure out how to turn off all the fancy mood lighting in our modern apartment. Snug in my king-sized bed, wrapped in luxurious bedding and surrounded by fluffy pillows, after one last check on my iPad for recent emails, I drift off around 1:30 am, my son already asleep in the next room.

Life is GOOD. Mission accomplished. The adventure in Malaga has begun!

Waking Up in Malaga

My body is going to take a while to adapt to this nine-hour time adjustment. I have lost track of whether I am ahead or behind the rest of my world, so I am going to have to play it by ear. And ear it is! My first awareness of morning, Spanish time, is hearing the birds chirping happily outside. It's a good start to the day, and one that becomes the norm in our temporary home. We don't know it yet, but the 'considerable' expected construction noise that afforded us our 20% discount on the apartment will be competition for the birds, but this won't happen until Monday.

I have read that there were additional Roman and Moorish artifacts collected from the construction site outside our window and they are going to be housed in a new museum one day. I wonder if any were related to the long and bloody siege of 1487 when Malaga's Alcazaba was reconquered by Isabella and Fernando, ending Moorish control in the region. This building seems like it might have been precisely in the middle of it all if the clock could be momentarily turned back several hundred years. The thought is tantalizing, and the historical novels I have read in preparation for this trip add color to my imaginings.

Johnny is awake a bit before me and snaps a picture of the Alcazaba in the dawn light from our small balcony. I am so glad he manages to record that moment in time. Now, still jet-lagged, he has gone back to sleep. We have to rendezvous for our tour at 10:00 am, so we probably should look at options for a quick breakfast beforehand. We won't have time for a leisurely sit-down one at a café.

I remember that Thomas said there is a breakfast place that opens early on the corner of the Plaza. I decide to test my new lift-riding skills and ability to use the key on my own to get back into the building. I venture out toward the BrunchIt shop I happen to notice, to see what I can find. It might not be the one Thomas intended, but it is open, at least.

The sign out front says: 'Please wait to be seated.'

But I don't want a seat, just an order to go. I see others leaving with little white boxes, so I figure it is possible to do this. I hesitate, then follow other foot traffic inside and hang out by the cash register, which is next to a glass case housing a variety of enticing breakfast pastries.

After a couple of awkward minutes, me in my blue jacket, shuffling from one foot to the other, not completely sure this is where I should be standing, the smiling attendant behind the counter asks me what I would like. For all the hours I spent studying ahead of time, I cannot bring a single word of Spanish to my lips.

In English I ask for coffee, and point to croissants in the glass case, making a motion with my hand that I would like two. I feel like such a dunce. The attendant behind the counter says what sounds like, "Do you want Nutella on the croissant?"

I say no, or maybe I say, just on one. It is Day One and I still plan to follow my sugar-free diet, but Johnny might like it. She intuitively boxes up my order to go, and as I am served two black coffees, I ask for cream. After a bit of fussing and more

It Started with Malaga

mixed language dialog, she pours some milk into a third cup and arranges it all in a convenient cardboard tray.

It is a half a block and across two low-traffic streets, both of which are monitored by crossing lights, to get back to the apartment. I learn, for better or for worse, that at least in this part of town nobody waits for the light when there is no traffic around. By the end of the week, I will still wonder if I am breaking the law or being rude by following suit.

I feel quite proud of myself to get it all back without spilling anything, past the locked front door, into the elevator, up the marble steps, and into the room with the key. I do it all without having to set anything on the floor, because the cups are sitting in a small holder torn from a bigger size, although I am still balancing the cup with the milk in it. When I get the croissants unwrapped, one is plain, and the other is stuffed with ham and cheese. Hmmm … I thought she asked me if I wanted Nutella. Now I wonder if I got someone else's ham and cheese.

Johnny is awake. "Cool, thanks for getting breakfast."

"Do you want a plain croissant? Or do you want ham and cheese?"

Silly question. "I'll have the ham and cheese. Thanks, Ma."

The croissant is fresh enough though I miss a little butter. I am happy that the coffee, though a short one, is tasty enough and I wish I had another. My paper cup only half fills a ceramic mug from the cupboard, which is amply stocked with a variety of sparkling and trendy dishware, most of which we will never touch.

Johnny Facetimes his family back home and it all connects quite well. It's good to hear their voices and see their smiling faces. Technology can be absolutely amazing when it works.

"Hi, Daddy! Hi, Grandma! Where are you?" The three grandkids – eldest girl, 13, middle boy, 10, and the littlest girl, 6 – bounce in and out of the frame. Finnigan the dog is in the middle of it all. Jane is sitting at a tall table in the background, nursing a coffee.

"Hi kids, I miss you already. We're just about to go for a tour to a castle. I wish you were all here." That's what everyone says, right?

"Daddy, we won our soccer game!" says middle boy, excitedly.

"I'm going to be in a parade with my flute," chirps eldest girl, proudly.

"I wrote a song and played it on my purple 'kulele," says littlest, shyly.

"She really did," says Jane. "She even wrote her lyrics on a piece of paper and then sang along."

James and I have been encouraging all the children to play music, and the littlest seems likely to be a rock star when she grows up, though all the kids seem musically inclined. When a child just has music in their bones at an early age, you can see it.

"Can you sing it for us now?" asks Daddy.

"Next time," answers littlest, suddenly coy.

"We can see the fortress from our window," offers Daddy.

"Send pictures of it, okay?" middle boy urges.

We send the kids the picture of the castle taken from our balcony. On the left side of the image, you can see the edge of a building like ours, with laundry drying here and there on the rooftop.

They all talk for ten minutes or so and then it's time to disconnect.

Since the meeting point for our first tour is a fifteen-minute walk away we finish our breakfast, apply sunscreen to our cheeks and noses, and head out. We loop down the marbled interior steps around the lift housing, past the Escape Room sign again.

Relieved to exit to the lobby, I promise myself from here on in I'll use the lift both ways. I am dizzy enough with all the jigs and jags of travel without adding to the condition deliberately.

I know from exploring on Google Earth prior to the trip, that the 'calle' – the Spanish word for avenue – near BrunchIt is about a half kilometer long and will lead to the calle near the port. This, after a right turn, will lead us to the rendezvous point near the McDonald's. As I pass BrunchIt, I turn and take a picture of our apartment building with its signature peaked red shape on the side.

The Google Walk of this area had at one stage given me grave concern. The pictures were so old that the decrepit poster lined buildings that once flanked my building had made me wonder what kind of neighborhood I was booking myself into. It turns out that what I had seen were the remnants of an ancient cinema that in its time would have been a silver-screen treasure. Long since torn down, the site has been replaced with temporary fencing that boasts block-long murals picturing the best of the Malaga fair and other annual events. This road and the plaza are quickly becoming my familiar territory, and I feel just a little bit smug to have such an address as Calle de Victoria.

Calle de Victoria, a road built for traffic, bends into the wide, tile-paved Calle Alcazaba at the BrunchIt corner, and the rest of the calle all the way to the Malaga Museum is primarily for pedestrians. This span is flanked by well-kept buildings, shops, restaurants, the Teatro Romana (Roman theater) built under Emperor Augustus in the first century BC, and even the entrance to the Alcazaba that we will return to later. This makes for a captivating stroll and one that I will enjoy many times over the next few days, getting to and from tours and just wandering.

As we reach the lower end of the calle where it meets the road that runs along the Calle Cortina Del Muelle, which borders the impressive Parque de Malaga, we veer right past row upon row of motorcycles parked along the street. Later, when he looks at the pictures, my husband wonders where all the owners are. I suspect they are mostly working in the tourist industry, shops, restaurants, museums, transportation, or perhaps one of them is attending the small curb-side shop along the way where we will buy ice cream later.

As we enter the park, we walk in the opposite direction to a straggling group of about twelve to fifteen people, who are following a man with a lanyard around his neck.

"Hey, Johnny, I hope that wasn't our tour." I've planned and double-checked, but I am immersed in a foreign land, and I worry I will have unfortunate surprises.

"Well, what time is our tour?" At least he left his earbuds at the apartment today.

"Pretty sure it said 10:30." I really need to have more faith.

"Well, I wouldn't worry then. Relax." He looks at me curiously for a minute and smiles.

This is the first tour of many for me, but an important time for Johnny because he will be off to Marbella tomorrow, so I really want things to go well today. Five minutes later, we find McDonald's and the door next to that, which is the address given by the tour company, so this is reassuring.

But it is around 9:55 am and I don't see any group, certainly not like the group we passed, so I hold my heart in my throat just a bit.

Unfazed, Johnny asks, "Can I get you another cup of coffee? I'm getting one for myself."

"Sure, that would be great. Please ask for two creams." All the while hoping the line is not too long. I never get over the fact that Spain doesn't use cream in the coffee, just milk, but I am sure it is better for my health.

I spot another couple sitting in the outdoor seating area. The woman is wearing a sleeveless, breezy cotton dress, and the fellow is in short sleeves.

"Are you two waiting for a tour?" I hope I don't look like a fool, with my fuzzy hair and comparatively overdressed for the warmth of the day in my blue jacket and black pants.

Big smiles. "Yes, we are. Hello. You too?" There is no mistaking the Irish accent.

"Phew," I say. "Is it the tapas walking tour? We are, too. My son has gone inside for coffee. I was worried as I passed a tour a few minutes ago and thought I might have mixed up the times."

"Well, this is where we were supposed to meet, and we were wondering the same thing. We hope the guide shows up."

Okay, so I'm not the only worry wart, but I do need to relax. The hard part of the trip is behind us and the rest is just the adventure. We are here in Malaga. If one thing doesn't work out, there will always be something else to do.

We introduce ourselves and learn that our tour companions are Victoria and Andy from Belfast, and they are as friendly as anyone could hope for. I am suddenly back down to earth. What was it Tom Petty said? *Most things I worry about never happen, anyway...*

When I was booking the tours, I was on a bit of a splurge because the accommodation costs were going to be quite light compared to what I had originally anticipated. I was happy to get the exact type of tours I preferred, all small groups and exactly when I needed them. I didn't worry too much about the price. It all seemed so exotic in the weeks ahead when I was planning.

To our relief, like an apparition out of nowhere, our guide shows up at 10:00 am on the dot and announces he is Paco. He informs us there are just the four of us for the tour. If I had chosen a less pricey tour, we might have been in a large group like the one we passed on the way. I'm glad I chose this one.

For a start, a small, semi-private tour like this is handy when one of the participants is held up for a couple of minutes in the line at McDonald's getting coffee, as there is no risk of getting left behind.

Johnny returns with the coffee, and we head off with Paco to the Cathedral to walk around the outside of it. The plan is to then head to the Alcazaba, returning to the Cathedral for an inside tour later, because it is Sunday and we cannot interrupt the Mass.

11

Paco's Keys to the City

When we reach the Alcazaba there are literally hundreds of people waiting in line outside. Paco turns to the four of us and instructs, "Follow me closely."

We weave through the crowd right up to the entrance and then we are inside. Just like that. I feel like we are on a TV show, or some kind of celebrity, because we don't have to wait with everyone else. This is what 'skip the line' means, and yes, we paid for skip-the-line tickets. But Paco, his father and his grandfather are all long-term Malaga residents and consequently, he is well known around Malaga, so I have a feeling that it is Paco himself who is the ultimate skip-the-line pass, as if he has his own keys to the city.

I am glad about not having to wait in line because it is getting quite warm in the sun. Also, my new slip-on shoes are reminding me what being broken in on a NINE-MILE Day actually means. I am wishing I had brought my grubby walking shoes along. But it's too late now, and I march onwards and upwards. And upwards it is!

We go through the first of three doors or gates, shaped like a key at the top.

Paco says, "See this door?" as he pulls it open. "Behind here are the original nails." I take a picture and think I will blow it up later so I can see what he is talking about. We surely would not have opened that door ourselves. He must have special permission to open it, maybe to impress us. The bricks and tiles are beautiful and our heads spin to see it all.

My balance seems off though, and I soon realize I need to also keep my eyes on the floor. There is a lot of uneven ground and little steps here and there that are unexpected. Four times, I nearly trip or fall over because of one of these steps. We are covered for travel and health insurance, but we sure don't want to have to use it, and I can do without the pain of a twisted ankle.

We follow the wide path upwards, in awe of the fortress's construction. We are walking on historic ground. Paco tell us that, of course, none of the pretty flower gardens would have been here back when this was an active fortress, and no food was grown here either, because of the difficulty of bringing water in. In the 1400s, when Queen Isabella's army finally conquered the fortress, it wasn't by sneaking over any of these walls or barging through any of the narrow gates. It was by laying siege for months and stopping the flow of food and supplies from getting in. Her army probably camped out on the ground where my apartment was built.

Part-way up we are shown a pit that is covered with a grate, and Paco explained that this was a prison for those considered bad guys. There are two more gates that would have been impossible to breach as there are steep slopes leading up to them. Hot oil would have been dumped from above on anyone foolish enough to try, so in addition to the thick, solid construction being a deterrent, the slope itself worked in favor of the defenders.

The Alcazaba is a crown of Malaga, and it has an impressive and worthy history. If you have Thomas's book you can read a digestible historical timeline that I won't, for all I am trying to take it all in, attempt to repeat.

On our climb to the top, we see a beautiful and ancient marble bathtub, just one of many historical pieces still housed at this ancient fortress. It is a marvel how all of this has survived over time. At the top, there are stunning, well-preserved ceilings and a room that houses a model of the entire fortress structure.

Paco questions us, "Do you know why the ceilings are so pristine and beautiful?"

Hearing nothing in response, he offers, "They are too far out of reach for anyone to touch them and, being on the inside, are protected from the elements."

At least one of us should have thought of that.

There are also examples of pottery in some of the rooms, but by now I can't really see the displays – or much of anything else for that matter.

By the top of our climb, my face has begun to sweat like a hidden spring, and the sunscreen I'd applied earlier is seeping into my eyes, which are now stinging. In recent years, I have become increasingly sensitive to any type of perfumed lotion on my face. So, eyes watering steadily, I squint at what I can see, and vow to go without sunscreen for the rest of the week. I peer between the slits my eyes have become to see what I can of the far-reaching views. Everyone else 'oohs' and 'aahs' at the bullring, which we are high above, but I must admit I haven't spotted it, because I am almost blinded. Even before we get to the top of this mighty fortress I am looking forward to the tapas portion of the tour.

At the very top there are more dark rooms and some have samples of pottery found on the site, which are if great interest to me, but I can't see most of it. I vow to look it up online later.

Johnny takes my arm, so I won't trip over cobblestones as we wind our way down to the exit. It has been an ambitious climb for Day One, but I am glad to have seen the inside of Malaga's mighty fortress. It would have been a regrettable shame to have missed it. I will, however, enjoy the night-time exterior view of it immensely every evening while walking to and from my apartment on the nice, flat, tiled street.

For an April day, it is remarkably warm, and I note to myself never to come back in mid-summer. I also notice that in Malaga, not just the tourists but all sensible women wear a light cotton dress on a warm day in April. Unlike stubborn, unconforming, pants-loving me. I'll think about a dress, too, if there is a next time.

After successfully ascending and descending the Alcazaba without falling over, I am more than relieved when we are led to an inviting little restaurant with a nice, clean '*baño*' (bathroom, pronounced 'banyo'). It is now around 12:30 pm, the perfect time for lunch in this cozy little place. Our table, which has been pre-set for the group, is laid out with small plates and tall wine glasses. We order and are served a bottle of *vino tinto*, as well as water for the table. The wine is tasty and Paco, who tells us he is eighty, has some as well and reports, "If the guide drinks the wine, it is a sign it is good wine." Soon, a plate of appetizing-looking tapas arrives, some made with salmon, some with shrimp, and some containing fruits such as raisins and pear.

We offer Paco some of our abundant food. "No, thank you, my wife would kill me because she will have food waiting for me when I get home. If I ate on all my tours, I would be too big to walk. I don't want to ruin my figure," he chuckled. I joke to myself that perhaps the same does not apply to how much he has to drink. But no, in all seriousness, he has just a little of our wine. Paco assures us it is okay to scrape the goodies off the top of the tapas if we don't want to eat the bread, and we follow his advice. How did he know? Well, it is Day One and I am still thinking of my usual low carb diet. We will see how long that lasts.

I glance around the restaurant. There is a painting on the ceiling, a spin-off of Michelangelo's *The Creation of Adam*, which I saw in Rome in 2019. One small difference, though. In this rendering, right where Adam's fingers touch, there is a tumbler of beer.

I point this out to Johnny, who chuckles and says, "I wouldn't mind drinking beer, rather than wine."

"Hold your horses, kiddo, that's for another city at the end of the week." I quip. We are having fun, and I am cherishing the moment.

After we've eaten, we head off to the next tapas joint. This one is outside, under a sail shade cloth. There is a cool breeze, and it is now quite pleasant to be outdoors. Another bottle of wine, water and some more tapas are ordered, and because Andy is an athlete and not drinking except for water, the rest of us have extra *vino tinto*.

After all the busy weeks spent preparing for the trip, the travel itself, and the morning's tour, it feels blissful to be sitting here enjoying the experience and each other's company. I'm spending precious time with Johnny, we have new friends from Belfast, and this memorable moment is also full of anticipation for the rest of the week.

As we chat, Victoria describes Belfast as *a small, little place where everyone knows one another* – so if we ever go to Belfast, who knows? Imagining being in Belfast and running into someone you met in Spain. Well, sometimes real life is stranger than fiction indeed.

Eventually, though, this pleasant session ends, and we wend our way through the fascinating, narrow and mostly self-shaded streets to our next stop, the Cathedral of Malaga.

It is a short, and mostly level, walk to get to the cathedral. We have already seen the rear side of this massive structure as we walked around the outside prior to heading for the Alcazaba fortress. Paco explains now what we are looking at. Gazing at the back of the cathedral you can see three massive arches, in each a display of religious significance. The arch on the left shows Mary in Ascension, and the arch on the right shows Mary in Assumption. I am not a Catholic, so I may have this wrong, but in one display the angel is above Mary, as she is informed that she will mother the Child of God. In the other instance, Mary is above the angel, because she has Jesus inside her as her unborn son. These are surely things we tourists would not have noticed had Paco not pointed them out to us.

It is one thing to gaze upon this product of mankind's hands, and quite another to imagine the actual building of this monument, the actual steps in the making. What did it look like as it was completed? Could the builders fathom the reach into the future they were building, how lasting it would be? There is no spare ground here. The road meets the building's walls, every inch consumed; no measure of space wasted.

When I was six years old and living in pre-1962 World's Fair in Seattle, I remember seeing a half-built Space Needle. This image has stuck in my mind all these decades. The image was impressed even further as, a couple of years later, I had a pencil sharpener shaped like the Space Needle, and it broke in half. I thought at the time, that's exactly what the actual structure looked like as it was being built. But recognizable as the completed Space Needle is, it does not compare to these ancient structures I am witnessing today. How I would have loved to read an account from some child or worker who witnessed the actual building of these icons.

Outside the cathedral, hundreds of people are lined up at the front entrance, waiting for the Mass to finish.

Paco instructs: "We will wait for Mass to end. Meet me back here in fifteen minutes under this orange tree." What a treat. Cut loose with just the right amount of food and wine in the bloodstream on a beautiful sunny day.

I wander down an adjacent cobblestone street, Johnny following, and am drawn inside a tantalizingly inviting pottery shop. I spy a lemon-colored plate that will end up plaguing my thoughts all week, begging me to purchase it. Instead, I buy a couple of small pottery containers that I will use for keeping jewelry. This will add to my collection begun in Malta, where I purchased small decorative boxes for my treasures back home. Sandstone for Malta, marble for Rome and Athens.

Time flies when you are shopping.

Before I can even think about finding another *baño*, it is time to meet Paco back under the orange tree. "You cannot eat these oranges" Paco explains. "They are too bitter. But they are not all wasted. Malaga sends 30kg of these oranges to the Crown of England each year for the Queen, and now the King, to make marmalade." And again, "Follow me closely."

Paco weaves his way to the front of the line and around the iron gates toward the entrance. I feel conspicuous that we are heading into the cathedral ahead of the couple of hundred people snaking their way down the calle in a long line. Not only are we allowed in first, because we are with Paco, but we are the only people inside the cathedral for at least 20 minutes. I have a vague feeling of what it must be like to be a celebrity and, although I feel uneasy, my weary feet and curious mind are not troubled.

We walk in a large circuitous counterclockwise route around the cathedral and are overwhelmed with the abundance of ornate religious artifacts. It is cool inside, a refuge from the sun, and the stained glass is beautiful. It is quite overwhelming.

As I gaze at acres of some kind of golden artifacts, I wonder, *Is it gold leaf? Is it real gold? How can there be so much gold?*

This is something I have no knowledge of. Just one of a million things to research when I get home. Where did all the gold come from and how was it applied so profusely on all these religious treasures? I had asked myself this same question all the way from Malta, at Christmas 2018, to Greece in July 2019, and to Rome in August of that same year as I visited elaborate and historic cathedrals. It is notable that all this gold from the past has survived time. I suppose it is protected behind all these pointed metal bars and gates, too far from human hands to be soiled, stolen or rubbed away.

This is Queen Isabella and Kind Ferdinand's cathedral, built between 1528 and 1782. You don't need to understand all of it, just feast your eyes.

Paco tells us stories about some of the objects, and later we try to sift out what is true and what is Paco folklore. Although I am not Catholic, I do recognize the object that is the Confessional, but I had never before heard the story of why this is built the way it is. It seems the structure must have a partition between the confessor and the priest, so women will not be able to be amorous with the priest. They can only speak through the grate, nothing more. I suppose, even then, it wasn't the truth that was important as much as it was others' perceptions of what you might have done. Remember, this is Paco's tour, so what Paco says must be true.

One of my favorite items is a small marble seat, worn where the body would rest if someone sat on it for decades on end. Paco tells us this is where what we might call the night watchman would sit with some kind of weapon – perhaps a sling shot? – so he was armed against any cats that might try to come through the cathedral doors. I am glad that my quickly snapped picture on my iPhone 10 captures a decent image. Later, I wonder if the story about the little marble seat and the man keeping the cats out is true, or if it is Paco spicing up the tour for us.

It Started with Malaga

Near the end of the tour, we are guided into the choir area. It reminds me of when my high school choir sang in the Cathedral at Corvey, Germany, back in 1972. I am not expecting to be taken back to that time over fifty years ago. I mention to Paco and the group that I saw something like this all those decades ago in Germany, and in a kind of language communication vortex, Paco emphatically denies that this could be true.

He completely misunderstands me and thinks I said I saw THIS very spot in 1972 and insists, "No, you did not". After a few awkward exchanges, the other members of my group understand that I was talking about another church in another country and that I did see something resembling these choir stalls. In fact, our high school choir had been given the honor of being able to go inside the stalls to sing, something I will never forget.

Later, Johnny recounts that Paco had two other odd misunderstandings with tour members during the day and had been quite insistent in those instances as well. This is a testament to the challenges of language limitations, and a tiny bit to the personality of our tour guide, who makes me jump when he suddenly barks, "Take off those hats!" to two young men who are wearing baseball caps inside the cathedral.

But for our dollar, I have eaten well and experienced wonderful company on a lovely spring afternoon in Malaga. I have witnessed more history than I can absorb, more beautiful art than I can appreciate. I am more than ready for a small siesta back at the apartment.

At 2:43 pm we five pose for a decent selfie, then Johnny and I say goodbye to our new friends, Victoria and Andy from Belfast, and our colorful tour guide, Paco, from We Love Malaga.

Outside, the one completed cathedral tower reaches for the sun while the uncompleted tower keeps everyone guessing as to the real reason it was not finished. One popular story is that the funds to build the missing tower were spent to help the Americans in the War of Independence; an alternative story is that the funds went to build roads in the region. Whatever the truth, we are joining the masses of those who wonder, having now personally set foot in this majestic historic structure.

12

Port Business and a Coincidence

After our epic tour, and still replete with wine and tapas, it's wonderful to get back to our apartment to enjoy a short siesta, Spanish style. It's also delightful to be able to do this so close to all the action. I am in love with both the convenience and comfort of our Calle Victoria temporary home.

This time, even Johnny takes the lift to our floor.

I am absolutely whipped. It is around 3:00 pm, a perfect time for a siesta, and I will drop without one.

I sleep hard and well. I wake up at 4:45 pm, still feeling like I was 'shot at and missed and sh@t at and hit' as my hubby likes to say, but within about an hour of waking, after puttering around in our apartment, we are ready to go again.

It only takes a few minutes to collect what we want to carry. We don't want to rely on the app to get back inside, so we are particularly sure to take the keys. We leave our passports behind, but we have pictures of them on our phones just in case, and we make sure we take only one credit card each in case we are unlucky enough to be pickpocketed, something we've been warned about. I make sure to wear my purse in front of my body and permanently clutch it. I have to say that not once in the entire week do I feel like someone is trying to rob me – perhaps because I have equipped myself with this preventative stance, who knows?

I am ready to leave the evening's activity to Johnny.

"Where do you want to go, kiddo?"

"I was thinking of the port. Is it far?"

"Not far at all. We were nearly there when we met for the tour this morning. I'd love to go down there so I can find my way there and back more easily when I'm by myself."

We head back past the Roman theater, the entrance to the Alcazaba, and the Malaga Museum (which, sadly, I never manage to explore on this trip) down to the garden area along avenue Paseo de la Parque, which follows the portside.

Just fifteen minutes from home, I am reminded of the day's indulgences. "Sorry to say, I need to find a *baño*," I report to Johnny.

"Isn't that one over there in the park?" My gaze follows his and I spot what appears to be a public washroom housed in a green, box-type structure near a playground area.

We cross the road to check it out. I am skeptical of using a public *baño*, so I am not all that disappointed when we see it is locked and closed, apparently out of order.

"You know, Johnny? I'm a lot more comfortable stopping in at McDonald's, even if I have to buy something to get into the can."

"Okay, let's head that way."

I remember that when James and I were in the city of Valetta, Malta, in order to use the McDonald's *baño* (the only place that had one) we had to buy something and then use the code from the receipt to enter the stalls. It's fair enough, I suppose, since the public spaces are so tight and valuable and, as in Japan, this makes a place to sit a marketable commodity. (Maybe I accidentally made a pun on the word commode?) So, when we get to this McDonald's, I go in and walk up to the counter.

"Hola, can I use a *baño* if I buy some *agua*?"

He replies cheerfully and emphatically in broken English, "No, no, no, of course," and he motions toward the stairs going up to the second level.

Ha! Another check mark for Malaga's status as Spain's most hospitable city. It may seem a small thing, but to me this reinforces the fact that we are visiting Malaga at a sweet time when both tourists and the related industry they bring are welcome.

I contrast this with visiting places like Las Vegas, which is surely an example of regional authenticity gone wrong. Nothing about Las Vegas is much about the ground it was built on, or the history that brought it to this day. And to be fair, for the tourist, it probably appears that Las Vegas didn't have a lot to start with, but for what they have built from neon and steel – although at least now it has some good sports teams. (Go, Golden Knights, 2023 Stanley Cup Champions!) So, when you visit Las Vegas and after you scratch the neon surface just a bit, there is not much there but dust and heat, ants and scorpions. Malaga, on the other hand ... well, the more you dig the more is revealed, though like an onion you will find parts that make you cry.

I feel very lucky to experience Malaga at this point in her history, when to the visiting eye, she seems to be full of happy people, both locals and visitors, who just want to go out to visit, eat and sip wine. Those on duty in the serving industry seem happy with their lifestyle and what these times bring for their own hopes and dreams.

I don't know about you, but when I have company coming over, this is mostly when I vacuum my floors. Right? Now that I'm retired, it's a good thing I have occasional guests, because I might not take care of this household chore otherwise. But

Malaga ... Malaga pressure-washes many of its plentiful and beautiful tiled streets every night. I notice this right away, because although it has not rained, there are patches of wet when I go out searching for coffee in the morning. In my short experience to date, it is rare to see a cigarette butt or trash on the streets at all, because this is attended to in a timely manner. To me, this is yet another example of the welcoming attitude, one that shows a healthy pride in what visitors experience and, indeed, in their own home and history.

Bodily needs relieved, we exit and cross a wide, traditional street, busy with cars and buses, unlike the streets we have walked to get to this point. We find ourselves near the Tourist Information Booth and I take note of this resource for later. We had gone a little bit out of our way to stop at McDonald's, but now find ourselves, quite by accident, at a much better spot to access the port promenade from the west end.

Along the seaside they have built a modern pergola-type structure that is flanked on the left by pop-up shops selling crafts, and on the right by the sea itself. As we pass, we see flamenco dancers performing, surrounded by a large circle of onlookers. The modern look here is in sharp contrast to the area from which we have come, so we are seeing another side of Malaga. There is a gentle breeze coming from the ocean.

Johnny and I continue along the wayside, snooping here and there among the stalls, until we eventually reach an area where the path makes a 45-degree turn – and so do we. We see the big colorful cube that marks the Centre Pompidou, and we walk up the ramp to get a closer look. It is much bigger than I had imagined from the pictures. We take a selfie with it in the background, and I snap a shot of Johnny standing in front of it so later we can remember how big the cube is compared to a human.

I have the niggling sense that this is not really Malaga, that Malaga is back in the historical center, but after a while time I warm up to the area. This modern part of the city has been planned well. Johnny and I continue along the upper street above the pier, as we can see the lighthouse in the distance, and we want to see it up close.

A lighthouse is a big part of the history of any town, and not least Malaga. This one, La Farola, was constructed in 1817, replacing a wooden lantern from a hundred years earlier, and has its origins in the time of Queen Isabella.

It is interesting that most lighthouses are prefixed in the masculine and named 'faro', but this is one of two in Spain with the feminine gender 'farola'. I have not yet learned the reason for this, but I have read that this structure may someday be turned into a port exhibition. I do remember that Thomas had written that the lighthouse is a good viewpoint for the port, so we make our way to the very end of the promenade to see for ourselves. At this point in the evening on a Sunday in mid-April, we are the only people there. I take a shadow picture of Johnny and myself against the backdrop of the lighthouse at 8:17 pm, exactly 24 hours since our plane's wheels touched down.

Standing here and surveying the vast seascape, you get a sense of the bona fide business of Malaga – the seaport. We have read that this is one of the most important ports in the Mediterranean and, in fact, we can see a large container ship just arriving.

"Mom, check out that huge ship. It's going to dock here at the port. I wonder what ship it is?"

There are tugs moving the ship to line up with the far pier, but we can't quite make out the name, although we can see it is the Maersk line.

"Maybe we can get a picture of the name if we take a photo with the focus as far out as possible." My prescription glasses help me see long distance, but the ship is too far out.

"Let's try. I know how to look that up on an app and we might be able to see where it's from and where it is going."

In a miracle of global connectivity, I am able to download this app to my phone, while standing at this far point in my world. I suppose the 'ether', where all this stuff comes from, has no particular home, and any place is as good as the next if you have some kind of Wi-Fi or cellular access to it. You just need hold your lips just right and it works.

"Wow, I can't believe this app downloaded with me standing out here." I marvel.

This falls into the 'sometimes things that seem like they should be easy are not, and other times things that seem like they should be difficult are easy' category – like instantly getting Euros out of your bank account while at an ATM 5.300 miles away from home as the crow flies. That seemed even more of a miracle twenty-eight years ago when I did the same at a market in Kuala Lumpur in Malaysia while on a work trip for my college in Canada. (Sadly, that was another one of those stories that never got written!)

Even though my iPhone is ancient, we are able to zoom in and take a photo. This reveals the name of the ship, which is Maersk Hidalgo, call sign 9V5600. Apparently, it originated in Singapore and its last stop was Morocco. The app tells us that it has just arrived at the Port of Malaga, and we can see for ourselves that this is true.

Mentally calculating with hand gestures, Johnny says, "That ship must be bearing at least 2,000 containers. I wonder how much will be loaded here? And will they load some back?"

That's a lot of containers. Will these all be unloaded and discharged throughout Malaga and Spanish parts unknown. By train? By truck? And what exactly IS all that inventory? We can only imagine.

We decide to circle back on the lower promenade and find a place for refreshment and tapas where we can watch the tugs do their work. I am glad to sit. We settle for Cerveceria La Surena, at the very end of the pier, where Johnny has a beer while I order a single-serve bottle of red wine, and we share a plate of *tortillas de camerones* – all for €9.50. I take a picture of the receipt so I can remember where we were for future reference.

We eat and drink gratefully, enjoying the respite from walking. We are surrounded by what appears to be locals, families and children, all enjoying the evening breeze and pleasant weather.

It has been a full day, so after watching the operations of the ship for a while – it is now secured to the port with the boom overhead ready to unload containers – we decide to head back to the apartment. We retrace our route, but now on the lower promenade level, closer to the sea, and eye the huge luxury yachts moored along the pier. We pass several more shops and restaurants and notice one with a life-sized black-and-white cow in the doorway. Johnny wonders out loud what that's all about. It is just one more mystery at the moment.

Leaving the pier, we cross the busy road to walk back along the full length of the Parque de Malaga, and eventually find the crossing in front of the City Hall that will take us to our street.

Johnny says, "Let's get an ice cream, okay?"

"Yes, I'm all in." I take a picture as he orders our treats. I choose the Double Gold Caramel.

Of course, I've known all along that he'll be going off on his own tomorrow, but right now it really hits me how much I'm going to miss him. He is going to be meeting people he doesn't even know tomorrow, for a brand-new job, and has an important presentation to give during the week. I can't imagine what it feels like for him, now that the main purpose for the trip is nigh upon us. This most likely will not be the last time that I can make such a purchase during a walk in Malaga, but it may well be for him.

We cross the wide road in front of Malaga City Hall and retrace our steps back up the calle past the museum, the Alcazaba entrance, and the Roman theater, all now on our right. We confidently make it back to our apartment to freshen up before we head out for a proper dinner.

We had earlier passed El Pimpi, a famous restaurant in the area, and we decide to see if we can get in, although I've heard that you often need to make a reservation. It is now 9:00 pm, an appropriate time to eat in true Spanish style. The restaurant is only a short walk away from the apartment and we have other options on the Plaza if we are not successful.

El Pimpi is at least partly owned by Antonio Banderas, a well-known Spanish actor whom everyone but me seems to know of. It seems the part of my brain that should remember the names of famous movie stars must have been swamped at some stage by other vital information – perhaps the names of all the students I've taught, or the books I've read. Or even by all the places I've lived, totaling over thirty by the time Johnny's dad and I bought our first house when I was just twenty-one. (But that, too, is another story!)

Of course, by the time this week is over, I have looked up Antonio on Wikipedia, and I'll possibly remember who he is for a while – no reflection on him.

The reputation of El Pimpi has preceded it for me, as I have both read about it and seen clips of it on YouTube. I had vowed that since it is close to my apartment I would visit it, and we are in luck. There is about a 10–15-minute wait, but it promises to be well worth it, so we stand in line and take in our surroundings.

As we are waiting to be seated, the people behind us strike up a conversation with us and the fellow asks us where we are from. Washington, I tell him, adding the words 'State' and 'in the Pacific region of the USA'. Being 6,500 miles from home by airplane, I don't assume that people will know where Washington State is.

It Started with Malaga

The fellow, who later tells us he lives in northern Spain, says immediately with a big smile, "I know Spokane, that's where I'm employed!"

"What?" You could knock me over with a feather, perhaps not surprisingly considering what a big day we've had.

"I work for Pyrotech, in Spokane Valley. It's to do with metal powders and connected with Alcan."

"No way, really?" How crazy is that?

"I was supposed to go there, but then Covid hit and the trip was cancelled. Have you been here before?"

"No, this is our first time, but I saw the restaurant on a YouTube so I knew it was a great place to eat. We are so happy to get in tonight. I can't believe you work in Spokane. That is such a coincidence."

"There are four of us who live here in Spain that work there. By the way, El Pimpi is a multi-roomed restaurant, and all of them are worth seeing. You should go in and check around all the different rooms."

"Are you sure?"

They won't mind. We come here a couple of times a year, whenever we are in town."

Johnny acts on the suggestion and I just wait in line to keep our spot, chatting with our new acquaintances.

We end up at different tables in different sections of the restaurant and I never see these two again, but while Johnny and I are waiting for our meal I look the company up on the map and discover that his work site is within four miles of my home. So, I learn something about my own hometown that I did not know while standing in line at a Spanish restaurant! This is just one of the ways in which I learn this is a smaller world than I ever realized, even in Malaga, Spain, a place I had never heard of six weeks ago. In fact, I start to feel like everyone knew about Malaga but me. Was my work head really that far buried in the sand? Ah, the world is a marvelous and large place. I am glad there is always more to learn and experience.

It is an absolute bonus that we managed to get into this famous and popular spot just on a walk by. We use an app to order a daily special, *Campero Pimpi*, grilled red prawns, and chickpea stew, with a beer for Johnny and a *vino tinto* for me. Even after such an epic day, our meal lives up to the standard we have come to expect in Malaga.

As we wait for the waiter to bring the bill, we talk about the food and drink and then broach the subject of the week to come. "Tomorrow should be interesting when we meet Grandma's backgammon friend, Lori."

"Yes, it certainly should be. It's amazing they have known each other online for over twenty years. I never learned how to play backgammon. Are you excited to meet your group in Marbella?"

"For sure, it should be good. I know some of the guys from Switzerland. My presentation is on Thursday. I never knew I had to do it until last Friday, but I'll sort it out. It feels like a test."

"How much time can you spend with Lori and me tomorrow?" My gut wrenches just a bit.

"Well, I'm going to take a taxi back to the airport and the company shuttle will pick me up around 2:00 pm, so I will leave you guys by 1:00 pm at the latest." That's better than I had originally thought, which was that he would leave in the morning. I am grateful for a bit more time.

Finally, we track down the server and ask for our check. For all my Spanish lessons, I still can't bring forward the words to ask for this in Spanish.

Before we leave, Johnny snaps a picture of me in my blue jacket in front of an open window, and although I am not at my best – well, shoot, my hair goes crazy with humidity – he declares I can use it someday on the back of my yet-to-be-written book. I still have the photo, but I don't know if it will end up on the back cover of a book. We will see.

By 11:30 pm we are back at our apartment. I find myself already hoping to return to Malaga another time, but there could never be another first day like this one and we have certainly experienced it with the upmost enthusiasm, curiosity and energy. My bed, at last, is a welcome sight. Fitbit says I have walked 21,687 steps and 9.15 miles. And the week has just begun.

We Meet Lori

True to what we have been told, the warm-up of motors begins at 7:30 am, and if my alarm hadn't woken me, this surely would have. Other plings, bangs and knocks start around 8:00 am. It doesn't bother us and is a rather fascinating front row seat to Malaga's evolution in the 21st century. Johnny notes that the multiple metal tubes swaying from the crane's hook are hovering just above the workers below, but they are so busy they don't seem fazed by the motion above.

I am so happy that Johnny can accompany me to our rendezvous with Loretta, otherwise known as Lori. Lori is my mother's backgammon friend whom she has known online for over twenty years. Lori is the reason why my 88-years-young mother (who lives in Canada) had already known the name Malaga six weeks earlier when I told her what my plans were.

"Malaga?" she had texted. "I have a friend who lives about an hour from there."

I think to myself, *What else have I missed?* Always late to the party.

So now we are going to meet Lori, our date having been organized via text messages some weeks ago.

I am a planner, as you may have guessed if you have read this far. I have often felt that there should be a word or phrase in the English language for the disparity between the vision of ease in plans made ahead and the reality of those plans coming to fruition. Maybe we could think of it as 'Planning Divergence Factor, or Pladifa, for short? I'll be thinking about that for a while, since the phenomenon does arise quite frequently when one is travelling. Indeed, I achieve this state a few times during the rest of the trip.

Johnny and I are too late to have breakfast prior to meeting Lori, and we launch ourselves out of our apartment around 9:45 am. We are feeling a smidge more acclimatized than the previous morning, having accomplished nine miles of adventure on the previous day. We look for a pastry shop with coffee. We see one, the pastry tantalizing La Canasta, but it has a long lineup, so we pass.

Although we have plans to meet Lori at 10:00 am near where we are staying, we have not hashed out an exact spot. Lori has said she will use public parking, and I am worried as to where this might be. I hope I at least get a text from her so we can prevent a big mix-up with the meeting point. I dread this turning into a 'Pladifa'-type situation, but I remind myself that I should have more faith in human nature and ability. After all, I am not solo in this challenge. I have my brilliant son Johnny by my side – and that turns out to be a very good thing.

Somewhere along the wide, tiled calle next to the Roman theatre, we get a message from Lori. It turns out she has parked conveniently near what we now know, after discovering it the previous evening, as The Cube. Unbeknown to us, however, is the fact that the underground area has more than ample parking, so she is already parked and headed in our general direction on foot. Now we just need to find her.

She texts me to ask if I have WhatsApp, because through this app she can track our location if we share it.

This is not the first time in the past few days someone has asked for my WhatsApp contact info. And I don't think I have it. However, Johnny does. He gets Lori's number from me and connects. Soon, they 'see' each other's location and we continue toward the port area from where she is headed.

The Plaza de la Aduana slopes slightly downhill from where it departs Calle Alcazabilla, and a pleasant breeze stirs the warm sea air. We wander along now familiar territory, past the ice cream bar, and along the tiled promenade alongside the Paseo del Parque. The pedestrian walkway borders Malaga's beautifully planted and maintained public gardens, the Parque de Malaga, that lines the avenue that parallels the port which is on the far side. It is a glorious place to meet a new friend. Before long, we spot a smiling blonde woman in a breezy dress waving from a half-block away.

We move toward one another and meet halfway. It feels like a scene in a movie, an epic moment! We three are closing the gap of a long-distance friendship, albeit a couple of generations removed, 6,700 miles around the world, 22 years after it was first made, on a tiled Malaga pedestrian walkway with the taste of salt along with something floral in the air.

Introductions are made, and we all hug.

Lori kisses me on both cheeks and says, "Get used to that. It is how greetings are done in Spain."

Okay then. I can adapt. We pose for a selfie, which I send to my mother back in Penticton, British Columbia. We are nine hours ahead of her, so she is still asleep, but when she wakes, she will be thrilled.

It turns out quite serendipitously that none of us have eaten, and the common need for sustenance provides us with direction. Lori and her husband have a favorite breakfast spot up the Calle Marques de Larios, so we reverse our tracks and head south-west along the garden paths that border the calle.

Lori explains some of the park's features as we are nearing

one of her best-loved features, a circular tribute to all the towns in Malaga province, with tiled plaques around the perimeter. She points out hers for Alcaucín, and we see the one for Marbella. I take a few pictures and later observe that they are all tagged Parque de Malaga. It is beautiful here. I cannot help but consider what impressive foresight it took for the city to build this stunning garden where the port meets the city. It is excellently maintained, and a tourist could ask for nothing better.

Lori, smart lady that she is, is wearing a sleeveless print dress on this warm April day. I have a hunch I could learn a lot about life in Spain from her. She and her husband, Paul, are British, but they bought a house about an hour's drive away from Malaga and moved here ten years ago. My mother has shown me pictures of their place, situated in the countryside among the olive groves, the mountains in the background separating the village from Granada.

I give Lori the package of signature Spokane-made soft peanut brittle I'd brought from home. I offer to carry it for her, but she says it's no problem and stuffs it into her roomy handbag.

We chat happily as we wander along the plant-lined path, dodging the occasional puddle from where a watering hose has leaked. We know that just a few weeks earlier there were torrential and unusual rains, but the weather right now could not be better.

We all share various details about our lives, and Johnny and I talk about what we have seen in the city so far. I get the impression she is keen to be a good welcoming committee and show us around, and although we have already seen some of the city, we don't care if we see some things twice. We just got here, after all. Johnny and I are all eyes agog as we walk along, taking everything in. We finally arrive at the restaurant, which is welcoming and comfortable. We have our pick of the tables. The music is too loud, perhaps to invite attention from the street, but we ask if they will turn it down and they do.

Johnny notes: "This place has a British influence."

Lori, surprised, looks around as if this never crossed her mind and says, "Really? Do you think so? We just feel comfortable here."

Later, we conclude that because she feels so comfortable there and is so familiar with it, she simply doesn't see the British connection. We, being new to it, immediately notice the contrast to the Spanish locales, but we are quite happy to be here regardless and proceed to order some food.

We all decide on French omelets, which we find are outstanding. Ordering coffee is a continuation of our education in coffee Spanish-style, but we end up with Cafe Con Leche, the first time I have used that term. I need two large cups to satisfy my coffee cravings.

The cost, although perhaps a little pricey for Spain, is far less than what we would have expected to pay back home – just €35 euros for the three of us, including second coffees for Johnny and me.

Lori assures us the restrooms are clean and modern, so we climb a flight of stairs for the Ladies room and Johnny continues up an extra flight for the Gents. As we descend, we notice pictures of the Queen on the wall behind the pool table. Yep, definitely a British influence!

When I look it up later, the name of the cafe is 'John Scott', and it is owned by a Swedish company. In a coincidental quirk, I later find out that it was quite appropriate I learned how to order coffee here, as the establishment that had been there previously, Café Central, had been there for over 100 years and had long specialized in coffee. A lot of people were very unhappy when it closed. It may well have been that nasty pandemic that did it in.

Perhaps this controversy is one of the reasons we have our choice of tables – or maybe we are just eating at an odd hour for Spanish custom. Whatever the reason, to us, brand new to the city, it is a lovely spot to share a meal with our new British friend.

❋ ❋ ❋

Appetites satisfied, we wander back toward the Plaza de la Merced, so we can show Lori our apartment and Johnny can do what he needs to do to make his getaway to Marbella on time.

I am fascinated by the butcher shops, and I take some pictures to send to our butcher friend Brent, a friend of my son Jay's, who owns Doug's Homestead, a butcher shop in Kaleden, British Columbia. It is still very early in the morning at home, but I know ever-energetic Brent gets up at the crack of dawn – a good and necessary trait for a butcher.

I am particularly impressed by the large ham legs with the black hooves, which I am told means they are Iberian ham, which is delicious. A bit of research reveals that this kind of ham is very special, as it comes from pigs who feed primarily on acorns, and chestnuts. When I send the photos to Brent, he responds that he will catch the next flight to Spain.

Eventually we make it to the Plaza de La Merced, which I already think of, after less than forty-eight hours, as my neighborhood. Although Lori is aware of Picasso's birthplace on the corner, she did not know that his bronze statue is also here, situated on the end of a bench so those who are so inclined can sit and have their picture taken with him.

I have been waiting for a moment to do this and the time is right. We get a great photo on this beautiful sunny day with the scent of the early-blooming purple jacaranda trees on the breeze.

I mention to Lori that the obelisk in the middle of the Plaza is a memorial built over the bones of forty-nine men (including Robert Boyd, whose name will become more familiar later this week), who died alongside General Jose Maria de Torrijos for trying to overthrow the absolutist regime of Spain's Fernando

VII. They were caught and executed on December 11, 1831. (One particular picture of the plaza, with the purple-blossoming jacarandas and the memorial obelisk, ended up becoming the permanent screensaver on my iPad which then morphed via the works of a graphic artist into the cover for this book.)

The Plaza de La Merced is abuzz with happy people, both locals and tourists, who, by all accounts, simply want to eat and drink and talk. I fit right in, as this will soon be my focus. The entire preparation and execution of this trip has been built on the premise that I would be solo for the days in the middle. And the time is approaching.

The three of us make our way to the apartment and squeeze into the little lift so we can proudly show Lori our temporary home. She loves it, and fiddles with the remote for the air conditioning on our behalf, as we have been unable to make it do much of anything. The weather has been just a smidge on the warm side of perfect, so we haven't tried too hard, but we are appreciative. Johnny packs up only the items he needs for his four days in Marbella.

I am as prepared as I can be for this, but there is no escaping the sense of loss when it is time for him to depart. It is a bonus hug from the universe that I have Lori's company for a while longer this afternoon. We pile into the tiny lift again, now with the added luggage, me eyeing the load limit posted inside. I hold my breath as we descend, math conversions from kilos to pounds bouncing in my brain. With a landing bump, we are back at the lobby level. I tap the buzzer on the wall to unlock the lobby door, as if I had done this every day of my life, and we belch out onto the sidewalk.

We say our goodbyes, then Johnny stops next to one of the building's columns to wait for his Uber to the airport where he will meet with his shuttle to Marbella. I capture a photo of him and his suitcase, and remind myself, *This boy is a grown man. He can take care of himself.*

Lori and I walk away, and I try not to look back too often. But my heartstrings are tugging at my eyeballs, so resistance is hard. As soon as we cross the street, though, the bus stop shelter blocks our view.

Even though he is a grown man with a family of his own, I am still the proud mom of that little boy who has grown into the capable person that he is today. My teaching career took me from Canada to Japan for an entire year, to Singapore and Malaysia for short trips, to California and all around the USA, and then to Europe with my professional organizations. I should not be surprised that my youngest son is following the travel-with-work tradition.

There is one big difference though. My traveling was a means for my brick-and-mortar colleges to reach out in the world. Johnny's company is truly global, based in Switzerland, so he works at home by himself and then travels to clients and company events. It's a completely different model from what I knew for thirty-six years.

14

Kindness Rises Like Cream

"Well? Where shall we go now?" my new friend Lori asks. "We still have the afternoon. I have some things to do tonight, but I have a few hours before I have to drive home."

I am thoroughly enjoying this time, and ripe for exploring whatever there is to see. "I'd be happy to wander back through the historical district and then down toward the port if that's okay. That way, we can end up near where your car is parked. There's a lot of interesting shops along the promenade that I passed by too quickly last night when Johnny and I walked out to the lighthouse. Would that work for you?"

"Sounds great. Paul and I love walking along the port promenade. And I often take my kids there when they're in town. We can wander through the historic district on our way."

"I'm grateful we have more time. Who knows what we might find along the way?" Exploring with Lori feels so natural, as if we are neighbors who have known each other all our lives and are out on the town for the afternoon. A new city to explore … and a new friend. What a gift the universe has offered up to me.

Having decided on our general route, we turn and cross the

plaza. There is a maze of crooked cobblestone streets in the historic district, so we choose a new route down one I don't think I have seen before. Near the corner, we spot an antique store and are drawn to check it out. The ceiling is high and, as we enter, the walls are wide apart. There is one narrow path between piles of curiosities stacked from the floor right up to as far as they won't tumble. Near the back of the store, the walls close in so they are nearly touching each other, forming a narrow hallway to who knows where or what. A person could spend hours in a shop like this, pieces of Malaga history stacked high, each with its own historical scent. You never know what you might find. I browse with curiosity for what qualifies as good old 'junk' and antiques in Spain.

I suddenly remember that Johnny has been looking for a sword-type souvenir for middle boy and I spot something. It looks like a small sword, and it is enclosed in a leather sheath that matches a leather handle.

I'm not sure if Johnny has even had a chance to reach the airport, but he won't be driving, so I text him. "I might have found a small sword for middle son. It looks really authentic." Johnny is quick to respond. "Oh? Hi, that sounds awesome. Can you send me a picture?"

"Okay, it's about 14 inches long and it has its own leather sheath."

As I check it out, though, I grow concerned. I don't think it is a toy. "He wouldn't be able to play with it or really do much with it until he is an adult, but it looks like it is a true souvenir of Spain," I message Johnny. I think to myself maybe this is more a souvenir for my husband than for my grandson. I need to find something special for James who, not least, encouraged me to make this trip.

The daddy Johnny responds tentatively, "Well, I'll text Jane about that. I'll see what she thinks." I slide the casing off and see that the blade is quite sharp and comes to a point at the end.

It Started with Malaga

There's pink grease on the blade. Perhaps to keep it from rusting? It looks a bit like blood at first, but that's just my imagination, right? What kind of grandma am I?

"No, skip it Johnny, I'm sorry. I don't think this is what you are looking for. Are you at the airport yet?"

"Just about. I'll text you later. Thanks for looking."

The reality is that this is an actual real sword or dagger ... I'm not sure what it should be called. But it is certainly far too sharp for a child and, frankly, it looks like it may have been used! I did NOT just make up an excuse to text my son, who departed 15 minutes ago. Did I?

My husband would probably have loved such an artifact as a souvenir, but I fear it might attract some attention in my baggage. It is beautifully worked, both the handle and the case. As I study it further, I begin to worry that it might have too much history – or even ghosts – attached to it.

Now that I've held this historical curio in my hand for five minutes, I begin to sense a mood of darkness. Uh, nope. I lay it down to take a picture and then put it back where I found it. I have just had an intimate moment with a piece of Malaga history about which I will always wonder. Did I project that mood? Or does this weapon have a history I don't want to know about? Maybe we should keep our shopping to the outdoor, crafty-type shops for the rest of the afternoon.

Lori and I wriggle our way back through the musty piles of story-telling treasures to the door and out into the street.

As we wander through Centro Historico, Lori points out to me that, because of the drought, many of the fountains do not have running water in them. I see this to be true over the next several days. There are so many fountains in Malaga, but for now they are all dry. I decide to make my shower just a tad shorter in the morning.

Eventually we wander back through the Parque de Malaga. There is a small stream, too big to step over, alongside our path and this, at least, is running. We are close to the sea, but this must be fresh water. The sun seems to be perpetually turned on and the sky is a palate of blues.

"I really love this park. What a great idea the city had to build this. If I come back some day, I could just sit on a bench here and people-watch." Lori agrees and says she and Paul like to come to town and hang out in this area, too, and that she has brought both her son and her daughter here from time to time when they have come to visit from England.

Along the modern-looking port promenade, I find a shop where I had seen the small, multi-colored plate on Sunday while Johnny and I were exploring. It is decorated with a Picasso-stylized young woman. I buy it to fill the last empty spot on the shelves James built to frame our electric fireplace in our master bedroom back at home. The last plate I'd bought had come from Alaska while hubby and I were on a cruise for our 25th wedding anniversary exactly one year ago. While I don't regret that we made that water journey together, even though we both got Covid for the first time at the end of it, that cruise was the polar opposite of being in Malaga and experiencing all this history and culture.

Lori and I have refreshments at the port, me a glass of *vino blanco*, and she something soft as she must soon drive for over an hour to get home. Her son is flying in tomorrow and as an accomplished baker and cake decorator she has plans to create something awesome this evening to welcome him. Sipping my wine, we share more than a few stories as if we have known each other forever and are just catching up. I feel I have made a true friend. She invites me to come and stay at her place sometime. She shares pictures of a beautiful apartment in her basement that opens outside to a pool that she and her husband Paul added after they bought the place. How did I get so lucky?

I declare I will indeed come back some time and take it in all over again – perhaps to enjoy this next visit to Spain at a bit of a slower pace. I say this as a courtesy, but in the back of my mind I am already grasping for a good excuse to actually do it. We hug at The Cube, take a selfie, and then she disappears through the entrance to the carpark. I'm left standing there, frizzy hair tossed by the wind, hoping with all sincerity that this is not the last time I meet her in person.

🌸 🌸 🌸

As I walk home, I reflect on my first Monday in Malaga. I consider the blessedness of the birth of a new friendship, particularly one with no requirement to compare any political notes.

My mind drifts to this tricky subject. There is a voice inside me that wants to talk it out, but in everyday life it seems there is always someone to tell me I am wrong, interrupting me before my first thoughts on the topic are complete.

I believe the media is the culprit. I have all but stopped following political news broadcasts, with no loss at all to my well-being. The essential highlights are unavoidable on my devices as it is. I don't need to seek out any more than that.

It's my belief that most people have a lot more in common than not, but it does not seem to serve the powers that be for us to think so. That's what living in the USA, the country of my birth, these past twenty years has taught me. Canada taught me something, too, as did Japan, but those are the stories I never wrote, and the U.S. state in which I was born, Washington, is my home base these days. (Note here that the Los Angeles Dodgers are my new favorite baseball team, the Seattle Mariners coming third after the Toronto Blue Jays!)

But back to the news. If there is a storm on the radar, I want to hear about it. If a hero saves a victim in need, I cheer. If someone achieves an inspirational milestone, I want to hear about it. Yes, if Kate conquers her cancer, I will be happy for her.

What does *not* add value to my life – the one in which there are no guarantees – is a relentless pounding of negativity and a crescendo of constant fear that is all what we get from following politics these days. I do not believe that my neighbor, who may or may not vote for the same candidate as me, is someone who will run me over, rather than help, if my car breaks down on the side of the road. Or deny me a plant shoot from their garden if I am expanding mine.

We all have hopes, and dreams, and reasons why we believe what we believe. But at the heart of it, we all want the same things. Trouble is, you can't find a place to talk about real issues anymore. Misunderstandings build, fears grow more horrific, and the gap between humanity widens. There are things we need to know, of course there are, but *please* just give me the facts, and let me decide for myself if I need to move to higher ground.

By now I have read enough about Spain's history to know that this country has been far from exempt when it comes to voices being silenced. History is inescapable.

'Oh no, I've said too much. I haven't said enough.' The words of an R.E.M. song James and I love to play in our room with the red flamenco dancer, and sing when we drink tequila, comes to mind.

Does history repeat itself again and again until we are forced to learn? It is not an original thought, and maybe that's why we don't take the question seriously. But I have waxed too philosophical, and I hope I have not lost you! What *was* that wine I drank at the port?

Still, these questions lurk in my fuzzy head, both tainting and inspiring my next step, which is the urge to buy a bottle of Malaga wine and head to my apartment for a siesta.

I have just experienced the goodness of another human being, the willingness to befriend and be part of something akin to a cosmic essence of kindness. It has been an incredibly special occasion and one that I will cherish. My life and my whole being is all the better for having met Lori, who gave of her day to a near stranger and her son Johnny.

I take heart that in this world good will prevail after all, no matter how hard the alternative pushes.

Okay, I've said my piece as best I can, and with the best of intentions.

My last picture of the day with Lori was taken at 3:01 pm.

15

Victoria's Secret Meeting Place

Truly alone for the first time, I make my way back along the port, the Parque Malaga, the wide tiled calle past the University of Malaga, the Museum of Malaga, the Alcazaba entrance, the Roman theatre, and El Pimpi. By now I am in sight of my familiar building with the red brick shape on the side where once another building stood.

I imagine I will relax in my cozy apartment and sip a glass of the bottle of Malaga wine I'd bought. My fridge is empty but for the bottles of water I purchased at the Indian food takeout. If I was going to be living here longer, I would be eating from that takeout as the smells emanating from it are delicious, but there are just too many other options, and I am in Spain, after all. I want to try *Spanish* food.

I cross the street, offering a nod and a smile to the proprietor of the antique store at the street level of my building, who has a fan blowing cool air in from his open doorway. I open the outer lobby door with my key and head for the lift.

Back at the apartment, tiredness hits me like a ton of bricks. It is definitely time for a siesta. But before I fall asleep, I decide to create a WhatsApp account – and guess what? It seems I already created one five years ago and have never used it since.

The sound of the workers and machines outdoors does not bother me at all, and it's amazing how much better I feel after an hour or two of sleep. My feet no longer hurt, and I am ready for another adventure.

Tonight is the evening tapas tour, and I feel sufficiently adjusted to being on my own to be able to look forward to meeting a group of new people and exploring new places. The *Genuine Malaga Wine and Tapas Tour* by Spain Food Sherpas begins at 6:00 pm and we are to meet at Calle Marques de Larios, 18, to start. It will end near the Plaza de la Merced, near my apartment, around 9:00 pm. Perfect.

By now I am confident I can find the place and Google Map indicates it is near the intersection Johnny and I used yesterday to cross over to the port. I wander in that direction, still not 100% sure of where all the little streets twist here and there, but knowing I will get to the spot eventually, which I do.

This is the first time I have attempted to meet with someone on my own and on arrival, I can't see a single sign of any group resembling a tour. The address seems to be a Victoria's Secret store! Panic washes over me, jolting me out of my prior contented mood.

Perhaps my error is in arriving early? I spot one young woman looking at her phone as if she might be checking an address.

"Are you waiting for a tour?" Her eyes widen as she looks up from her device to check me out and bolts in the other direction. I assume that my English startled her. I feel bad to be that person she is afraid of.

And then I just feel lost. Is another case of 'pladifa' rearing its head already?

I suspect I resemble a deer in the headlights myself for ten

It Started with Malaga

minutes or so, because while there are many people coming and going, not a single soul looks like they are there for a tour.

I frantically consult various resources on my phone, my map, my ticket, my email about the tour, and check inside the store just in case, and finally I see two ladies standing nearby looking as lost as I feel.

"Are you waiting for a tour?"

"Yes, we are, and you? The tapas tour?" Thank goodness. This pair, who are from Yorkshire, are indeed waiting for the same tour.

"We've been wondering the same thing. Where is everyone? This is where our phone led us." They introduce themselves as Sandy and Sue, and for once I remember the names for five minutes after learning them.

"Well, at least there are three of us now," says Sue. Finally, someone besides me is dressed in slacks and a shirt. I am wearing my blue jacket as usual, and it seems they had thought I might be the guide.

The real guide turns out to be Gabbi, who shows up with a clipboard, cool and fresh in her pretty sleeveless dress, and right on the dot of 6:00 pm. She assures us we are in the right place. We suggest that it would be helpful if there was a sign to indicate this was the tour starting point. A poster, perhaps – or anything at all.

Gabbi tosses her blonde hair and chuckles. "We're considering moving the start point to the tourist information booth across the street, but that hasn't happened yet." She counts her flock. "We're missing two. Does anyone know where they are?" Another tour go-er says, "Those two are coming from the beach, so they might be late. They are trying to get here, though. Can we wait a few minutes?"

Sue is noticeably irked. When the tardy two show up, ten minutes later, and still dragging a sandy beach towel which they try to stuff into a bag, Sue is not shy at coming forward. "That's the way it is with the young people these days, they just think everyone should wait for them," she complains.

Sandy: "It's true, but just let it go."

Sue: "Well, I think we should have left without them ..." It takes a while for her to get over this, but the wine helps.

The next day I learn that anybody who has been in Malaga for more than a day knows that almost all the tours start at Victoria's Secret. I am happy to be informed of this, but it would have been less unsettling if there had been something written aside from just the address. Being from the states, I am not used to Spanish-style addresses, and it takes just a split second to flip from being confident that I'm in the right place, to being certain that I am not. My stomach juices are the tell.

Right now, though, I am ready for the wine part of the tour and am getting chatty with Sandy and Sue, if not yet the seven other people who will be my companions for the evening.

Everyone finally accounted for, we traipse off like geese following the gander to the first stop – the oldest wine bar in Malaga. Gabbi tells us it is 180 years old and so well known to the locals that it doesn't even have a name outside the door. I imagine the changes these walls have seen over time, the people coming and going for all occasions. This is the Antiqua Casa de Guardia, a bustling place where we are served three kinds of the traditional sweet wine of Malaga. The wine is decanted from large brown barrels and served by happy mustached men in white aprons.

We stand at tables at the street end of the tavern, sipping the wine and sampling green olive, sardine and pearl onion tapas on skewers.

The wine is served at room temperature and has an interesting flavor. I find myself longing for an ice cube in each, but it is better than some of the expensive dessert wines I have tasted back home. Maybe I could acquire a taste for it. I enthusiastically down the sardine-wrapped olives. At home, 6:30 pm would be dinner time, but here in Malaga it is just time for a tapas snack.

There are entrances on three sides of the bar, which is probably not as small as it feels but is so filled with people it seems cramped. The flow of people in and out on this warm spring evening is constant.

Sue disappears for a bit to find the *baño*. I am surprised that I don't feel the need, but figure that all the walking today has evaporated any extra bodily fluids right out through my skin. It is good that this is our first stop, I muse, since it is the most famous and the most important wine bar in the history of Malaga, but as the night goes on, I will be begging to sit down.

We manage to pose for a group photo, and I hand Gabbi my phone so I get one, too, as sadly, most people never share the photos they take on their phone when they say they will. At one stage I notice the time is 6:37 pm. Back home it is 3:37 in the morning and everyone is asleep. Here in Spain, I am just getting warmed up for the evening's adventures.

I capture a couple of photos of the barrels and the tile work as we exit out the back door, on to our next stop. Naturally, a couple of people start off in the wrong direction and need to be herded back. "This way, please!" hollers Gabbi, and the goose line threads forward, with Sue, Sandy and me near the front.

We pass the market, and I think to myself, *Ah, so this is where it is!* I am really looking forward to visiting it, but this is part of Thursday's plan.

Following along, we reach the next restaurant, Mesón Donde Carlos, and I realize I have not paid much attention to where we are going. This middle stop is on the outskirts of the historic area as I know it. Inside, we are seated at a long table and offered a type of vermouth that is foreign to any vermouth I have ever tasted. It is tasty enough, nicer than I expected, although not necessarily something I would have sought out.

I am trying to take it all in, as I don't want to forget anything, but the more I experience, the harder it gets.

I need a word to describe what I decide is 'sensory input overload' but it comes in degrees, so I also need a way to measure this condition. Being on the cusp of 69, I continually experience learning, unlearning and learning again, on an increasingly notable basis. My brain doesn't ask me what should stay and what should get sloughed off; it just does it, sometimes leaving me in a memory vacuum. I'm sure it has nothing to do with my bad DNA and my twin APOE4 genes – which put me at an increased risk of Alzheimer's – or at least, I hope not. I choose to be optimistic.

I decide am going to make my new word 'sensoload' and I am going to rank it on a scale of 1 to 10, with 10 being the most egregious instances of forgetting or not retaining information, and 1 being the least.

As I sample the vermouth, I experience *sensoload*. I can taste the sample in the moment, but later I cannot recall the flavors. As vermouth is not all that important in the grand scheme of things, I rank it at 1 for the flavor.

As time goes on, I chat with more members of the group, each increasingly friendly the more we imbibe, though Sue is still irked. I discover that they all, except for myself, are from England. We have several more tapas, in the form of olives, ham and cheese, and are offered another type of wine. This time I choose a *tinto*.

At the third stop, where unfortunately I do not make a note of the name, there is a mix-up with the seating for our table and we wait a couple of minutes while they find us a bigger table. By now, everyone is jolly well on their way to being relaxed and even Sue has finally forgotten her irritation.

Because everyone else is with someone, I wait until everyone is seated so I won't mess up the plans for friends to sit together. It doesn't matter to me who I sit next to as I can chat with anyone – and I do. I need to be nudged on more than one occasion while deep in conversation with the person on my left, when the smiling waiter is waiting to hand me something. We are served a kind of creamy soup and are offered yet another variety of wine, and again I choose a *tinto*.

This is not intended to be a historical tour, but along the way Gabbi mentions this and that, and we see a lot of interesting shops selling flamenco dresses, pearls and all sorts of Spanish treasures. Somewhere along the way I spot another large plastic cow in the entrance to a shop. I snap a shot for Johnny so I can text him and explain that the cow is the icon for a trendy but inexpensive curiosity shop for all ages called *Ale-Hop*, which later research reveals is based out of Valencia, not a dairy. It turns out that in addition to laying claim to being the most photographed cow in the world, since 2001 when the family business was founded, there are 250 shops across Spain with another 55 in Portugal, Italy, and Croatia. It *was* the only cow I photographed in Spain!

The late afternoon has arrived at the 'golden hour', just before sunset. The city is beautiful and as we cross Calle Marques de Larios again and amble through the Plaza de la Constitucion, the light is perfect for photos. My entrepreneurial nature is piqued, and I suggest to Gabbi that they plan a tour for this time of the day that takes in strategic points for photography opportunities in this magical golden light.

She says she will mention it to her boss, then gives me her card and asks me to contact her later to talk about it. Maybe the entrepreneur in me just wants to find a job here! Later I reflect that her tour company seems to have enough going on and doesn't need new strategies to pull in customers, as from what I can see they have a steady flow already, so I never do get back to her.

I can see we are heading as promised in the direction of my corner of town near the Plaza de la Merced, and, in fact, the last stop is just a short distance away from the corner opposite Calle Victoria. This is El Chinitas and it turns out to be the most comfortable of the evening's venues. It is too early for the dinner crowd, so we have the place to ourselves and can relax.

Here we are wined and fed a full meal – and it is delicious. This time, the wine is passed around by the bottle, with these being replenished as needed, and several courses of food are served. I regret I did not take photos of them all.

I pass the time having a conversation with the self-proclaimed nerd on my left about my earlier woes trying to use a popular blogging platform prior to the trip. He knows all about it, and says the platform was its own worst enemy when they stuffed it with too many options. More often than not, the new user is overwhelmed and gives up. His buddies chide him a bit for bringing the topic of work into their fun night out. I have to take the blame for starting that conversation, but I learned something. I'm not the only one overwhelmed by that particular platform.

By now it feels like we're just one big happy family enjoying a special occasion together – and after all that wine, for just these few hours we are. The evening tapas tour has been a success.

It is 7:37 pm when we enter the restaurant and, somehow, suddenly it is 8:57 pm and the tour is over. By now I am confident in finding my way back to my Plaza, and I bid farewell to my companions and set off happily. By the time I cross the Plaza de la Merced, it is just after 9:00 pm and the plaza is beginning to buzz with activity.

I am ready for my apartment. Tonight, I start my habit of having a cup of the lemon-ginger tea I've brought from home and a piece of Spokandy, the local hometown mint I picked up at Seattle airport. I PJ up and fall into bed to catch up on emails and WhatsApp messages and make notes about my day – which feels like three packed into one. I check my Fitbit and see that today I have walked 18,009 steps and 7.5 miles!

Tea drained, I confirm the location and time – 10:00 am – to meet for tomorrow's vineyard tour and set my alarm on both my phone and my iPad to be doubly safe. No sleeping in for me.

Johnny has texted me a shot of his room's ocean view with the words, "I made it". I send a thumbs up.

16

A Visit to a Pretty Vineyard

I have been sapping my energy to the nth degree these past few days, trying to take in as much as I can. A pattern is evolving: siesta in the afternoon, eat dinner at 9:00 pm, go to bed late, review plans for the next day. Then, if I wake up in the middle of my night, it is a good time to chat with people back home – when it is their evening and my 3:00 am.

If I can't sleep, sometimes I write in my journal. In the morning, I often wake up five minutes before my alarms go off.

I surmise that even if my alarms didn't go off, the noise of twenty workers, one giant crane and some sort of impact drill will wake me. I try to count the laborers one day, some barely visible even below the rebar down in the looming hole. Pling, pling, bang … something pounds into a rock somewhere. I resist an urge to wave at the crane operator, whose vehicle is balanced on a narrow ledge across the gaping hole, its large hook filled with cargo sometimes dangling not far from my balcony.

The shower is modern, concrete and glass. At first, I think there is no overhead fixture and assume I will have to make do with the handheld showerhead that clips to the wall at waist height. In a 'blink' this takes me back to my days in Japan where

I sat on a low stool to shower. Today, I turn a mysterious knob and am instantly rained upon from the ceiling. The water is cold at first, so now I am really awake. I choose to wear something that goes with my blue jacket again today.

The Brunch-It restaurant has coffee-to-go ready and I grab a cup of cafe-con-leche to drink on my way, but otherwise I do not eat before the tour as I worry about getting carsick.

Feeling more familiar with the area by now, I opt not to take the most direct route to the Plaza Marina where the group will meet in front of the Tourist Information booth. Five minutes in, it dawns on me that this might have been a mistake. Some streets look familiar, others not so much. All I can do is walk in what I think is the correct direction and hope for the best. I have a moment of panic when by 9:50 am my surroundings don't look as familiar as they should.

Dang! I should have just gone via the familiar route. Instead, I have made things difficult for myself. I have just ten minutes to not be late. Finally, the tiny calle I'm on emerges adjacent to the main street, Calle de Larios. At the foot of this famous street, just a few steps away, a large crosswalk leads directly to the Tourist Information Booth. It takes me just six minutes to reach it. Another case of 'pladifa' has been nipped in the bud. Phew.

I meet the other participants, who are already waiting at the meeting point – all women, and *all* in light and breezy dresses. One of these is a perfect lemon color with a green leaf print. As for me, I have my blue jacket with pockets, which will keep me from losing my phone.

There are eight of us, including the driver, among them two cousins who are close to my age. One has lived in the area for 31 years and the other visits frequently from England. What fun to be able to do that. There are four other young ladies from the United States, but from further east; one is from Alabama and the other three are from Minnesota.

We head underground to a giant car park. After a small delay while I search for bathroom facilities in a sketchy location, the driver assuring me that they can wait, we load ourselves into the air-conditioned van for the 45-minute drive to the hills.

The cousins have claimed the front seat for the same reasons I would have, a history of car sickness. I sit in the second-row middle seat and there are just two of us in a spot made for three, so it is quite comfortable. With the AC on just enough, I am happy to say my stomach does not give me grief, even on the winding paved roads or the bumpy dirt ones we encounter as we get closer to our destination.

This was going to be a crucial factor in my enjoyment of the day. I had been worried that the situation might change with the consumption of food and drink, but I am happy to say things remain trouble-free. I make sure not to fiddle with my phone or try to post anything while traveling and decide our guide, Laura, is a pretty good driver.

All my family know I am a nervous passenger, and they quietly forgive me for my quirk. In order to explain, a slice of yet another unwritten story begs for a shoo-in here:

🌸 🌸 🌸

Four years ago, I accompanied Johnny and his family on a road trip, trailing behind in my own vehicle as I get car sick in the back seat, for what should have been a fun weekend. When we all lived in the desert, everything was at least 70 miles away. The theme park known as Six Flags isn't necessarily my cup of tea, but I had agreed to go along to help with the little ones who were too small to ride the roller coasters.

We stopped en route for a while, because Johnny and family were thinking of buying a new car and they wanted to test-drive a white SUV we saw at a car dealer. It was near dusk and dinnertime by the time we were done, so we decided to stop at Outback, a steakhouse just one freeway entrance further along our route. As we accessed the freeway ramp to continue to the dinner stop, eldest girl, who had decided to travel with grandma after the stop for the test-drive said, "Let's say a prayer for all the people driving on the road …" and proceeded to recite a short prayer. We both said "Amen".

Within a few seconds, as we were travelling well behind the pack, Johnny and family were lost in a blur of red taillights.

A black car whipped by me on the left and was soon up with the pack. The car took the far left of three lanes, then passed a car in the middle lane, then cut back in too soon. This sent the car in the middle lane into the driver's side of the SUV in the far-right lane – and that car was my son's.

As this was happening, I was screaming, "NO, NO, NO!" Then I stopped, because eldest girl was in the back seat, and I didn't want to make this more traumatic for her than it already was.

I'll never forget the sound of eldest girl blurting out "That's my family!" as we both watched the scene ahead of us unfold.

As Johnny's car lost steering and headed for the dust, it rolled three times, blew out all the windows – there was glass and personal belongings strewn for 200 yards – and came to rest upside down with everyone hanging from the roof by their seat belts.

I didn't know it at the time, but Jane was in the back seat with the two-year-old middle boy and five-month-old littlest, still buckled in their safety seats.

I drove around the scene and pull over on the shoulder. Shaking in every cell of my body, I called 911. The people on the end of the line were hopeless. For all I knew, I had just seen my son and his family die. Fortunately, several other people also called it in, so my frantic call was not all the rescue team had to go on.

From behind me, safely belted in her car seat, eldest girl, who had somehow been able to turn and look directly back at the scene from her seat, said calmly, "It's okay, Grandma, they're all out."

Johnny and Jane had been able to crawl out of the completely wrecked vehicle and quickly release the kids.

The front passenger area, where Jane *would* have been if eldest had been with them instead of me, was totally crushed. There were cuts, bruises and sore joints, and the kids were flown off by helicopter to Children's Hospital of Los Angeles to be on the safe side, but fortunately, there was no serious injury.

The next week, they went back and bought the car they had test-driven 15 minutes before the accident.

Ever since witnessing this, I have had my own post-traumatic stress response to traffic, particularly when a vehicle is turning in or out of a lane ahead of me. Even four years later, I have a heart-pounding physical reaction just recalling the moment from the safety of my home as I write this, even though I know it all ended well.

Ya, I am still a nervous passenger.

🍇 🍇 🍇

When I attest to the safe driving skills of our guide Laura, it means I am truly impressed. Not only can she drive well enough to keep me comfortable and all of us safe, but she also chats the entire way about the history of vineyards and the wine industry around Malaga all the way back to the Phoenicians.

I remember this much.

In the beginning, the purpose of wine was simply to make the water safe for drinking. Water was not abundant in Andalusia, and what was there did not run as freely or abundantly as was required to keep it fresh. Early wine was bitter and stinky but was tolerated for serving as an antiseptic. In fact, Laura explains, to drink the ancient wine you would have needed to plug your nose. Far from being a pleasant accompaniment to a nice dinner, wine was used by the Romans – and, indeed, peoples all over the world – purely to sanitize the water.

Romans had the technology to build aqueducts and this helped ensure that vineyards grew abundantly in the region. Indeed, vineyards were so important to the Romans that the nearby city of Ronda had its own coin imprinted with images of grapes.

By the mid-1800s, a blight caused by the grape phylloxera insect, which originated in England and was transferred in the roots of vine plants by ship from the Americas, had resulted in huge upheaval to the industry.

"Vine roots had been transported back and forth for 400 years, so why did the blight suddenly take hold in the mid-1800s?" Laura queries.

None of us have an answer. Not even a guess.

"Well, the bug that ate the roots had a life span of three months, and prior to 1850 the time to cross the 'pond' took four months. With the invention of the steam engine, it took two weeks, so the little blighters were still alive and well when they arrived and thus destroyed all the vines in Europe."

This is just a tiny piece of what she tells us, but my *sensoload* kicks in and, although I listen intently, I can't keep up. I gaze out the window as we swoosh by mile after mile of rolling hills planted with olive trees as far as the eye can see.

After 45 minutes of driving, we arrive at our remote location. I am refreshed to be out in Spain's countryside. Large concrete trestles, perhaps the same ones I had seen from the plane, are incongruous in the scene that is acres of vineyards surrounded by lemon groves. The bright green of the vines, yellow lemons and the stunning blue sky contrast sharply with the brown earth.

We climb out and Laura offers us umbrellas, sunscreen and water, as it is quite warm now. I take some water, and belatedly realize how nice the umbrella would have been for protection from the sun as she launches into more of the history of wine.

(Tip: When the guide suggests an umbrella for shade, there must surely be a good reason to take one.)

Apparently, our pretty little vineyard was founded by two brothers who reclaimed the land and converted it back to grapes from the lemon groves. It rests on a gently rolling hillside, perfect for the red grapes that are grown here. The surface of the fields is clay, but the protected roots grow abundantly in the rich soil about a meter down. Laura tells us that the red grapes like the slope because Mother Nature wants them to grow up tough, and to grow long roots that will fight for the water. She also wants them to learn to shiver at night and sweat in the day, so this particular variety can only be grown at specific elevations where the temperature swings from day to night are just right. All of this makes for good skins, which are used for the *'tinto'* part of the process that turns the wine red.

The white grape crops are off in the distance, lazily spanning a flat field. White grape skins don't factor in the final product, so they don't need to get tough.

It strikes me as ironic that I had to come all the way to Spain to learn these delightful facts. I hope I will remember them correctly. But then again, I have never before met anyone like Laura, who is training to be a certified wine sommelier specializing in all aspects of wine and food pairing. I am grateful that she is sharing her passion with us today.

The air smells like honey from the flowers coming into bloom and the thousands of lemons that drip from the trees lining the vineyard. A trendy insect 'hotel' sits at the top of the hill encouraging the right kinds of flying things to frequent this organic plot. After a walk around among the various types of grapevines and a fascinating lesson on wine growing, we head back to the van.

Laura says the wine cellar, 'Bodegas Perez Hidalgo C. B.', where we will enjoy the tasting is just five minutes away. If I am going to be car sick, it will be now. We wind through one country lane after another, then into the village, where the streets have been formed from ancient goat trails. We arrive at the 'white houses village' of Alora. I check my phone and see that the journey took more like fifteen minutes than five. I need the *baño*!

Laura leads the group to a cozy and quaint setting right in the wine cellar where they make the wine. Here we are presented with the most delicious wine pairings I have ever experienced. We eight ladies, quite formal with each other until now, open up considerably while supping samples of six different wines matched with the most perfect accompanying tapas. It is lovely.

In the midst of it all, I become Instagram friends with the four young American women, Stephanie, Ashley, Sophia, and Angela, who now 'follow' me – and me them. My grandson, Peter, had told me I needed Instagram, and now Ashley helps me with my settings so I can advance my understanding of how it all works.

Now thoroughly loosened up, several of us confess to Ashley – who is the one wearing the lemon-and-leaves print dress – that we are jealous of her perfect choice for the day. She says she picked it up at a Malaga store, off the bargain rack. What luck!

Chatting like the slightly drunk happy people we have all become, apart from the driver, of course, the trip home to Malaga seems to take next to no time.

Back at the drop-off point, we take a selfie, and I then confidently meander back to what has become home where I conk out for a two-and-a-half-hour nap.

17

Friendships in the Moment

When I wake, the workers and their corresponding noises have disappeared. I peer out over my small balcony to see if there is any noticeable change below. It occurs to me that the six giant cylinders spanning the massive hole are not, as I first assumed, pipes for electrical or water. Duh, these are some kind of giant presses, several feet in diameter, spanning the project widthwise, and this is what is keeping the walls from caving in. Walls upon which my six- or seven-floor apartment building is directly resting.

The same is true on the other side of the project, where there is a massive multi-floor apartment building. The realization gives me a sensation of vertigo, and I go back inside, locking the patio door behind me – against what, I do not know. It would be impossible to access the room from outside, being four floors up.

My laptop is plugged in and resting on the glass tabletop just inside the door, and I take care not to trip over the cord. My Surface Pro has not had much attention these past few days. I had thought I would use it for keeping my journal, but last night I had written a whole chapter on my phone. It is going to be full of typos. I sit and type for a while, jotting down the events of the past few days.

I get a text from one of my young wine tour friends and they ask if I remember where the rooftop bar is that the guide recommended. I don't, but I text Thomas, who responds with a list of good choices, and I forward it to them. They thank me and say if they find a good spot they will let me know and maybe I can join them. There is some kind of sports activity happening tonight and they are hoping to catch that on the local station, too. I smile to myself, happy that I have connected with this youthful energy and that I am now more *with it*, with my very own Instagram account and 'followers'. I'll need to be creative and post now and then, I guess.

My stomach talks to me a bit and I realize that I have only eaten tapas, albeit generous in quantity, for the entire day. It seems as if all I have done is eat and drink since I arrived in Spain. I have quickly adapted to the siesta custom and the habit of eating later in the evening. Malaga seems to pull me in that direction so easily, as if some sort of Malaga-based clock activated in my brain when I stepped out of the airport, just as my phone changed time zones when I set it to Barcelona time.

It is just Tuesday night, and I am torn between the pleasant feeling of having my long-made plans come to fruition, and the uneasy feeling that time is passing too fast to take it all in.

I am rested from my siesta and the sky is darkening, the air cooling a bit. It is surely time to enjoy an evening meal, Spanish-style. It is perfect timing, just 9:00 pm.

The odd little lift is becoming familiar to me now and I exit my apartment building with confidence, tapping the button on the wall to unlock the outer door just in time for me to reach it instead of fumbling with the key. In just three days I have developed a comforting sense of belonging. I no longer imagine that people will think it odd that this woman emanating *soy de norte americana* exits in her blue jacket and inevitable black pants looking like she has business to attend to. I always try to look like I know what I am doing, even when I don't.

Outside, my temporary neighborhood, complete with jacaranda trees and obelisk, has come alive as if it has popped out of the screensaver image that I set up on my iPad a few weeks back. Tonight brings me to a moment I have been visualizing for weeks. This is when I finally get to experience dinner on the Plaza de la Merced.

Being a Tuesday night, the Plaza is buzzing, but not so much that I fear I will not find a seat.

Although the little tapas restaurants are visually separate establishments, it appears some may be from a common chain, as I see the words '100 Montaditos' on some of the sandwich boards boasting menus. As I expect to have a similar taste and value no matter which place I choose, I am selecting from the half dozen or so establishments by which one offers the most advantageous seat for one person. About halfway down the promenade, I am in luck!

There is an empty table with a Plaza-facing view, and next to it are a couple of ladies who look like they might be chatty. I am still unused to dining alone, and I want to have the opportunity to chat with a fellow diner, so I make a beeline for that seat.

I sit down and scan the menu. The chicken Caesar salad looks good, especially with a tapa order of garlic shrimp, this latter becoming my signature order along this strip of eateries.

The ladies, who are from England, are polite but not at all chatty, and as they are finished eating they soon leave. Oh, well. I can people-watch. I order white wine instead of my usual red, and now that I am *educated* on Spanish white, I enjoy it immensely.

After a few minutes, another female patron takes a seat at the next table and after she orders I strike up a conversation. Her name is Carrie, and she is all the way from Australia. It dawns on me that she would have traveled in the opposite direction around the globe to arrive at this place. This is her first solo trip since her husband passed away a year-and-a-half ago. She plans to meet her daughter and her grandson in Barcelona in a few days' time. They had been together in Switzerland a few days ago, introducing the two-and-a-half-year-old grandson to her late husband's family, and she shows me a photo on her phone of the group at a picnic table in the Swiss Alps.

We share stories over a glass of wine and I have a feeling she, too, is happy to have someone to chat with over dinner. When dinner is finished, and she gets up to leave, she gives me a tight hug. I have told her I am writing a travel journal, and she has expressed interest in reading it, but although I share my email address on a napkin, I do not hear from her again.

It seems Malaga has plenty of women travelling solo or in groups, and although there may be men doing the same, I probably wouldn't strike up a conversation lest I give the wrong impression, so I can't really say. I am learning, however, that solo travel is a 'thing' – something I have never considered before. As for me, I can think of a few friends I would like to bring back with me, though they are all so different from each other I'd probably have to bring them one at a time. It seems impossible that even with all I can pack into these seven days, after all the study and planning, this could be my only trip to Spain. Would I come back solo if it were the only way?

Meanwhile, the night is beautiful, the air sweet, and the jacarandas are starting to bloom. I look out at the soft darkness of the Plaza and know that this is one of those moments I will step back into from the future, wishing I were here. In a kind of brain boomerang I leap forward and then back again in time to my seat.

I am sad that I know it can't last, but in this moment I am very satisfied to be here. Malaga is everything I expected and more. But this is, after all, only the evening of Day Three, and tomorrow marks the halfway point.

Now that I have Instagram, I text my virtual guide, Thomas, to report on my success at finding dinner in the Plaza. Now that he is only an hour out of my time zone in England, he gets my message at a reasonable hour. He is still up, and texts me back that he is having a glass of something, too. He sends a picture showing my text to him on his computer, complete with glass of wine, so in a sense we have a 'salud' to the success of the trip to date.

But it has been a long day and tomorrow's tour starts at 9:30 am, so now I head back to the apartment, which takes all of five minutes to get to my door with its inviting welcome mat. I turn and snap a photo of my seat before leaving.

After my lemon-ginger tea and Spokandy mint, I fall asleep right away. However, I wake around 2:30 am. My Fitbit app reports that I have made 65,236 steps in the past week and already walked over 27.5 miles. I am getting around six hours sleep a night, in addition to my siesta, so I am managing.

I wonder for a moment about the braces holding up the walls below the foundation of my building. Then I realize I don't know where the fire escape is. Hmm ... Well, the entire building, walls and floors, seems to be made of concrete, so I suppose I am safe. Too late to start worrying about that sort of thing now. I don't have a hard time telling myself to go back to sleep, at least for a couple more hours.

My notes say it was early morning when I finally purchased our return train tickets to Granada for Friday. Given the length of the day prior, and the fact that I am still jet-lagged, this may explain why I had to correct my ticket twice to get it right. First, I booked the ticket for the *following* Friday when we would be long gone. Then, when I corrected this, I booked it for a.m. instead of p.m. and only noticed when it uploaded to TripIt and placed what I intended to be the return ticket AHEAD of the morning ticket. The online train aggregator program, Omio, let me sort it out, but I then had to correct a different error, noting

Johnny as the senior for the €6 reduced fare, instead of myself. This boo-boo weighs on me, but I will leave it for the moment. It is something to solve by the light of day.

※ ※ ※

I always wake up in good time, just before the alarm goes off, despite being awake for a couple of hours during the night. At home, hubby likes to stay up late, so whenever I wake during the night, being nine hours ahead of him, it is usually a good time for a text chat. I am not the sort of person who endlessly calls home when she is away, but it is nice to check in and just give an update at some point each day. We have a short but pleasant exchange, and he then goes back to watching his show.

What I have not mentioned is that yesterday I squeezed in a call to my tour guide for today, Juan Diego. The reason I was nervous about this is that while I'd been organizing everything back home, I had not been able to purchase an actual ticket from their site, www.voilamalaga.com. It is the sort of site that has a lot of good information, and as soon as I had found it, I'd wanted to book a tour, but the page where you submit a request for information never seemed to work for me – perhaps because I was accessing it from North America.

Thomas had encouraged me to email the outfit directly, which I had done, but now all I had was a brief email dated April 1, more than two weeks previous. This contained a short message confirming availability and a link to a meeting point. Instructions were included to pay cash at the start of the tour, but it didn't state how much.

Now, I don't think I'm a gullible person, although I suppose I am a trusting one, going on instinct and good vibes and the seeming respectability of this well-designed website, all about locals who really love their city and boasting good reviews. But for me, a solo woman in a foreign city, to just show up on a corner somewhere and dish out an unknown amount of cash to a man I've never met, based on an email that is more than two weeks old, I needed more clarification.

I acted on my instincts, and the solution was an easy one. The fine line between worry and joyful anticipation was, in the end, just a WhatsApp call away. I called the number listed after his name in the email and, thankfully, it worked and my guide-to-be answered the call. Easy-peasy. He confirmed that, yes, he would meet me at 9:30 am the next day, which is today, and the cost was exactly what it says on the website for a one-person private tour, €120.

Okay, then. I am willing to do this and pay this price, because the Spanish Civil War is something that piques my interest, as you may remember from my pre-trip reading list. In fact, it has more than piqued my interest, out of all the history of this city, and I will continue to read as much as I can about it. But today I will walk some of its 85-year-old history.

It is a very recent history when compared to the Roman Theater or the Alcazaba, both of which are visible from my balcony – so recent that I expect most of the residents of Malaga, young and old, have some personal or family memory of those harsh times. Yet they have come through it, rebuilt their lives and their city and show up for the tourists with the warm welcome I have been enjoying. How could I possibly ignore this indelible piece of the mosaic that is Malaga?

The meeting point for the tour is 1.2 miles by foot northeast along the foot of the hill upon which the Alcazaba and the Castle of Gibralfaro sit. I plan to have breakfast first and hire a taxi to take me to the meeting place. But the hour is earlier than when I usually head out, and my handy BrunchIt breakfast joint is closed. They are still setting up, not ready to serve even a coffee to go. It is best just to keep walking and see if I can find a place to eat along the way.

It is the opposite of my original plan, to eat and ride. Instead,

I walk and risk not eating. But I need to be adaptable. Not for the first time, nor the last, I regret that the miscellaneous parts of coffee-making devices in my cute apartment have not provided me with the chance to drink my coffee at 'home' before I set out for the day.

At the start, it is the same walk I have made several times down toward the port area, but this time when I reach the Avenue de Cervantes just ahead of the Parque de Malaga, I turn left and on the north side of the street head along the front of City Hall. I will eventually pass the Biznaguero Statue, although I don't yet realize what this is, and then the famous fountain.

Just beyond, where the avenue joins a traffic circle with the Paseo de Parque and connects with Paseo Reding (though I don't yet know what that it is, either) I see the office for my property management agency. Since I didn't stop for breakfast I have a bit of time, so I call in.

A young, smartly dressed woman looks up from her computer and smiles. "Can I help you?" She seems to be the only person on duty, though the place is filled with comfortable chairs, presumably for guests. I sit for a moment.

"Oh, hello, I'm Karen, and I'm renting one of your apartments just up on Calle Victoria. I just spotted your office on my way by. I am on my way to a tour, but I have a minute so I thought I would drop in and introduce myself."

Inwardly, I wonder if people in Spain have seen the name 'Karen' as damaged as it has been in the west. I seethe that in this day of cancel culture and intolerance, somebody, somewhere, started a nasty rumor that to be a 'Karen' is to be ... well, I don't want to perpetuate it here, but it isn't a nice thing. How dare they 'steal' my name and make it something to ridicule! I have never been a victim of this vilification personally, so most of the time I don't even think about it. But when I do, it makes me angry. And this makes me sad, because I can't even say so, or I would be fulfilling the prophecy. Argh!

No wonder I am happy to vacation in Europe. This and a lot of other reasons, as I am discovering.

"Welcome, Karen, thanks for stopping by. I am Cynthia. It is nice to meet you. I do remember your emails. Would you like a bottle of water?"

"That would be great. Thanks so much. I was going to stop for coffee and breakfast, but my usual place wasn't open yet. I am loving the apartment, but the parts for the coffee maker don't seem to add up to one working device." I appreciate the water, although I don't realize just how much until later when I have neglected to buy another bottle for my tour and there is nowhere along the way to remedy the situation.

"How long are you here? Is everything going okay so far?"

"Oh, yes, I am having a great time and loving Malaga." I am aware that I interrupted her work, and I don't want to be late for my tour, but I clear up a couple of questions about storing the luggage on Saturday before we fly out.

"Just bring your luggage by when you check out of the room, and pick it up before 8:30, okay?"

"Oh, that's perfect." We'll be taking the bus to the airport and our plane doesn't leave until around midnight. Leaving our luggage here for the afternoon would be great, because I'm sure we will have last-minute exploring to do. "Thanks again," I say.

I say goodbye then continue making my way eastward along Paseo Reding. I don't even notice that further along I pass the Centro Cultural la Malagueta, which is located in the refurbished bullring. A bullring looks a lot different at eye level compared to the view from above, although I remind myself I never saw it from above either when I had the chance thanks to the sunscreen in my eyes.

I am focused on my destination, which seems to move further away as I walk. My bottle of water is soon drained. The streets look different, less touristy and less for show, but the bustle of activity is much the same on this weekday morning.

My next surprise is St George's Anglican Church and cemetery which appears suddenly on my left. A friendly-looking caretaker notices me pausing on the sidewalk and in perfect English greets me. "Come on in. You are welcome to look around."

"Oh yes, I would love to, but I am already on my way to a tour. I *will* come back later, though. Will you be open this afternoon?" It is an unexpected connection for a moment in time in a strange place, and I think to myself that, yes, this is a promise I want very much to keep.

"Oh yes, we are open until five. I hope I see you later. Have a nice day." I don't know it yet, but my next sip of water will come from this friendly stranger, hours later.

Juan Diego Tells a Story or Two

My destination meeting point is Paseo Reding 66, which I suspect might be the famous Hotel La Caleta, built in 1919 with 100 rooms. I have read about in some of the books I pored over, primarily my favorite of Joan Fallon's: *Spanish Lavendar, Love in a Time of War* which is set in February 1937 Malaga.

I arrive perfectly at the coordinates given in Juan Diego's email, but again there is nobody here and no sign on the street that this building *is* the hotel. The building is beyond a locked gate, secluded and expensive looking.

My missed breakfast and lack of coffee are a mild distraction, but I see a streetside newsstand across the road. I cross over and decide to have an ice cream bar for breakfast. Failing in my Spanish communication once again, I use my phone to indicate the picture of the Caramel Bar I'd had on Sunday night, but they are out of stock. I decide on a Strawberry Delight that is so delicious it makes me happy there was no caramel. Today, I will discover that an ice cream bar can go a very long way as an energy boost!

I have been eating enough to last me two days ahead, so my

missed meal really isn't a problem. The perplexing thing is – as my husband will tell you that I am always harping on about staying hydrated – that I don't consider buying another bottle of water for the morning walk. *What was I thinking?* I suppose I thought I might be able to buy one along the way, as in every other tour, but this tour is of a different nature, through residential areas, and I should have known better.

Having snagged my Strawberry Delight Bar, I get myself back to the meeting coordinates and, just as I am licking the last bit off the stick, a fellow I recognize from his picture on the website shows up. It is Juan Diego, carrying a large red book.

He approaches me with energetic steps. I am the only other person on the street. "Hello, are you Karen?" I wonder what he thinks of my frizzy hair flying in every direction. "Yes, and you are Juan Diego? Thanks for setting up the tour. I'm really looking forward to it."

"No problem, I am happy to show you around. We are going to walk up these streets to the top. It is quite hilly. I am going to tell you a story along the way, okay? This is just one perspective of the Civil War. There are many, but this one is the perspective of the British people who lived in Malaga back then."

I nod and smile, trying not to miss anything he says, but his voice is soft and, obviously, English is not his first language. I suddenly remember about the payment and offer it. He smiles and tucks the Euros away in his pocket. I wonder how often he gives tours and how else he might supplement his living.

"Do you give this tour often?" I ask curiously.

"Well, yes, I did just last week for a guy who asked for the whole thing in Spanish. Do you speak any Spanish?"

Gulp. "Oh, I am working on it, but sorry, I really don't." It would certainly have added to the richness of the experience if I could have conversed with Juan Diego in Spanish, but this is not to be.

He opens the big red book, which is full of text and pictures.

He confirms this *is* the Caleta hotel in front of which we are standing. He explains that he will tell me the perspective of a British man, Sir Peter Chalmers Mitchell, author of *Mi Casa de Malaga*, or *My House in Malaga*, and that if Sir Peter had not written his story, then much of that time and perspective would have been tragically lost to Malaga's history. *(Note to self on the value of recording memoirs.)* Sir Peter stayed behind, not least to protect his home and garden while most of the British fled Malaga via Gibraltar at the outset of Spain's Civil war. This is actually a story I have read before I left home, but now I am standing right where it all happened.

Juan tells me there are also multiple Spanish perspectives, and one that stands out for Malaga is the voice of the working people, the poorer class of this city. He reveals that he used to include this perspective in the tour, but it required a trip to the poorer areas across town which added a couple of hours and made the tour far too exhausting.

Right now, we head out for the walk, past some lovely old trees that we try unsuccessfully to identify, and up the slight incline at the lower limits of what is a hillside, to our first villa. We will march on like this for two-and-a half hours, with many memorable villas on display, many of which once served as embassies. I am acutely aware that my knowledge of this particular aspect of Spain's history is new and limited, so I listen carefully as I am keen to learn.

We climb higher and higher, pausing here and there along the way for Juan Diego to read from his large book. He fills in the gaps from time to time with his own story, which I will get back to in a bit.

By now my overworked legs are screaming at me, telling their own story, and it isn't pretty. Finally, when we stop, I ask if it is okay if we sit down on one of the many benches that line the streets at intervals under the towering shady trees. Happily for me, we get a bit of rest by doing this as the climb gets steeper.

Some of the homes from Sir Peter's story are gone, as some were burned down during the war, and others were simply rebuilt, but many of the little matching houses that the servants would have lived in were spared and remain to this day as they were originally constructed.

Eventually, we reach the Castillo Santa Catalina, where a fortress was first built in 1624 by order of King Philip IV. Among the ruins a castle was built to modern standards between 1929 and 1933 by French architects Levard and Lahalle at the instruction of the owner, Marthe Guilhou Georgault, a French woman who added her own interpretation to the architecture, and her husband Manuel Loring. Together they were Count and Countess of Mieres, Spain.

This castle complex has now been turned into an elite hotel, and as we pass through an area where guests are having lunch on our way to a spectacular viewpoint, Juan Diego explains that this is why he can only bring a maximum of four people through at a time – so as not to disturb the guests. He takes a few pictures of me against the panorama that is Malaga, the port and the sea, and I take one without my bedraggled self in it.

The breeze is perfect, but it has been quite a climb, and we are not yet at the summit. Later, I check out the hotel online and add to my bucket list to one day spend a couple of nights there. *One can always dream. Perhaps I will meet my editor there and we can get to know each other in person, together solving all the world's problems… or maybe just working on a memoir together, inspiration blowing in on the sweet Mediterranean breeze.*

After a very pleasant and much needed rest on the wall overlook, I surreptitiously deadhead a red geranium or two as we pass, as I know the plant will grow much better without the wilted piece. It feels nice to leave my little touch on things in this exotic place as we head along on our walk.

It takes another fifteen minutes or so of circling up the winding streets before we come to one of the most written-about homes in *My House in Malaga*, from which Juan Diego is reading sections, that of Sir Peter's wealthy neighbors. The Bolins resided at the Villa Las Palmeras and this estate is still intact. Juan Diego tells me that Tomas Bolin was descended from a Swedish entrepreneur, John Bolin Kruse, who arrived in Malaga at the beginning of the 19th century. John's father was a wax trader, and according to Juan Diego popular thought is that some part of the family became a jeweler for the tzars of Russia. Thomas's wife, Mercedes, was even richer. She owned a shipping company and a large share of Banco Bilbao.

They lived at the villa from the year it was constructed, 1924, until 1964 when he died, except for a period at the beginning of the Civil War when they were turned out and had to run for their lives, and the villa was temporarily turned into a hospital. If you read Sir Peter's book, you will see that the Bolins, husband and wife, and indeed their nephew Luis who was Franco's chief propagandist each had their own very complicated roles in this time period under Franco.

What amazes me today is that their villa is pretty much standing as it did back in those days. My imagination fills in the people moving around this beautiful property, husband and wife and five daughters and all their household staff, visitors coming and going, all before the times of trouble. They surely loved living here.

There are a couple of royal-looking peacocks strutting about, and we get a great shot of them. The peacocks clearly care nothing for Civil War history and roam here like they own the place.

We sit on the wall above the chapel area, and Juan reads more of the story while I marvel inwardly at how, just decades later, I find myself immersed in the middle of this tragic history. During the war, Thomas was on Franco's side, whereas Lady Bolin was suspected to be sympathetic to individuals, such as the household staff, who were on the side of the republic. She and her five daughters were thus considered to be a threat to Franco. It seems Sir Peter had been instrumental in harboring Lady Bolin, who he describes in his book as a Monarchist-Catholic lady, whereas Sir Peter himself, although he tried to be true to Britian's non-intervention pact (which in itself had a big historical impact), was friendly to the opposite camp, the republicans, and was eventually at risk of losing his own life.

He did manage at one stage to get back to safety in Britain, Juan Diego goes on, but for the love of Malaga, he came back to Spain bringing medicine and supplies for the villa hospital. It's a complicated story and hard to digest, even though I read the book once before the tour, once after, and am having parts explained to me in context on this day.

It is important to add that we also visit the Official College of Architects building which was is housed in a mansion on top of a hill, built in 1922 by Fernando Strachan. We are able to go inside, as it currently houses day offices, many of which are open this Wednesday. More importantly, it also has a *baño* we can use.

As at last we make our way back down the windy roads toward the starting point, we pass through more beautiful, tree-lined streets, and the home of a man named Porfirio Smerdou (1905-2002), a Mexican politician and diplomat, who served as honorary consul of Mexico at the outbreak of the Spanish Civil war. He was able to secretly harbor refugees from both sides of the political scene in his home, sometimes up to fifty at a time, ultimately protecting an estimated 600 people. He was honored with a plaque sometime in the early 2000s, placed outside the property to be viewed from the street. I take a photo of the plaque and the blue building set behind the fence. When I get home, I see that the original home was torn down and a new one built in its place, but I do not know the details of the modern building.

Once again, I am happy at the occurrence of more benches to rest on as we descend to the point where we had started out two-

and-a-half hours earlier. As I bid him goodbye, I let Juan Diego know that if he has Part 2 of the tour on the menu by my next visit to Malaga, I will see him again.

Although Juan Diego had told me that his grandfather's bones were among those of hundreds of thousands of others who were executed and buried in mass graves during the Civil War, I hadn't asked him too much about it. Later, I regret that I hadn't asked more questions, so I send a follow-up email, as he had invited me to do before we parted. I also take the time to post a tour review, all of which give me an opportunity to delve further into his passion for the Civil War.

My review is as follows:

Juan gave an excellent Civil War walking tour. I read the book 'My House in Malaga' by Sir Peter Chalmers Mitchell a couple of weeks before visiting Malaga, and this book along with others piqued my interest in the Spanish Civil War and, more specifically, the people of Malaga's experience. There is much to see and appreciate as a tourist in Malaga, but by investing time in the not-so-distant history of the Civil War, I feel that as a visitor my appreciation for the people of Malaga is much richer. We walked through the very streets and looked at the very homes that were referenced in the book, and aside from the natural beauty, which was abundant, the historical pairing was superb. This is an incredibly special tour that I am so grateful not to have missed. Please remember to take a bottle of water as there is some climbing. Thank you, Juan. I look forward to the tour part two from the other side of town next time I visit.

Some email correspondence followed:

Juan Diego: *I'm very glad you enjoyed it so much. About my interest about the Civil War, I guess it comes from the very same history of my family. When my mother was born, her father had already died in the war, as well as all his brothers. She lived in a village and the majority of men were killed.*

Me: *Does this mean she never knew her father? So sad. Can you tell me any more of that story?*

Juan Diego: *My grandmother was wearing black while she was pregnant and had to work a lot for raising my mother and my uncle. They had to cope with daily life practically alone. My grandmother tried to recover her husband's corpse, but her mother-in-law didn't want to as she had to pay a lot for that, and they didn't have that money. So he is buried in a common burial in Ronda, but we are not sure where exactly. My father also joined that escape on the road from that little village, called Casares, and the whole family arrived at the limits of Malaga. He was 3 but he remembered it vividly all his life. He had 7 siblings, and all walked about 60 miles, but at the end they turned back.*

Me: *Did they turn back because things were bad in Malaga? What did they do next?*

Juan Diego: *I don't know why they turned back. But what I do know is that when they returned, they had looted their house, no food, no mattresses, etc. Then they realized some neighbors who stayed had stolen things from everyone. But you couldn't denounce. Now they had to shut and obey. There is a chance for identifying my grandfather's remains, but it is difficult, and politicians*

are right now arguing about it, so I don't know. Some families have already recovered their deads, but there are too many. My parents died both.
Best regards, Juan Diego

I wish I could understand it all better, but it is a history that is still new to me. Then I remember: *It is exactly the same for people near my age in Malaga.* They wouldn't have learned about it in school because for forty years of Franco, what *was* taught was what those in power wanted people to believe. Isn't that what the victors always do? Is this not true everywhere?

The people who did know more, the parents, didn't talk about it for fear of reprisals and consequences. In the documentary I watched later, one fellow said, "It is one thing for people to die in a war, but when the war is over, to continue to die just for thinking differently – that is where everything that wasn't already wrong becomes off the charts." What I am thinking is multi-generational tragedy.

I think back to my tiny concern about the ticket for this tour and meeting a stranger – Juan Diego – and realize that of the little I've needed to worry about regarding my safety, the very least of it was my time with the man who just wanted to tell the story.

Echoes of Malaga's Dead

I am full emotionally, so what better time to visit a church and a graveyard. Right? The return trip, which will seem shorter for having travelled it once, will bring me to the church gate. It is appropriate that I will now visit the graves of some of the people whose 20th century homes I have just passed along the avenues, or even whose gardens I've wandered in.

I can see the sea off now to my left, and I recognize that there are some famous beaches in the area I have read about. At one point, I start to jog down what is just a short block so I can see the famous Malaga beach up close, but my legs plead otherwise, and as I still have a lot to do, I turn back. The beach will have to wait for the next visit and a time when I can, hopefully, taste the salted sardines. I will go back, right?

As I retrace my steps, I notice the bright and colorful bougainvillea which is abundant and fresh due to the rains that occurred a couple of weeks before my arrival during the Holy week and Easter celebrations. It is everywhere, adorning the buildings and the supporting wall that keeps the upper hillside from collapsing into the street. I spot some restoration work taking place on an old building and wonder at its history.

I have a sense of walking backward through time, against the stream of refugees that exited the city on foot along this corridor in the opposite direction back on February 7, 1937, as Malaga succumbed to Franco's army at the end of the Civil War. I can almost feel their presence as they pass me by. Men, women and children, often barefoot, headed for Almeria, 200 kilometers up the coast, a destination that will take them ten days to reach if they are lucky.

Many won't make it, some being defeated by illness or exhaustion, others blown to smithereens by enemy ships that cruised in from the sea close to land and set the ships' weapons to target those moving slowly on shore, carrying their only possessions and with absolutely nowhere else to turn.

I absorb some of their desperation, but I also tap into their strength. It is a sensation I won't forget any time soon.

I think to myself that all anyone can do is remember, and we can only remember in context of our own being – so perhaps I am giving back a little bit of life to these souls by simply 'remembering', in my own human way.

I may be an intruder in their history, but my heart is filled for their flight; so perhaps compassion is the ultimate translator, timeless, and they are reaching out to me instead of the other way around. My feet have sturdy shoes, after all, and I am walking *toward* Malaga's center, not away from it for the last time as they were.

※ ※ ※

I keep thinking I may inexplicably have missed the gate to the cemetery, and that it is further back than I remembered. The entrance finally reveals itself although until you are upon it, you might never expect it to be there. Aside from a welcome gatehouse (first built in 1856) just behind the entrance which is guarded by lions on large pedestals, the access drive and pathway leads sharply uphill. I am determined not to be dissuaded from my plan to explore, but first, I enter the gatehouse and see there is a small fee, which I willingly pay as it supports the cemetery upkeep.

The cheerful attendant I had seen earlier provides me with a glass or two of water, and I feel foolish as it is obvious to her that I have been walking all morning without a supply. She chats in Spanish with another visitor, and I know they are commenting on my lack of foresight. Isn't it funny how you can sometimes tell by the tone, even if the words do not compute. I experienced this during my year in Japan back in 1994-1995. Of course, that is another story. But it is one similarity, and it is a significant one.

When I spent a year in the 'east' I felt I had never learned so much about the 'west', because when you investigate a foreign land and culture, inevitably you are contrasting it continuously with your own. This cultural reflection is happening again as I experience Spain. The lady who gives me water also offers a cemetery map in English, showing where some of the famous people are buried, so off I go, refreshed by a short break.

I am about to wander through the only Protestant cemetery in the region and, indeed, the oldest such cemetery in Spain, established in 1831. I have read that prior to this cemetery, Protestants – as they were considered heretics – were unceremoniously buried, only after dark, or buried vertically with just their heads above the sand at the seaside. The establishment of this protestant burial ground and the original chapel came at the persistence of William Mark, British Consul in Malaga from 1824 to 1836 who was disgusted at the treatment of non-Catholics at the time.

The road to the gravesites wanders upward through pleasant gardens of well-kept trees and flowers. There is a small bench to one side and I consider sitting on it to rest, but then realize it is ancient and has been placed there for show. While the bench could no doubt tell a long story of its own, I do not want to intrude on that history. In any case, I would have to step over a small drainage ditch and into a thick tangle of ivy that looks like it has not been disturbed for a very long time. As I reach the flat expanse at the first level built carved into the hillside, I notice there is a lot of tiny cobblestone work around the gravesites. I see a woman is working with cement to inset some of these stones around a grave from a bucket beside her. There are a multitude of large white tombs and also some more modest, and I take my time reading whose final resting place these are as I stroll along.

At the far end to the east of the plot is the small church. Flanked by large columns that support a covered area with benches on either side, the main door opens to the back of the church and empty pews. It seems like a good time to sit and reflect on the morning, as well as my life in general, and I rest here for a while. I can't help noticing the contrast of the simplicity of this small Anglican church to the vast and golden Catholic counterparts I have seen, filled as they are with artwork and tombs – although in all fairness these have been cathedrals, not your average neighborhood parishes.

This small building really needs no guide, as its purpose is obvious, and one can enter with ease. As far as religion goes, I am Anglican as much as I am anything, although my days of attending church regularly ended a couple of decades ago when we moved to California from Canada. There were no Anglican churches near where I lived in California, or in Washington, and I never did make the adjustment to the next best thing. So it has been a while since I have sat in an Anglican church, and I never imagined it would be in Spain. It feels good – not least for my legs and feet – and I have passed the point of looking forward to breakfast, or even lunch. That ice-cream bar is really doing its job.

It is just after noon, and I realize that this is the half-way point of my time here. I am already jealous of the days gone by and greedy for the next few.

When I exit the little church and try to get my bearings, I check the map the caretaker lady gave me, but it is confusing until I realize I have it turned the wrong way. I adjust it. I am looking for a couple of graves to try to find out more about their roles in Sir Peter's story. This gives me direction and a reason to keep exploring.

There is an arch leading to an even higher level of the cemetery, which I learn is the original and oldest plot, so I head for it.

Just beyond are graves that are covered in seashells. I have read that these are often the final resting places of children who died from tuberculosis and fever. At other times, the seashells are used when the identity of the buried is unknown. I have also read that the use of seashells is as close to a burial at sea that a land grave can provide. Another clue is in whether the seashells are turned up or placed face down, though my research has not fully explained the significance. For now, all I can do is look and take a picture or two, and I manage to get a nice close up. What fascinating stories these shells could tell!

I see the grave of little Violette, who was just one month old when she died.

Then, yes, nearby ... here it is, the grave of British subject, Robert Boyd, who was executed in 1831 at age 26 for accompanying General Torrijos in his insurrection against King Fernando VII. While his bones are here in the cemetery, the rest of his comrades are memorialized in the obelisk back at the Plaza de la Merced.

I find it fascinating to learn that Boyd's was the first grave on this site and William Mark personally saw to his interment in the then primitive cemetery he had fought so long to establish.

It is becoming increasingly hot as I wander along, and the

sun is borderline burning. I've taken my blue jacket off and am now carrying it over my arm. I am exhausted, but I am determined to experience as much as I can. I am enraptured to be plodding around on this ground that I had only read about just a few weeks ago from my home so far away.

Stepping even further up the path, my eyes taking in the details of the more interesting gravestones – names, dates, records of lives lived – I finally come upon the graves of the British author, poet, and hispanist Gerald Brenan (1894 – 1987), known as 'amigo de Espana', and his wife Gamel Woolsey Brenan (1895-1968), both of whom played a part in Sir Peter's story.

There are weeds around the graves and I reach down and pull out a few, and then wonder if she, Gamel, would have wanted it so. I do it out of respect, then, because I have lived in the desert, a niggling part of me muses that even a weed is a sign of life winning over death in the dry stones and heat. There is no grass covering these graves. It's too late to put the weeds back, though. I feel I have left a touch of myself once again and hope it would have been okay with the resident.

Mission finally accomplished, I wander my way downhill until I come across a grave that, though it would normally only be significant to a member of the buried person's family, is special to me because of the date. On a large slab near the path is carved: *In Loving Memory of our Mother – Ethel Mabel Miles, born July 3, 1880 Toronto, Canada. Died April 17, 1964, Malaga, Spain* – exactly 60 years ago to this day. Below this is inscribed: *And our Father, George Gordon Miles, born February 16, 1878 Toronto, Canada. Died December 27, 1938, Toronto, Canada.* Underneath this: *Beryl L. Lawrence and Peggy Miles.*

What an interesting coincidence and curiosity. Did they transport his bones 26 years after his wife died so he could be with her in the hereafter? And why did he pass so young to begin with, and so close to the time of the Civil War? I'm not sure I will find anything about this grave online or in any of the record books, but it does hold a mystery, and I am glad I spotted it.

So far, I have done all of this on the nutritional boost of just one ice-cream bar and a few cups of water, which has at least prevented me from needing to find facilities at every corner. But now it is time for me to head back to familiar territory as the urge will soon be upon me. It is a lot easier following the wide path winding downhill through the cemetery, and out to the street past the gatehouse, than it was climbing up. I smile and wave at the attendant and make a silent wish that I will return some day for a service in the church.

As I wander a few blocks in a south-westerly direction back past the property management office and the park, I pause to appreciate the statue of the Biznagas man, who stands as a symbol of Malaga. I don't actually know exactly what it all means at the time, but after posting a photo on Instagram, Thomas responds and fills me in.

It seems the 'biznaga' is a flower that is man-made from the stem of a thistle and the flowers of jasmine. Later in my stay, I find a biznaga lapel pin and buy it for myself. When I wear it for the first time, I realize it is infused with the scent of jasmine, which it still holds to this day. This delightful symbol of Malaga has become a cherished souvenir, and inspiration for the chapter separators in this book.

Nearby, in the park, is a beautiful fountain and I admire this, too, as I plod my way back through the Jardines de Pedro Luis Alonso, which lies adjacent to the city hall in the shadow of the Alcazaba. I am grateful for the refreshing surroundings, but I don't linger unnecessarily. My apartment and a siesta are waiting.

Before I retire for the afternoon though, I find that BrunchIt is now open, and in some kind of magnetic pull to the familiar, when I could have tried something new, I go in and order a late breakfast and a coffee. One reason I choose this venue is because I know the coffee is good – in fact, I order two – but I also know where the facilities are here.

Foodwise, I am torn between a kind of Eggs Benedict and another egg dish that appears to be drowned in a local type of yogurt sauce. I go for the latter and it satisfies my tummy, though the eggs, surprisingly, are served stone cold.

As I sit by the window looking toward my apartment building over the busy street corner that I have now crossed so many times – and not always with the traffic lights –, the coffee makes up for the cold egg dish. I am more than satisfied with my morning's explorations, but I am ready for a siesta. The photo I snap of my breakfast tells me it is 1:58 pm. I am right on time. I arrive at the apartment and there are no more photos taken until 5:35 pm when I am dressed for flamenco and dinner.

An Evening of Flamenco

By the time I have puttered around the apartment for a while and indulged in my much-cherished siesta, I am rejuvenated. My legs and feet have rebounded to the point that it almost feels as if I haven't yet walked on them today. I suppose I am becoming conditioned to the additional exercise – or at least I try to convince myself this is true.

I could not have planned better than to follow up such a serious and thoughtful day with a dive into another cultural mainstay of Spain, the flamboyant dance called the flamenco. I am looking forward to being entertained, and to dressing up in some of the nicer clothes I have brought with me that are a bit different from my usual daytime uniform.

I choose a black-and-gold outfit I bought for my Malta trip back in 2018-2019. One wonderful thing about retirement is that, since I spend so much time in my PJs and don't need any clothes for work, the old wardrobe lasts a long time and I don't get tired of it. James and I don't go out much these days – our prime source of entertainment is playing music at home – so we rarely have the need to dress up. I also switch from my flat walking shoes to my comfy sandals, which, surprisingly, are as good as gold for walking. Admittedly, I wouldn't want to wear them to climb an uneven slope, but on clean marble-tiled streets, they are fine.

The weather could not be better; it is simply perfect. Even when I'm out walking or sitting in the sun for an extended period, I am never too sweaty or uncomfortable – although my hair has gone for a wild circus ride because the breeze from the Mediterranean Sea is just humid enough to dance with my slight natural curl. My purse is small, so I tend not to carry a brush around with me, and often when I see myself in the mirror at the end of the day, I wonder if people think I am a crazy lady because of my untamed locks.

But I always do my best to look respectable, at least at the start of an adventure, and in this case I am very much looking forward to some tasty food and pleasant entertainment. I have not yet mastered the bus – it will be another 24 hours until I can make a successful bus pass card purchase – so because of this, and partly from time constraints, I plan to take a cab down to the restaurant, which is just past the Centre Pompidou Malaga at Alegria Flamenco y Gastronomia. I bring this up on my map and attempt to hire a cab from the ever-present line-up on the Calle Alamos.

Sadly, the taxi driver does not understand my failing Española and I decide not to try too hard to get my message across, because it is a beautiful evening and against all logic, my legs and feet are energized, and I know I can handle the walk.

So once again, I head for the far end of the avenue and the Parque de Malaga where I will head east. My phone tells me it will take just 16 minutes to get to the restaurant, which means I will arrive a full 30 minutes ahead of the dinner schedule.

The walk is truly lovely, and instead of staying on the wide marble walkways sandwiched between the park and the avenues, I choose the flat dirt pathways that take me inside the park itself. I stroll through the groves of trees, over little bridges and under

It Started with Malaga

towering palms. Birds flutter above me and I feel refreshed. This is an absolutely marvelous environment to be set inside a city, and it is so well maintained. I reflect that if I were to be around for longer, I would just go and sit in this area one day and watch the world go by. I pose for a few 'shadow pictures' of myself, a habit I started back when I was a single mom with three young boys. It was an uncomplicated way to get pictures of us all before the ease of mobile phones. You don't need a second person to take a picture of your own shadow, and in a shadow picture, my age and double chin are not revealed!

Even though I dawdle, I have found the Alegria Flamenco Gastronomia by 6:05 pm, and with the ease of someone who is a lot more confident than she was a few days ago. I am the first person to arrive and am given my choice of seats. I choose a nice table just inside the front entrance, where I am able to breathe the fresh air from outside and near enough to the action to people-watch. The servers are very attentive, and after I have located the facilities for immediate and future reference, I am invited to order my dinner. The menu offers a choice of tapas, main courses and desserts, as well as a selection of beverages which are cleverly presented on the label of a repurposed wine bottle. This menu won't blow away.

I choose the ham and cheese tapa, which turns out to be enough for a meal on its own. I send a picture to Jay and his butcher friend, Brent, and they text back that they want some, too. This moment turns out to be a pivotal factor in a purchase I will make tomorrow, and one that leads to much speculation for the rest of the trip, but I will leave that for now. Meanwhile, I order a traditional fish soup for the main, and a lemony cheesecake for dessert.

Having had a moment to relax, I decide to try my Spanish – checking it first on the translator app on my phone – and ask for some water, please. To my astonishment, I am delivered mineral water in a beautiful cobalt blue glass bottle. I check online and I see that back home I can order six of these for US$35, but the container will be blue plastic, not glass. I wonder if these bottles are recycled. Does the restaurant return them to the manufacturer? I never do find out the answer, but when I ask the somewhat amused waitress if I can keep the bottle, she confirms that I can. This bottle does stay with me and makes it all the way back to my breakfast nook table, where it will be a perfect vase for some of my prized daffodils every spring. (Later, Johnny tells me he went through at least twenty of these beautiful bottles during his stay in Marbella, and he is happy I saved one to take home.)

After an enjoyable dinner, it's time to find my seat in the show room. As I had signed up early and online, my ticket is numbered, which gives me free access to any of the seats. I choose one in the front row, but not right in the middle. Later, a couple sits down to my left, and the senorita of the pair is coughing a bit. It makes me nervous, as I do not want to get sick.

I smile as non-aggressively as I can, while moving my backside to the next seat, leaving one between us. She smiles back and says, "*Oh, no, I am not contagious, but I just have a persistent cough that I live with.*" I do not know her name and do not ask, but I mentally assign her as my Spanish Desiree. I do understand that people can have coughs that are not contagious way but nevertheless, since there is nobody who needs the seat between us, I stay where I am for the show.

Unfortunately, I do not have a small bottle of Fireball to remedy her situation as I would with my friend of the same name if I were at home and she were visiting. Desiree, if you are reading this, I know you will smile.

The show kicks off with the guitarist playing a soft melody. His skills are showcased, and rightly so, before any of the others join in. Then he is accompanied by singing, and I am mesmerized. More entertainers quietly access the stage from a side door, and after a bit they begin to dance. I have never before seen flamenco, live or otherwise. The precision and technique that is displayed seems beyond possibility. I don't know how they do it. I find myself wondering what the real meaning of the dance is. This dance looks like it is a tale of new love, or at least a tease of romance, and is very captivating. I wonder if the dancers have been doing this since they could stand, and what kind of training they have had. How many years does it take to master this art? Cameras are permitted, without a flash. I consider taking a video, but I feel it would be rude, and I also really want to witness this through my own eyes and not through a camera lens. I settle for three or four still pictures, which are not very clear because of the lighting – but that's okay, the memory is seared in my heart.

By the end of the show, I am almost in a trance, as if hypnotized by the movements of the bodies and the magical sound of the guitar. The guitarist has no accompaniment but the voices. It was all absolutely enchanting.

My photos indicate that the cast took a bow at 9:09 pm. We had sat down at 7:30 pm, so they had been at it for over 90 minutes. I stand for an ovation, but the rest of the crowd remain seated, although they clap appreciatively. I don't care that I'm the only one. Maybe a standing ovation is not a thing here, but if we can sit for 90 minutes while they do this for us, I can certainly stand by myself as I applaud for thirty or forty seconds. What a way to top off the day.

On the way out, one of the singers, Maria del Mar Fernandez, is selling her CDs for €15. I buy one and she signs it 'To Karen' from Maria. As I am walking back to my apartment, I realize I don't even have a CD player at home anymore, but then I remember I do have one in the car. The following week, on my birthday, my husband and I listen to the entire CD on repeat while we drive to a couple of appointments and then, later, to dinner. On the back of the CD is the handle for her Instagram account, so I now follow her and at one stage messaged her to say that I enjoyed her CD. I am just sorry that the guitarist did not have a CD too, as I would have snapped it up in a heartbeat. Or maybe he does, and just did not have them for sale at the time. I'll have to text Maria and see.

Later, back at home, I am sure to post a review. I have finally discovered how to do this on Google Maps. I find the restaurant on the map, select the name, and this brings up an opportunity to review. I mention this here in case I am not the LAST person in the civilized world to understand that this is possible. I leave a five-star ranking and the following words of appreciation:

I attended this solo and had a great experience. The tapas itself were enough for a meal. The show was amazing and since I bought tickets ahead online, I had the best possible seat. My only regret is that I didn't capture even a minute of video for my husband back at home, because although cameras without flash were ok, I thought it would be rude to take a video and I wanted to enjoy this authentic show through my own eyes, not a camera lens. I did buy a CD from Maria del Mar Fernandez after the show and I am so glad, because I can listen to this beautiful music in my car back in Spokane Valley, Washington, USA and remember my time in Spain fondly. The dancing and the guitar were superb. I wish I had a way to listen to the songs and guitar again.

Within a few hours they reply:

Your kind words mean the world to all the people that work in Alegria Flamenco. We strive to give the best service, and the artists perform with soul and passion. It is very much appreciated that you took time to give such a wonderful comment. We look forward to your next visit!

Kind regards.

※ ※ ※

All that is left of this day is to walk back to my apartment and tuck myself into the comfortable bed and accompanying four pillows that I have come to love settling into at the end of the day. This is now my fourth trip either up or down the avenue past the Alcazaba and the Roman theatre, and the walk back is as pleasant as the earlier walks. I just love how it all looks when it is lit, and by now I am amazingly comfortable with Malaga at this time of night and in this area, which is still full of happy, chattering people on this beautiful April evening. All that's needed to make this epic day complete is a cup of lemon-ginger tea and a Spokandy mint.

Tomorrow I have another tour at 10:00 am, this time a participatory one – a paella cooking class. It will be my last day solo, as Johnny will reappear on the scene early Friday morning so we can catch our 9:35 train to Granada.

My Fitbit reports that I have walked 18,819 steps and just under eight miles. Every step was worth it.

Postscript: When I have been home as many days as I have been away, I message Maria using Instagram, translating my request into Spanish using the app, asking if she can tell me the guitarist's name. She replies that it is Ruben Lara. I search on Instagram and find him! Of course I do; he is a star. I am now listening to his five-minute track named Jara, recorded in 2022. Wow. Malaga keeps on giving.

Lost ... and Found!

I wonder to myself if time passes more quickly when the days have been long anticipated. My well-spent days are passing far too fast, as I suspected they would – my Malaga time a currency, the toll collected each day by the setting sun. Although I haven't overbooked myself, I truly couldn't have squeezed in anything more without running myself ragged. It has been a bit of a balancing act keeping my physical being prepared for the next adventure with just enough sleep and time for the well-earned aches to heal, but I feel I have planned it well.

I wake up each morning to the sound of the workers getting busy outside and am still resisting the urge to wave at the guy in the cab directing the very large crane across the gaping hole outside and below my balcony that will one day be filled with a new hotel. I hope it will be a Marriott, and that I'll have enough points to enjoy it one day, but otherwise I wish it were just going to be a park, because it really is going to ruin the view from the apartment.

This morning, as I ready myself for the day's activities, I am acutely aware that the trip is winding down, and with tomorrow being the day to take the train to Granada, there is just today and one other left to explore Malaga. *Don't think about that right now,* I tell myself. Looking around I realize I will never use the microwave or the oven, or most of the lovely dishes and ample pots, pans and kitchen gadgets, all of which seemed attractive amenities at the time of booking. The various pieces in the cupboard that are supposed to make up a coffee pot never do puzzle themselves together to be workable for me, but I have been managing okay with the kettle and my lemon-ginger tea at night.

I decide that tonight will be the night where I tackle using the cute little washing machine that is tucked under the kitchen counter on the opposite side of the sink from the dishwasher. I have brought five of those new washing machine sheets, where you just throw one in and it dissolves into washing detergent. My interest is piqued to give them a try. I chuckle to myself that I have brought so many, as if I might have been planning to stay a month. I reflect that I have done well to capture as much as I have in the first four days, but now it is time to wade a little further into local domesticity.

This is going to be the day for challenging myself to become savvy with daily life Spanish-style, because what I don't accomplish now will have to wait for a second visit – and who knew when that would be? The washing machine is on my list of the advantages the apartment has to offer, and I want to prove to myself that I can operate it with just Spanish instructions. I mentally put that on my list for tonight.

The paella class tour is at 10:00 am so I take a shower and carry out my usual morning preparations. I ready myself for the walk with the destination mapped out on my phone. The phone is one gadget that has worked seamlessly in Spain. I have paid a flat US$10 a day for full use of calls and text for each day abroad, and this includes having cellular access to mapping and searching throughout the day even when I'm not using the resident Wi-Fi. I wanted to be able to track and be trackable, post and be notified, so this is one of those magical things that has gone smoothly, and for this I am grateful. Some things are easy when they might not be, it seems. And on the flip side, as I will discover this morning, some things are difficult when they needn't be, although they may still get solved in the end.

This morning, I head across the Plaza de la Merced – just because I can, even though it is quicker to go around it. I head down Calle Granada, which angles off from the other side of the Plaza. This is near the tobacconist shop, which I don't pay much attention to right now, although I will have cause to visit it later.

I now know there is a coffee and pastry shop down this street, and it is on my way to the tour meeting place. Later, I'm going to eat what I cook – for better or worse – but this morning I am not going to miss out on a coffee and pastry like I did yesterday. I have my fingers crossed that there won't be a big line-up, because I want to be at my tour location on time.

Well past El Pimpi and the Picasso Museum on the left, I find the La Canasta coffee bar on the corner. Finally, I can find something where I last saw it. This is a stand-up coffee bar with lots of fresh pastries behind a high glass counter. Today, I am in luck and there are just two customers ahead of me.

I am googly-eyed at the various choices and am just running out of time to decide, when the young blonde woman ahead of me, fluent with the language, orders a cafe-con-leche and a ham-and-cheese croissant. If I could spend a year here, as I did back in Japan when I was in my thirties, I would eventually be able to speak Spanish just as easily as she does, and probably go about my day with a of the same smug confidence at being so savvy in a foreign country. I'm sure she well deserves the attitude, and I wonder what her destination is and, even more intrusively, what she is doing in Spain. I would like to know her story. But she hurries off, no doubt to some important job where being fluent in both English and Spanish is a requirement.

It is now my turn and for the sake of convenience, I decide to go with the same order, though I wave and motion rather than verbalize it. For all my truly sincere efforts to learn enough basic Spanish to be able to do things like order a coffee and a bun, just about all I'd learned had already been displaced from my buzzing brain a couple of days before I'd left. I hadn't started soon enough for much to sink in. I decide I will take longer to prepare the next time. This potential *next time* seems to be a recurring theme. I just need a good reason for *next time*. In the back of my mind I keep running through scenarios, but I cannot quite put my finger on the one that will justify a return soon enough to satisfy my new obsession with this city. One week is not going to be enough; I know that much.

I now have my coffee and wrapped-up croissant, but there is no place to sit, so I continue on my way. I really don't want to eat while I walk, and come to think of it, I haven't seen anyone doing this during my stay. Around the next corner, there are some empty tables and chairs in front of a restaurant that is still closed. I hope I am not breaking local etiquette by seating myself at one to eat my fast-food breakfast. I take a picture for the record in this cute little alcove, and after about five minutes, I am once again on my way.

🌼 🌼 🌼

There are both usual and unusual sights to see as I make my way to the meeting point at the base of Calle de Marques de Larios near Victoria's Secret, where familiar ground gives way to places my feet have not yet travelled. I follow Alameda Principal to the west, which has a parkway median, though not as extensive as the Paseo del Parque that is a kilometer or so further east. I continue until my phone map tells me that my destination, Kulinarea Cooking School, is to the left on Avenida de Manuel Agustin Heredia.

I reflect that Manuel must have been an important person to

have the street next to the port named after him. (Later I research and find that he was one of the men (1786-1846) responsible for Spain's industrial revolution including steel and ironworks and the first blast furnace in Spain. The street is built on land reclaimed from the sea and once was the site of early 20th century Malaga fairs.)

I don't know it yet, but later I learn that I am walking through Malaga's 'Soho' barrio, which is a less developed neighborhood as it is off the tourist track. But not for long it seems. Antonio Banderas and his business partner plan to open an 8,000-square-meter cathedral of stage and culture, 'Sohrlin Andalucia' – a Performing Arts and Cultural Entertainment Centre – in the midst of these old industrial facilities and warehouses by the sea. With a main hall capacity of 3,500 people, an auditorium, training school and artist residency, the center will surely bring new life to the quarter. I wonder what it will look like in a few years' time and how many lives will be changed by the opportunities it will create.

The walk has taken longer than expected and when I reach my destination it is 9:57 am. The event starts at 10:00 and here I am.

But yet again, there is not another soul to be seen.

My stomach flips to see the sign 'Kulinarea' above two large plate-glass windows, but behind the windows are large metal shutters and they are closed.

I wish later that I had taken a picture, but at this moment that idea is furthest from my mind. The effect of the closed metal shutters is not at all inviting. I think to myself, *Ah, I am at the wrong place. I got something wrong.* My mismanaged Rome tour experience has reared its head. I can feel the kind of stomach acid that is generated by disappointment and anxiety starting up in my guts, and no doubt my troubling blood pressure has gone up, too.

I need to sit.

Next door to the cooking school, there is a coffee shop with plenty of tables, some empty, on the streetside. I could sit at one of them just for a minute to take stock. My brain gets fuddled when I am trying to sort out a problem and I need to use my phone for, not so good at it while standing on my feet. This is a problem that is going to take some digging to solve. Oh, I hate being late and I really don't want to miss the class.

The proprietor of the cafe sees me while he is cleaning off the sidewalk tables and scurries to make a spot for me.

Just then, an energetic-looking young woman arrives at the Kulinarea door, and in a flash, she is inside and has pushed a button and up winds the security screens from behind the windows.

I breathe a huge sigh of relief. It is 9:59 am and I have been flummoxed for all of two minutes.

I smile and nod to the cafe proprietor and hurry to let myself in the door behind the young woman,

"Hello, I am so glad to see you. I am here for the cooking class."

She smiles and takes a pause while she digests both my presence and my urgent outburst, "Oh, the tour starts at the market. You need to go up there to meet everyone."

Oh, my goodness. So, I'm not out of the water yet! I did know that the tour included the market, but nothing on my ticket or any of the messages that I can access electronically have indicated that that was the starting point. The only location mentioned in my correspondence is right where I'm standing. Fortunately, because of the Monday evening tapas tour, when I accidentally noticed where the market is, I know how to find it. The young woman makes a call, in part English and part Spanish. I gather that she is speaking to the tour guide and she lets him know that 'Karen' will be meeting the rest of the group at the market, and to look out for a woman wearing a *blue jacket*!

It Started with Malaga

I dash off, not quite running, but jogging the half-kilometer distance to where I should have been, and it is easily found.

But once I am there ... OMG, she didn't actually tell me *where* to meet the group. This is the most severe case of 'pladifa' yet.

I assume the meeting point is at one of the main entrances, but there are two of these as well as a couple of side entrances, and rows and rows of stalls lining the interior. I frantically circle between all these gates until at some point, growing more frazzled by the minute, I text Thomas, who has so far been on hand – albeit at a distance – for the entire trip should I need assistance. I'm not sure how he can help, but he might think of something. While I am racing here and there, looking for a group that I do not find, he finds the phone number of the outfit for me and texts it to me. I call and leave a message on my new WhatsApp account, but there is nobody answering.

My phone vibrates and a notification appears on my phone telling me that the tour has begun, and that I have missed it. What a letdown!

It is now 10:17 am and I pause to catch my breath at one of the main entrances. At least I can go back to the cooking school and not miss that part, but I am sad to have missed the guided walk through the market. I am sadly perplexed. There has not been one lanyard-wearing guide to be seen, nor a group of wide-eyed tourists such as myself.

As I pause for a moment near one of the gates, I see a woman and a man smiling at me. I smile back as we lock eyes. How can this woman be familiar? I do not know anyone in Malaga.

"Ah-ha, is that you?" We both speak at the same time. To my astonishment, it is my Spanish Desiree and her husband, who sat next to me at the flamenco show last night. How funny is this? I am running into someone I 'know' in the heart of the Malaga market, just as I might do if I lived here. Laughing, we pause together for a selfie, my first and only one ever with complete strangers, and they carry on.

I never do find out her real name or where she is from, but at a heart level we have connected as happy tourists, and it gives my somewhat discombobulated morning a bright spot.

※ ※ ※

A couple of minutes later, just as I am about to give up and head back to the cooking school, a friendly looking fellow, whom I learn is Javi, asks me hopefully, "Are you Karen?" I am flooded with relief.

Javi explains that the group had met just a short distance away. In fact, Thomas tells me that it is the corporate office for Spain Food Sherpas. It turns out that all the group has done is walk to the market, using a different route to the one I took, and they are just beginning the actual market portion of the tour. I have missed nothing.

Javi has approached every other woman in the market wearing a blue jacket, and the entire group of eight has been looking for me. What a welcome I get. Nobody is weird with me because I was the klutz that didn't start at the start. Good thing Sue isn't here, I think to myself.

Everyone is just incredibly happy I have been found. Suddenly, I am experiencing near-celebrity status. I am simply grateful to be found.

It turns out that the cause for the mix-up is that I did not sign up at the usual Spain Food Sherpas page because I was registering solo, and the site would not allow me to. Instead, I signed up at the actual cooking school site. This meant I had received the email sent from Food Sherpas yesterday to all the other participants confirming the intended meeting point.

If you ever have the good fortune to experience Malaga's impressive Mercado Central de Atarazanas, you will appreciate

It Started with Malaga

how fortune smiled on me that day. It is a large building frequented by many people and to be able to connect with Javi and the group seems nothing short of a miracle. I am so glad I wore my bright blue jacket and for the unfailing effort of Javi to find me.

Now that I can breathe, I can begin to appreciate my surroundings. There are stalls selling all varieties of fish, shellfish, fruit, meats, cheeses, vegetables, nuts, spices, anything a market shopper might desire. Ready-made sandwiches and other delights are abundant and the whole building is surrounded by places to sit and eat. Javi leads us to one particular stall where we are offered a large variety of goodies to sample: plain or spiced green olives, various types of Iberian ham, cheeses, almonds that taste better than any almond I have yet tried, and not least, the most delightful figs.

The smiling man behind the counter splits a fig, stuffs it with an almond, repeats the process and offers the stuffed figs to the group. This is the 'heart of Malaga' we are told, and with the downing of this morsel, my shopping monster is unleashed. I go first, loading up with many of the delights on offer.

In the back of my mind, I am seeing a red flag about taking Iberian ham back to the USA, but then remembered I had read somewhere that you can take a small amount for personal use if you declare it. There is a model airplane strung from the roof of the stall with the words, 'Vacuum Packed for Airplane'. My culinary desires are unleashed.

At Malaga prices, my bag is quite heavy for my surrendered €85. I will later wish I had bought a beautiful ripe red tomato to try. I do buy some saffron, though, and for this opportunity I am grateful. The price is significantly less than what I would pay back home – only €2.5 for half a gram – so I buy three packs, one and a spare for myself and one for a gift for Faye, who loves to cook.

I realize I will have to buy another bag for airport check-in. I want to go back and buy the platter I spotted a few days ago at the inviting pottery shop. I also have the 375ml bottle of wine that I have not yet opened. There is no time to sip luxuriously on Malaga sweet wine by the time I reach my apartment each night.

The market is a wonder to behold, so while everyone else is shopping, now that I have opened the floodgates, I have a good look around and capture lots of photos of the beautifully displayed wares. What a lovely resource for the people of Malaga.

Javi is an observant guide. My plastic bag of food is stretching from the weight of my purchases, so he offers to carry it inside his canvas tote and I accept. I tell myself not to forget he has it. Now we are on to the main event!

A Perfect Paella

Bedraggled as I am, I am happy when we arrive as a group back at what started as my personal meeting point for the tour. The Kulinarea Cooking School is already prepared for our class, with a long table set for us to enjoy the delights of our labors, and a parallel bar set up for us to prep and cook. All the ingredients and utensils we could need are beautifully arranged for our convenience. At the end of the room, near the windows overlooking the street, there is another table laden with olive oils and all the necessary components for us to participate in making traditional sangria.

Acutely aware that next week I will be back in the Pacific Northwest, and highly likely I will soon be back to chores like mowing my large lawn for the first time this spring, I am very much looking forward to the experience of making paella here today, thousands of miles away on another edge of the world. So much so that I had forgotten that this class also includes olive oil tastings, making the sangria, and the making of gazpacho.* I must admit I am not quite sure at this stage what gazpacho is. I

---

* All recipes can be found at the back of the book.

also appreciate the fact that I am going to be learning from an expert, because for so much of my 36-year teaching career I have had to learn things on my own. Happily, paella is not going to be one of my self-taught moments.

Welcome, too, is the opportunity to take things at a slower pace just for the moment and just *enjoy*.

I miss the sangria-ingredient chopping as there is a wait for the *baño*, but making sangria is not my primary focus of attention anyway. Sangria has always been a disappointment to me, as in spite of its reputation for being such a festive and joyful drink, it has never really done it for me. I'm quite happy that some of the other tour members are chopping the apples and peaches. I don't need to be in the middle of it. The choppers have attracted the attention of some passers-by who are interested in what is going on, and I feel very lucky to be on this side of the window.

While I watch and listen, I sample the three types of olive oil that are set out in little bowls by dipping bread into each. Each is a different hue of greenish gold and none of them taste anything like the extra virgin olive oil we buy back home – mine usually from Italy. During my sixteen years in California, I have tasted some lovely olive oils, but these here today make me feel like I have never really tasted olive oil at all. This is sad. I reflect that I have been focusing too much on price and not enough on flavor. Surely, I can do better for my tastebuds even if it makes a bigger dent in my grocery shopping dollar. I vow to mend my ways and choose different brands of olive oil in future for dipping or salads. At less than a week before 69, life is too short for just adequate.

I am about to get another surprise. I taste the sangria. It is sappy I know, but I could cry even now as I remember. I have never tasted sangria like *this* before! Now I know what it is supposed to taste like, and I am converted. I hope I'll be able to replicate what I have just imbibed. Fortunately for me, Javi later sends the recipes out to the group, eliminating the need to search on my iPad for random recipes. (In addition, Spain Food Sherpas has given me permission to include the recipe in the book, and you will find it, along with the recipe for paella and the gazpacho, at the back.)

Olive oils and sangria tasted, we are invited to be seated on the tall stools from which we will prepare the ingredients for the paella. I am shown my reserved spot where the portions have been laid out for my single meal. There is a threesome next to me, a dad and his two daughters, and the dad sits at the end. I am on his right and his two adult daughters are on his left. We are sharing a flat-top induction surface and our pans, slightly different in size as mine is for one and theirs is for three, are sitting in front of us. Little steel bowls containing squid, shrimp, sweet peppers and what turns out to be a cup of broth are laid out at each station, along with a stirring utensil and a small scale with a bowl for measuring the correct amount of rice. Up until the time we use the broth, I mistake it for a drink the dad has ordered, and he mistakes it for a strange drink of mine, so we have a laugh when we get to that part of the recipe and find out what it really is.

At the other end of the table, the gazpacho is being made and mixed in a blender not unlike my Nutri Bullet back home. Although Gazpacho can be a soup, it also works well in a thinner consistency as a refreshing drink, and samples are poured into small cups for each of us to try. Apart from being delicious, it is packed with vitamins and healthy veggies and I decide that, later, when I'm mowing my lawn, I will make some to bolster my energy. Although it is an acquired taste, I'm certain I can get quite used to it, and it's perfect for our looming summer back home.

Gazpacho sampled, the time has come to get to the business of making the paella. I'm sure it will be better than the dish we tasted on our first night in Malaga. Lucky me to have this opportunity to learn.

We start by removing the tails and thin shell membrane from our shrimp, but before we do this, we are asked to cut the heads off, making sure to leave the brain of the shrimp intact. These and the thin shells are collected in a bowl to be used to make a saffron fish broth for tomorrow's class to use. The chef explains that the brain adds a lot of flavor. I make a note in capital letters at her next instruction:

'NEVER SALT OR BOIL THE BROTH'

She smiles when she notices this note on my phone and explains that our grandmothers have been doing this wrong for all time. Boiling the broth brings out the nastier parts of the bones or shells – and, in this case, it might be mercury from the sea. The salt, she tells us, makes the water you are turning into broth denser and less able to absorb the good stuff.

Although it wasn't my grandmother who taught me, it seems I have been making my homemade chicken and beef broth incorrectly for decades. It's something I learned from a cookbook and in later years online, and without this class so many miles from home, I would never have known.

I mustn't forget to mention the pre-made and strained tomato sauce that is also provided for us to use with the paella. Our chef tells us that she makes a batch of this every Sunday by roasting tomatoes with salt for 45 minutes in a pan, and then straining them through a sieve to remove the skins and seeds. She suggests that if you freeze the sauce in ice cube trays you can use one cube per serving when you make a paella. I look at the amount of tomato sauce in my little bowl and deduce that she is using large cube trays and remember we have some that size at JO's Place. I see these large cubes later in various Malaga bars and wonder if this is a thing in Spain, or just a coincidence. It turns out, it is *not* a coincidence. It's actually common to see huge ice cubes in

Spain because it can get so warm here the smaller ones melt too fast.

Next, we are instructed to pour a tiny amount of olive oil into our pans and to begin searing the sweet peppers that we have chopped small, because this is our chef's preferred size. We then add our white fish, and when all is suitably tender, we add our seasoning which is turmeric and smoked paprika. Our chef likes her rice al dente, so now we pour the broth into the pan and wait until it is gently boiling to add our Bomba rice which we have measured out to 80 grams per serving. If we preferred our rice to be more cooked (and according to our chef, the dreaded mushy) we could have put our rice in the pan ahead of the broth and had a different result.

Somewhere in the process we have added the tomato sauce. While the broth is cooking the rice, we tuck the shrimp into the rice mixture, and it gently cooks itself. We cook on a medium heat just until the broth is absorbed, or until we begin to hear what sounds like the paella talking, when it starts to sizzle. We let it sizzle for just the right amount of time until it forms a crunch known as 'socarrat' on the bottom of the pan – meaning that the bottom layer is well done but not burnt. The chef comes around and turns down the heat during this last part.

Our paella is all but done and we cover it with a square of foil for ten minutes with the heat turned off for it to finish perfectly cooking. The large room smells delicious and our sangria glasses have been refilled, so we sip appreciatively while we wait.

Somewhere along the way, the chef tells us that if you are from Valencia, you have 100 rules for making paella, which can be viewed as either logical or suspect, depending on whether or not you are from that province. The rules include things such as 'the water to make the broth must be from Valencia'. Another rule is that only seafood can be used, never meat. We understand the message, loud and clear: Valencians believe they own paella. I'm pretty sure the rest of Spain can argue with that and win.

Here in Malaga, they clearly know how to make it, too, and the chef assures us that there are only three rules: 1. Make whatever kind you want. 2. Use water from any city. 3. Enjoy eating your paella!

And indeed we do and are provided with wine of our choice to accompany our meal while we are at it.

All that is left is to move this happy party over to the long table. At this point, groups at both ends want me to join them, so clearly no one is holding a grudge against the morning's missing Karen. I choose a spot in the middle. I know the 80-year-old dad and the two sisters are shore-hopping from a cruise ship docked out in the port, and I'm pretty sure another dad and his young daughter, who is not quite old enough to drink and doesn't really want to, is from England. The rest of us are from the USA.

The group of three have a challenging time finishing their portion, and they don't want to take it back to the ship. As almost of us know, cruise ships are loaded with food and usually there is no place in your state room to store it. I'm pretty sure the guide gratefully eats their leftovers. Mine is gone, to the last kernel of rice, and I am not left wanting. It has been perfect.

"Javi, this has been awesome," I say as I prepare to leave. "Thank you so much for carrying my heavy bag. And for not giving up on finding me. I am going to need another carry-on bag for all of this." I had seen some in a shop, but they were quite pricey.

Handing me my bag of treats, he smiles and replies, "This is a common problem for visitors to Malaga. There is a great place to buy one not far away. It is a shoe store, but they sell bags, and it is named Payma. I can show you on a map. Can you bring up a map on your phone?"

My phone still has juice, so I bring it up and he points out the location. It is just a little out of my way, a new adventure.

Lastly, I am sure to thank the chef. "The class was awesome. I will never again salt or boil my broth!"

I take my last photo of the event at 1:55 pm. I am ready to wander back to what I now feel is home, via my new favorite Malaga retail, which is Payma. After sharing a few hugs with my classmates – I am not sure I even know all their names – I depart into the sunny Malaga afternoon.

※ ※ ※

I make sure to log a review when I get home:

Javi was an enthusiastic and knowledgeable tour guide and translator. He even carried my heavy bag of treats I bought at the stall from the market to the cooking class. This class was an excellent experience. The only reason I could not give five stars was not at all about the content of the experience at the market and the class, which was FIVE-star. Both Javi and our chef were excellent.

It was because of the meeting point, which I did not understand at the beginning. There is a special reason for this that will not apply to all but did apply to my experience as a solo registration. At the time, the Food Sherpas site would not let me register as just one person. On the page I could only select 'two' or more. I used the Kulinarea site to sign up for one person. I understand that all the people who signed up through Food Sherpas did get explicit details for the meeting point I think by email as a reminder just prior to the class. The meeting point was not precisely at the market or the cooking class site, but it was nearby the market. I could not find any of the information on my ticket when I was walking to the tour. I ended up at the Kulinarea cooking class actual site at the start instead of at the spot near the market with everyone else. Nevertheless, Javi searched for me (the chef called him and said I was wearing a blue jacket) and I rushed the six-minute walk up to the market where twenty minutes later Javi found me, after interviewing many other women with a blue jacket. He went above and beyond so I did not miss my tour, but the information could have been better for my unusual solo booking.

They reply:

Hi Karen,
First of all we would like to apologize for the confusion with the previous information! The minimum number of guests for our food tours or cooking classes to take place is indeed 2. Kulinarea – the company that owns the kitchen – has since rectified the information that solo visitors get, so that they too can easily find the meeting point. We really appreciate you taking the time to write this review, and we will make sure to forward your kind words to Javi.
Thanks again, and we hope to see you again soon!

Postscript: Later, after they reply that they will correct the issue with the information, I try on multiple occasions to change the ranking portion of my review to five stars, but so far Trip Advisor won't let me. I'll keep trying. At least from the written review it is clear that I was very happy with the value and the experience. I was just rattled that it would have been easy for me to have missed out on at least the market portion of this event if I hadn't been persistent and kept trying to resolve the situation, and hadn't had the support of Thomas in the background helping me with the phone number. In the end, Javi found me, thanks to my blue jacket.

23

The German Bridge

*A*s I retrace my steps through Soho and across Avenue Principal and up another side street back in the direction of the market, my eyes are drawn to things I had not had a chance to notice when I was fast-tracking this route just a few hours earlier. I need to carry my blue jacket over my arm for a bit, as I have a long-sleeved cotton shirt on underneath, and it has grown warm.

I am happy for the zillionth time that I wore such my bright blue jacket today, making it easier for Javi to notice me among the crowds. The morning had gone marvelously from that moment onward. The class was a bargain for just €75, and I am full as I walk – in mind, body and spirit.

I wander inside the market and take in the various kinds of fish and seafood for sale. It is late in the day, so most of the vendors are closing and there is a lot of hosing down and washing up going on, but there are still plenty of transactions taking place. I suspect that the vendors have it all worked out, how to close and clean the stall, while being prepared to make a sale of the most popular items right to the very end.

Here is where I could have snagged a tomato, but I am

distracted from this thought, as I am still just taking in all the colorful sights. I hope to bring Johnny back here on Saturday when we cover the must-do bases for his last day. I suspect he will have seen nothing like this in Marbella, because even if there is a smaller version there, he has been busy with his company events, insulated by the architecture and mood of a luxury hotel.

I am so glad I chose Malaga for *my* days in Spain. Looking back, it is clear there should have been no doubt at all. Now, I can hardly imagine not returning.

This time, I have entered the market though the ancient gate where the sea used to rise in centuries past to this very spot, and I eventually exit through a gate with beautiful stained-glass windows. I turn to my left and end up at Plaza de Arriola. Now I am in new territory as I follow the map on my phone toward the Payma store, where I hope to get a bargain on a new bag to safely carry my souvenirs onboard the plane.

I walk in what feels like a northerly direction, but I am not sure because the angles of the streets are deceptive. The atmosphere of the street I am walking along changes to one that is less showy for the tourist and more practical, truer perhaps to the behind-the-scenes day-to-day life of Malaga. It is just a subtle change, as though I have walked behind the set to where the actors and actresses prepare for the show. But it is not shabby. I pass near a stop our group made on the Monday evening tapas tour. All is clean and in order, just as I have come to expect from the streets of Malaga.

I don't know it quite yet, but I am in for another delight, for me an accidental discovery, where this road meets what was once a mighty river, the Rio Guadalmedina. Is that the bridge from my online jigsaw puzzle? A few weeks ago, when researching everything Malaga, my online puzzle company had tossed up this bridge and I had completed the puzzle late one night when I couldn't sleep.

It Started with Malaga

The iconic sign mid-span says it is the Puente de Santa Domingo, then in brackets, Puente de los Alemanes – the second name meaning 'Bridge of the Germans' as it is popularly known. The bridge crosses directly to what I will soon read on the building is the Pasillo de Santo Domingo, the true name for the bridge crossing directly in front of this church. I am thrilled to find this landmark without even trying, as my days here are numbered.

I see another bridge a bit further north-east that will provide a convenient return to the east side of the river in the direction of the Payma store, so I venture across the iconic bridge that I pieced together as a puzzle not so long ago to have a closer look at what is on the other side.

I remember that this bridge was given to the city by the Germans, as part of their appreciation for coming to the aid of a German Navy ship carrying 470 sailors who were on their way to Malaga to pick up a diploma in 1900. On December 16 the ship, named Gneisenau, went aground in a storm just outside the port. Seeing this, many locals came to the rescue and threw themselves into the water to help. All but forty-two German lives were saved. Twelve 'malagueños' also died in the effort. The captain and chief engineer, along with the forty-two sailors are buried in the Gneisenau Tomb at the English cemetery I visited yesterday.

But the gift of the new Santo Domingo Bridge did not come right away, and this mighty river was not always dry. A few years after the shipwreck, on the night of September 23, 1907, a catastrophic flood destroyed bridges, buildings and the railway, and caused much other damage, too. The original Santo Domingo Bridge was wiped out, along with the others. The flood left mud and debris so high, some houses could only be accessed via their upstairs balconies. Twenty-one lives were lost in the flood event, and it took two months to clean up the streets. When the Germans heard about this disaster, they built the new bridge to help Malaga with the recovery. This is why the bridge has two names – its original name 'Santo Domingo' and 'the German Bridge', to pay homage to the Germans for their gift.

The 29-mile-long (47 km) Guadalmedina river, the source of this and several other catastrophic floods, has been dammed up to the El Limonero Reservoir and now provides water to the city. Although the reservoir's retaining wall is made of rock, the river itself now has a concrete bed, much of which has been filled with soil and planted with wildflowers. The result is very pretty at this time of the year. A comparatively small stream of water which must be underground at the point I am viewing still makes it to the port to dump into the sea, but it is nothing like the river that once was. Frankly, as a former California resident who has seen it all first-hand, I feel Los Angeles could take a page out of Malaga's book on the beautification of a dry riverbed. But don't mind me. I'm sure I know nothing at all about urban development.

Reaching the other side of the bridge, which divides Malaga East from West, I find myself standing immediately in front of another well-known landmark. The Church of Santo Domingo is a much damaged but now rebuilt Renaissance church that is home to several Holy Week images, including the famous 'Mena' crucifix. Pedro de Mena was the most famous sculptor in Spain after 1667, although, sadly, many of his works were destroyed during the burning of the churches and convents in the 1931 riots. Maybe I will learn more about those times if I am lucky enough to return for part two of Juan Diego's tour.

I don't know about these revered contents as I stand gazing, though, nor do I know at the time that I have just missed this year's celebrations, which took place in the week before Easter, when the sculptures depicting the Passion of Christ are paraded through the streets on the shoulders of forty-two brotherhoods.

Unaware of the historical significance, but charmed by the ambiance, I wander by the church, taking plenty of pictures. To

It Started with Malaga

my left I see a span of an area of Malaga that I will never get the chance to explore. Beyond that is the airport, to which I will soon enough be making my way.

I amble across the second bridge, which is more modern and made of steel until I find myself back in familiar-looking territory, even if these *are* my first steps on this exact street.

Just ahead I can see the sought-after Payma shop, for which my phone map has been of great assistance. As I enter, I instantly spot the bag that will be my chosen companion, and it is priced at just €49. It might be just a tiny bit big for a carry-on, but it has wheels and is a perfect size for my existing purchases and any I might add during my last few days. I tap my card and seal the deal. Ah, the joys of global credit. Both the bag and the price are perfect. When I am done with it, I may give it to Johnny, so he doesn't have to use the zombie apocalypse bag with the bungie cord next time.

I wonder if the large platter I'd spied earlier might fit in it? Meanwhile, my stash of ham, saffron, figs, and olives roll along tucked neatly inside, and I am free as a bird with no further luggage to carry for now. I am acutely aware that if there had ever been any doubt, I am giving myself away as a tourist, wheels clacking along on the cobblestones. But I don't spy any dirty looks. Hopefully the people of Malaga intuitively know I am just another visitor who must buy yet another bag to get everything home, and that I have contributed to their economy in thought, word and deed.

This is an afternoon of discoveries and surprises. In a little square I come across a human who is sitting on a bench that totally blends in with his body. The whole tableau has been camouflaged as a newspaper with a newspaper body, reading … a newspaper. This is one time when words fail me, but fortunately I am on the ball enough to take a picture. I'd like to put some coins in the busker's hat to show my appreciation, but to my dismay the only coin I have is worth just a fraction of a euro. I don't even know what this Spanish 'nickel' is called. It goes in the hat regardless, and the form motions for me to sit down next to him.

As I have no more funds to show my appreciation I do not sit, but I am impressed by the effort to create a work of art out of something seemingly so ordinary – a man reading a newspaper. I nod goodbye and keep going.

Around a corner and down the next cobblestone lane, I find myself in front of a real estate office. I pause for a few minutes to see what the market is like, should I ever get lucky with a lottery. On the flyers in the window, I spot some cute apartments and let myself dream for just a moment. The first flyer showcases a four-bedroom, three-bath 1970 apartment in Centro Malaga, 193 square meters for €1,485,000. The next is a 2024-built ground-floor one-bed, two-bath apartment at only €340,000 for 74 square meters. The last property is a two-bed, one-bath apartment for €365,000. They all look interesting. I am thinking that Malaga is experiencing the 'being discovered' uptrend, and I suspect that these are not bad investments for those who have the funds.

There are expensive-looking pamphlets displaying these and other properties sitting in a rack. I flip through one and consider taking it as a souvenir, then put it back. The business-sense side of me knows these are too expensive to be wasted as a keepsake and should be kept for the serious buyer. As I have not purchased even one of the lottery tickets I have seen marketed around town, I am not likely to ever be in the serious buyer category. Still, I wonder what the taxes are like, what the property values are compared to the countryside, and how easy it is for foreigners to buy here. I'm glad I saw that window. It has given me food for thought.

Although I have no idea where I am if I were called to name the street, I also find a shop that sells religious souvenirs. I am curious, so I go in. On a shelf is a beautiful little 3.5-inch porcelain doll of Santa Maria de la Victoria. It is the Virgin Mary with the Baby Jesus on her lap, and both are wearing crowns. I buy it for my friend Desiree back at home. Later, when I take the time to read the back of the little protective box it is in, though it is all in Spanish, I find I can understand most of it, having spent so many years in Canada reading French on every box and label.

I don't want to miss anything, so I type all the Spanish into the translating app, only this time in reverse, and to my amazement the Spanish in the app has autocorrect, which means that when I begin to type a Spanish word, the app guesses where I am going with it. How convenient.-I learn anew that September 8 is Malaga's festival day for Santa Maria de la Victoria and that she is indeed the city's patron saint. I carefully remove the figurine from her box so I can get a picture. My long-time friend Desiree is going to love her. I exit the store with the prize and continue on my way.

Around another turn, I see a building whose façade features a beautiful tri-color pastel geometric pattern, and I take a picture. Something about the pattern reminds me of a design I have seen here before. I can't for the moment think what it is, but it is very unusual and beautiful. I reflect that at least one place I have seen it is on some beautiful note cards. Later, Imake a mental note to come back one day and retrace my steps and pay more attention to what I have seen, because when I try to find this beautiful building on Google maps, I come up empty.

The quest for the platter I had seen on Sunday is now revived, and the task of finding the store again gives me new direction. I'm certain it was near the cathedral, so I head in that direction. All I need to do is go back to the cathedral and walk around the immediate area until I find it.

This is exactly what I do. But when I go inside to check out the platter and size it up for my new bag, I find it is too big. There is no hope of getting it home in the bag in one piece. I ask the clerk if they will ship it and get a quote. The price of the shipping is greater than the price of the platter, so for the moment I stand on one foot and the other revisiting all the reasons I love this platter, and weigh this against the costs.

The sales assistant then says he has a perfectly sized cloth bag he can give me, and he thinks it would work as a carry-on. I know better. This is not going to be at my side as I retrace my journey all the way back to Spokane Valley. And even if I were foolish enough to try, there is the matter of what we are now calling the 'Dublin Dash' layover, when every minute will count for the plan to work – which means finding a storage locker for it at the airport is out of the question. I also envision the small Horizon Airlines storage areas on the last leg of the trip. No, I can't take it as a carry-on. Maybe if I were just going to another part of the EU or England, yes, but not trans-Atlantic.

I circle back and look at the other pottery options. There is a fish platter, much smaller, in the same pattern, but it is not what I have set my heart on. Back at the counter, my hands resting on the precious platter that I want to own, its beauty crawls up my arms and into my heart. I make the leap and decide to go for it. I ask for it to be shipped.

It just took a while to process the decision, maybe three minutes. Kind of like the way the idea of the trip started out. Well, anyone following my Instagram now knows that the platter arrived safely about eight days after I did. The invoice says it is from Agent 15, Manuel, and one day I will figure out a way to send him a note thanking him for the complicated but thorough packaging he carried out with cardboard and about half a roll of packing tape. There is no doubt his attention and care ensured safe transit. I finally conclude I will just have to go back and thank him one day.

Considering the artistry of the plate, the selling price was low enough to begin with, I tell myself in an effort to justify the expense. I don't mind at all that I paid more to get it to me safely. It is already a family heirloom!

Meanwhile, there is plenty more adventure left in this day, so I move on. I head in the direction of 'home', which is now just a few blocks away, enjoying each step on yet another beautiful April afternoon.

As I am rolling my new bag along the cobblestones, probably looking like a lost tourist, suddenly through the window to my left I see a white-suited confectioner rolling out the most delicious-looking substance on a marble table. Then, neat and quick moves turn the slab into bite-sized chunks. The sight of it makes my mouth water.

There are tables nearby with pyramids of white boxes stacked halfway to the ceiling. That's a lot of inventory. It must be good. I pause for a moment and watch, resisting the urge to turn and take a selfie with the candy-maker in the background, as I used to do at the window displays at Disneyland to see if I could make the cast members smile. I don't know what it would be like doing that job all day long, every day. Do people notice your excellent craftwork? Or is it always about the candy? I like to observe the people, not just the product. What a happy purpose in life, making treats for others to enjoy. Focused as he is on his craft, I can't catch his eye. I'll have to go in.

This place must be popular. The entire inventory is candy, presented in rectangular boxes, and in a multitude of varieties. How will I choose? Ah, there's a try-me counter, and on it is a large glass bubble under which is a loaded tray. I move closer and just stand there staring. A small sign I am glad I did not miss says, '*Not For Self-Serve*, while another reads '3 for €21'.

A smiling young woman approaches. "Would you like to try something?"

I certainly would, but it's hard to decide. There are at least six kinds of candy on the tray. "Well, these all look interesting. Which ones are your favorites?" She shares her favorite three and I try each, then gaze stupidly at the rest, at a momentary loss.

"Try another if you like." I smile and point at another variety.

By now they are starting to all taste the same. So much for my sugar-free trip. Chocolate and nougat ... who can resist? Besides, Johnny says if I try, I buy. He is right about that.

I decide to buy the first three I sampled. James will love these. I'll bring Johnny back here if we have time on Saturday.

I take a selfie with the doorway to the Torrons Artesans Vicens candy shop entrance on my way out.

As I near my apartment I take a picture of that, too, knowing that soon all of this will be just a memory. Time is going way too fast.

I need to get off my feet, decide if a siesta is in order, and plan out the rest of my last afternoon and evening flying solo in Malaga. I am always more than happy to arrive home. As I press the button to call the quirky lift, I feel almost like a local and life is good.

Wet Wash and Dry Run

Back in my apartment I am tempted to have a siesta, but the pull to accomplish what I can on my last free afternoon is stronger. For one thing, I am determined to do some laundry. I have plenty for a load, and while I am not short of clothes, it will be nice to have everything clean for the trip home. The tipping point is that I really want to use a washing sheet, as I have purchased these especially for this trip.

How hard can it be to turn on a washing machine, even when the instructions are in Spanish? Some things are just intuitive, right?

I gather up my dirty laundry that I have been collecting in a bag, and for good measure also add the shirts and pants I have worn the most. So far so good. I toss in a washer sheet, choose a setting that looks to be around average, and close the washing machine door.

Nothing happens.

Having half-expected to encounter a mild challenge, I spend about ten minutes fiddling with all the settings, crouched awkwardly on the kitchen floor. Could the machine be out of order? When was the last time anyone used it? Perhaps, like the coffee pot, it is not functional, and nobody has reported it? I get an error code, *E30*. I turn the whole thing off and start again. Error code *E30* again. I decide to Google it, although I am skeptical of what I will find, so I slam the door and stand up.

Instantly the washer starts up. Can you guess?

The door had not been closed firmly enough on this little front loader. Lesson learned. Wow. That's pretty much a universal type error, and it almost got the better of me. I hazard a guess that if I stick around long enough in Spain, I will find more similarities than differences when it comes to domestic matters. Oh well, it is now 5:30 pm and it was 3:30 when I stopped to buy the candy, so clearly time is passing. I feel a sense of urgency to make the best use of the rest of it.

By now, my virtual guide Thomas knows that I am a little apprehensive about tomorrow's timetable. Johnny is arriving back early in the morning. He has to travel back by ride-share 30 miles from Marbella and he wants to bring his luggage to the apartment before we head off to catch the 9:25 am train to Granada for our Alhambra and Nasrid Palaces tour I have booked – at no small cost, as I'd bought them only two weeks prior. Thomas texts me and suggests that tonight I do a dry run to Malaga's Maria Zambrano train station, thinking I might sleep better tonight if I can put my mind at rest about the timeframe. I think this is a great idea as it will also give me the chance to ask about the tickets after mixing up who was the senior when I bought them.

When foreigners ride trains in the EU, the ticket needs to have your name and passport information on it, and you must be prepared to show that identification on the train. Thomas reminds me for the umpteenth time that I can buy a 10-pack of bus passes (good for up to a year) at the tobacco shop across the

Plaza, and even sends me a picture of it in case I can't find it. In truth I have passed it many times, though it had not registered, as there was so much else to look at. But today, having mastered the washing machine, I am ready to beat the bus system, so off I go, retracing my steps across the Plaza de la Merced and to the tobacconist, where I discover it is ridiculously easy to buy a pack of bus passes for all of €4.20, just as Thomas said it would be.

I head toward the bus stop that is just outside the door to my apartment on the other side of the street and wait for the next C1 bus to arrive. C1 will take me on familiar streets and then carry on a bit further to the station. Later, C3 will bring me back. I stand with the locals waiting for the bus and feel contented to know I have graduated to a greater level of ease for getting around Malaga.

At the same time, getting around by foot means more chance of coming across things you may have missed. There is a certain satisfaction in accidentally discovering things you have read about but not yet seen yet, as happened with the German Bridge and the Anglican Cemetery. Still, it is nice to have the option of the bus when time is of the essence, as it is right now.

The C1 bus arrives, and I find myself a seat at the front. It is empowering to ride the transit, and it's a satisfying ride. I enjoy the sights immensely, some old, some new, and we pass through the tunnel near my apartment for the first time. The tunnel exits near the property management office where we will store our luggage on Saturday, and I realize I can catch this same bus Saturday when we board with our luggage for the final leg to the train station.

I anticipate that the train station will be a major stop and that nobody with eyeballs could miss it, but nevertheless I keep an eagle eye out for the right place to disembark. Soon enough, the destination is reached. I hop off the bus with a light step and head for the main entrance.

Inside, the station is clean and modern white tile floors.

Vendors are selling tempting pastries and churros, and I can see various gadget shops on the far side, but more importantly, there is an Information Booth, and I head straight for it. The young lady there listens to my concern about my tickets and directs me to the Customer Service area, which is just a bit further along and on the other side of the building, ahead of the security area that serves those embarking on a train for regions out of town. This is where we will go to catch our train in the morning.

At Customer Service, out of eight or ten windows, there are five open. I join the ranks of those who are waiting to be served. After about ten minutes, I realize there is a number system. I am supposed to have collected one so I will know when it's my turn. I had thought it was curious that people were not standing in orderly queues. I see that the instructions for the machines where you collect your number are all in Spanish.

An elderly man standing nearby asks me if I am going on a train that is leaving in less than two hours, or one later. I tell him my train is for morning, so he shows me which button to push, and I get a ticket numbered 428. His number is 423. The people who are leaving on the trains within two hours are getting tickets numbered in the 300s. I see that the system is calling one party from the group that is leaving within two hours and then one from the group leaving later, in rotation, as customer service representatives become available. It takes around 35 minutes for my number to be called.

Meanwhile, I chat with the helpful man who is from Germany – in fact, a town named Rottenberg, a place I visited on that trip back in high school.

By the time the numbers get into the 415s and above, there are no more people leaving within two hours, so the numbers on the big screen advance quicker.

Finally, I am the next customer to be served. When I get up to the agent, I explain that I made a mistake when I bought my tickets to Granada through the Omio app site. Omio is an aggregator, like Google flights, which brings up all the possibilities for your search request and then lets you buy a ticket, but you have to make an account to do so.

I tell the agent that I accidentally identified Johnny as the senior and not myself. This error was then saved in the account, so the error I made on the ticket TO Granada replicated itself on the ticket for the return. I had saved €6 for traveling as a senior, but it was for the wrong person. I don't know what kind of complication this might precipitate, having never before traveled by train in Spain, and as a planner and a worrier, I want to sort it out ahead of time. No more 'pladifa' for me.

I remember that when I was traveling on trains in Italy the conductor's assistant had been grumpy with me and my companions, because we hadn't signed our tickets ahead of time. I don't want to be considered a bad tourist here in Spain, so I want to get the error fixed ahead of time. It will finally be Johnny's time to have some fun and see more of Spain than the beach of Marbella. We don't need complications.

The man behind the counter says he can't speak English well, so he uses his phone translator to assist the conversation with me. He tells me that he can't correct the error in Omio, as it was made online in my Omio account. Apparently, I can only fix it there (although I have tried, to no avail). Then he prints my tickets, both to and from Granada, smiles at me and tells me not to worry. I double-check. Nope, big smile and no need to worry.

Later, I notice he has printed the tickets with no names on them. Maybe this is the answer? As it turns out, tomorrow when we board the train, nobody even looks at the tickets. All they do is scan the bar code when we walk through the barrier to board. That's it. Again, just like one of my favorite Tom Petty lyrics ... *Most things I worry about never happen anyway.*

I head back to the Information Desk and ask where to catch the local trains, which is what Johnny and I will use to get to the airport with our luggage. I thank the young lady again and make my way to the spot she's indicated. It is down a separate corridor. I check out the machines where we will buy a ticket so I'll be ready for this event on Saturday evening. Local train tickets can only be purchased on the date they will be used, but at least I now know where to purchase them.

It has been a productive mission. I head out of the station to catch the bus home. Again, I enjoy the sights along the way, and this time I get off in front of City Hall and walk back up my favorite calle to the Plaza for a proper meal.

Being a Thursday, it is busier than it was earlier in the week. I don't want to take up a table for four, so I ask a server at a promising-looking café where I should sit. He shows me to a table at the back of the outdoor area, near a table where two young men, not much older than my grandson, Peter, are sitting by themselves.

A hostess leans over my shoulder between me and the boys and sets me up with a menu. I already know what I want, being hooked on Spain's garlic prawns.

"I'd like this order of garlic prawns, *por favor*, and a glass of *vino tinto*," I say, reverting to my usual shade of wine.

"Um, *something in Spanish* and, "No, that is not here."

"Oh, but I see it here on the menu?" She seems confused. I try to point it out to her, but she still doesn't seem to understand.

The young man seated on my left interrupts and speaks to her in Spanish. Smiling as he chats, he points out that they do have this dish on the menu and convinces her it must be available. She chats with him for a minute in Spanish and they both laugh.

Although I can't speak Spanish worth a shaker of salt – which, incidentally, I never once see on a table in Spain – it sounds very much as if she says, "You might have wanted some pretty girls to sit next to you, but instead you have a grandma."

I smile and think the same. Of course, she might have said something completely different, but it's funny how much a person can understand just by the tone of a conversation, even when they don't understand all the words. I don't think I have picked up *that* much Espanola in just five days, but listening is a lot different from speaking and I am certain I heard the word 'grandma'. I think to myself, she knows I don't speak Spanish, so she might have made a quip that would have been rude if I had understood it, but not to a fellow employee. I am not offended at all. In fact, I agree.

"I'm sorry, okay. *Si*." She takes my order. I am convinced my poor communication has caused the confusion. Reflecting, I wonder if I said shrimp instead of prawns, because at home prawns would have been much larger, although a lot more expensive and often less delicious, and certainly not cooked in flavorful oil like these are.

I smile at the young man. "Thank you so much. I've had that dish during my stay here and it is so delicious. I had my heart set on it. Are you from around here?"

"No, we are from the Netherlands, and my friend is visiting, but I work here part-time. I'm just off duty right now. She is new."

We chat politely for a bit. I savor the seafood and soak up all the cooking oils with crusty bread from a basket and feel a tiny bit guilty that the basket is empty when I am finished. Ah well, I won't get this at home.

I enjoy my dinner and a glass or two of *vino tinto* immensely and I can people-watch and enjoy the Plaza even though I am seated at the back of the outdoor area.

Eventually, after waiting in vain for the server to bring it, as I haven't figured out yet that I must ask for the bill or they won't bring it, I ask for the bill. I am astonished to see it is for a whopping €39 and appears to be for a lot more than what I ordered. When I ask about this, the server apologizes and comes back with a bill for a third of that and it lists only my own dinner and wine.

The young men next to me notice the exchange and smile. I say to them, "It looks like I was paying for everyone around me, not just mine."

Both young men turn their faces to lock eyes with me, "No, you were just paying for ours, too. She thought you were our grandmother."

Ah ... I see. The server did not say 'a' grandma, she said 'your' grandma She had thought we were all together. If I had known the error was for their meal, I might have been fine paying for it and I say so.

Of course, they say, "No, no. We can pay for our own."

As I stand up to leave, I add, "Well, maybe when I leave some pretty girls will come and sit down at this table."

The two handsome young men reply, "We hope so!"

Now my last mission is to see if I can find Malaga's famous ice cream place, Casa Mira. Johnny likes ice cream so I think he will want to try it tomorrow night after we return from Granada.

The walk is not far, just five minutes back down past the Roman theater, and soon this mission is also accomplished. The traditional Malaga ice cream I buy to round off my meal is both delicious and memorable. I eat it slowly as I wander back toward the apartment.

Feeling like exploring on the route back, I detour from the main avenue and head up a small side street that looks at first like it ends with no exit. However, by the time I get to that point, it jogs off to the right and heads into a quieter area. With the sky an indigo blue, the secluded mood is exquisite. I turn around and get a couple of pictures of a quaint-looking building. It is a good shot, as there are no other pedestrians, and I plan to frame it for my bedroom wall at home where I currently have pictures of Malta and Reykjavik.

As I walk the small cobblestone path, I notice a plaque on the wall indicating there is a five-star Michelin restaurant tucked along one side. I try not to gawk as I pass by the windows where the guests look to be enjoying a fabulous dinner. I am sure they have paid appropriately for their culinary masterpieces, and I hope they don't notice me peeking at them while eating in the street from a paper cup of ice cream.

This hideaway lane exits into a garden that takes me out in front of El Pimpi and to the area across from the Roman Theater. This is now my secret path to the ice cream shop, and I will bring Johnny this way tomorrow.

Turning toward home I pass a statue of Solomon Ben Gabirol, an influential 11th century Jewish poet and philosopher who was born in Malaga. I had taken a picture of this landmark while walking back from the bus earlier. This is another Malaga feature that deserves further research, perhaps while I wait for next winter to pass snug at home in front of the fireplace.

There are happy people dancing in the street over by the lookout to the *Teatro Romano*. This theater, millennia old, was only just uncovered less than 100 years ago. It consists of a semi-circle of multiple rows of stone seats and is even more magical lit as it is in the evenings. I wonder what else is below my feet. I don't think the underground parking garages extend to this area. I muse that we probably all stroll over more Roman ruins without realizing it.

It is lovely, and I am sad it is my only Thursday evening in Malaga. I take a photo, but it cannot begin to capture this 'all is well in the world' moment on a beautiful April evening.

Back at the apartment lobby ahead of the lift to my floor, I turn and take a picture of the lobby. Then I take a picture of the lift itself. It is just 10:03 pm and I know this sight will soon be just a memory. Later, I am sorry I never took a picture of the outside of my wooden apartment door with the little colorful welcome mat in front of it. I guess I will have to go back some day. *Keep trying for that,* I tell myself.

Inside, I unload the washing machine and lay the laundry on the fold-out rack I found behind the door in Johnny's bathroom. Now I am really feeling like a local. Not having a clothes dryer also takes me back 30 years to when I lived and taught in Japan for a year. I wonder if the clothes will dry before I need them again or have to pack.

I decide to give James a call, as up until this point we have just been texting once a day to touch base. It is early afternoon for him, around 1:00 pm, and he is in the middle of getting wood for the stairs project he is building from the back of the house down the slope quite steeply to the shop below. We talk for a bit, and it is good to hear his voice. He likes to hear from me, but I know he wants to get back to the job at hand, which has been slowed because of intermittent rain, so we don't talk for too long. If he had Malaga weather to work in, the first leg of the stairway project would no doubt have been done before I got home. But Spokane Valley is a long way from Spain, and the unusually wet spring weather at home is a few weeks behind the spring weather here on the Mediterranean.

Johnny has texted me with details of his arrival in the morning.

"Hi, what time do I need to be there tomorrow? I have booked a ride to leave Marbella at 6:15 am and should arrive around 7:30. I want to drop my suitcase off at the apartment. Is that okay?"

"That should work out fine. I did a dry run to the station tonight and checked out where to catch the train and which platform. I rode the bus and got us a pass we can share."

"Oh great, so I don't need to hold the car for us to go to the station then."

"Nope, I have it covered. See you tomorrow. I can hardly wait. Text me in the morning when you get close and I'll come down and open the door." This day – when Johnny can relax and enjoy now that his work commitment is over – is precious to me, even though it means our time is growing nearer to the end.

Fitbit says I have walked 15000+ steps today. This means it is truly time for lemon-ginger tea and sleep. What an incredible day this has been once again. As I settle into my comfy bed, I know I will be missing my Spanish home in just a few days.

Race to an Orange Umbrella

I am up early on Friday morning, although not as early as Johnny, who tells me later he has hardly slept a wink. At least he will be able to sleep a bit on the train, I tell myself, then remind myself that no matter how much I am looking forward to spending time with him, I'll need to be quiet and not rob him of his catch-up sleep.

In addition to packing up to leave his hotel, he was busy coordinating some planning on Thursday evening. His resourceful wife Jane had been researching potential tours for our Dublin layover – high priority tours to both the Guinness Storehouse and the Jameson Whiskey Distillery. Coupled with the need to get up early to meet with me and make it to the train, it is no wonder he couldn't sleep.

At 7:15 am Johnny texts me to tell me he is nearby and that the driver will now bring him around to the other side of the plaza, so I dash down to open the outer door. We ride up the lift together, me in my slippers. He deposits his one bag at the apartment, then we gather our things, head back downstairs in the lift and cross the street to wait at the bus stop for C1, along with all the locals who are going in the same direction. The quick photo I took records it is 8:06 am. The electronic notice board on the inside wall of the bus stop shelter alerts me that our C1 bus will arrive in five minutes, and it does. We all pile in, and for once I get a seat. Johnny chooses to stand.

We arrive at Malaga's modern Maria Zambrano train station early enough to have breakfast at a streetside cafe just out front near the bus stop. The portions displayed on the enticing sandwich board look more than generous, so we decide to share an omelet, and enjoy some churros – a Malaga must. It is 8:42 am when I take a photo of Carolina & Co. Café while we are waiting for our meal.

Over breakfast I prod for details of Johnny's work trip. "How did things go? Were you happy with your presentation?"

"Sure, it was all good, though it was a lot of early mornings and late nights. I met a lot of new people, but I'm happy to have a break from the work environment. I'm looking forward to the rest of the trip. I'm hoping to get a sword for middle son today if we see one."

"I'll keep my eyes open," I reply. "I'm happy to have you back at my side, too. It's been a wonderful week, but I'm looking forward to hanging out with you. I am glad we didn't order two breakfasts. This is plenty for me!"

"I agree. This is just right. What time is our train?"

"Well, it is just about the right time to head over there now. Let's go."

So far, everything has gone smoothly, but even though we appear to be in plenty of time for our 9:25 am train, I am nevertheless a little anxious about the possibility of missing it. The previous evening, the information agent had shown me where to go to catch our Granada connection, but we need to physically get to the platform – and before that we still have to go through baggage security. In Spain, you must have your baggage checked via an X-ray machine before boarding any high-speed train, and I am worried the process will hold us up. In my mind, if we miss the train, it will ruin the day, not just for myself but, more importantly, for Johnny.

Anxiety about little things going wrong and causing major consequences has plagued me for much of my life. I'm the girl who never knew she had graduated from high school in 1973 until nearly sixteen years later – all because of a clerical error on my transcript that resulted in my Typing Class grade being omitted from records of my required credits. Consequently, I always thought it was my only ever 'D' – in French, that precipitated the absence of a diploma being awarded, because my home room teacher was also my French teacher.

All those years later the error was corrected, just ahead of my teaching certificate graduation in November 1998, and although I was greatly relieved, I also cried many tears at the injustice I had unknowingly suffered. It goes to show you never know when just one moment of neglect will reach out and bite you. It was an important lesson and made me realize early on, just how vital it is to pay attention to detail, a habit I passionately took to heart myself and, hopefully, impressed on my students over all those years.

Incidentally, and perhaps interestingly, that French teacher always knew when I skipped class to hang out with the guy who would become the father of my three sons and my husband for a decade. Now that guy, Thor, is not only my friend Desiree's husband but also the drummer in our little living-room band back home. But I digress!

It turns out my worries about security are baseless. For some reason we are simply waved through, baggage and all, and we even have time to collect another cup of coffee from a restaurant inside the siding area.

When I am at the counter, I notice a tray of Malaga's own 'Torta Loca', a sweet treat I have been wanting to try. Inexplicably, I do not buy one, and later I never find another chance. When will I learn to grab opportunity when it is right in front of me? However, against all odds, there is a comfy leather couch at this café from which we can see the trains come in and leave, so we take advantage of our good luck and sink into it with a collective sigh to enjoy our second cup of coffee.

We're not out of the woods yet, though. After our coffee we leave our comfy seats and head in the direction of the platform where we expect the train to depart. I remember the digital sign ahead of security said our train should be on Track Five. An optical illusion has made it look like the train on Track Four is on our track. When we see it is not Track Five, we go back and sit down.

After a few minutes, a realization slowly sets in. Somewhere in a text or email, Thomas has mentioned that there are only two trains leaving Malaga Station within our time frame. Now I see there are, indeed, two trains taking on passengers – and neither of them is on Track Five. It turns out the sleek white Renfe train with the red stripe on Track Four *is* our train; the track has been changed at the last minute. We thank our lucky stars we have caught this in time. It's just another of a notable list of learning experiences we have had and will continue to have while traveling in Spain and learning how this country clickety-clacks along.

Happily, we still make the train with ten minutes to spare and all is well, but it underlines the reason why I secretly worry about minute details and how they can derail you (excuse the pun) if you get things wrong – especially in a foreign country.

Our reserved tickets indicate our seats are in the last row of the car, with our backs to the forward movement of the train. I always worry a little for my tummy when I find myself riding against the motion of travel. The seats are upholstered in a pale blue, two by two on each side of the aisle. We each have our own pull-down tray and a place to secure a water bottle. Our day packs can go above in the overhead rack, but we choose to put

It Started with Malaga

them under the seat in front of us in case we need to access them during the trip. I feel a wave of relief that we can just relax and enjoy the trip.

The train accelerates without a sound, and it is a smooth ride. We hardly notice the high speed, though we can see through the window that we are rushing by the scenery at quite a clip. As I expected, Johnny spends a good part of the journey asleep, and I remember not to disturb him by chatting. I also find myself dozing off from time to time, but when I am awake, I gaze out the window at endless hillsides of olive trees rushing by, nearly all the way to Granada.

The backward movement does not upset me after all. As this is a high-speed train, we arrive at 10:40 am, just an hour and fifteen minutes after leaving Malaga. If I had felt empowered by riding the bus, now I am Superwoman herself, and I begin to imagine returning to Spain and travelling by train a lot more.

We disembark at the small but well-lit and clean Granada train station, which consists of one long wide hall for passengers to queue along one side for their train and to pass through security ahead of boarding. This area is flanked on one side by a series of the usual rental car counters, which reminds me I am grateful we are able to get around by foot and bus. There is a cafeteria at one end and the exit to the city at the other, so we head for that exit.

Our first breath of Granada is just outside the station where a small circle provides space for multiple charter buses to park while they wait for their riders. Further up an adjacent street we will be able to connect with Granada's main road, so we set off in this direction. It feels good to be out and walking around again after sitting on the train.

※ ※ ※

I am following the instructions I've been sent for this tour, but I do have one small concern. A couple of days ago – and I will never figure out how this happened – I had received a call from a Spanish prefixed number and had answered it. The caller advised, in dodgy English, that my registered tour did not have availability for the timeframe I had booked and asked if I could arrive at either 11:00 am or 3:00 pm instead. You might remember that, prior to finding the City Pass ticket with a start time of noon that we plan to use today, I had booked a tour of just the Alhambra and the gardens, but not the Nasrid Palaces and this ticket was for 12:30 pm.

Since the only part of either tour that requires an exact time reservation is the Nasrid Palaces portion, I don't quite understand why they would call me about the ticket that did not include the palaces. I have left both phone and email messages with the Get Your Guide tour company where I bought the comprehensive Granada City Pass ticket every day since the weird call and have not had a response. All we can do is go forth in good faith. Having no response, I am worried that the Alhambra and gardens tour we are aiming for at noon will turn out to not be available until 3:00 pm. But worry is not going to solve this one. I have done everything I can.

I decide to give myself a break from worrying. Johnny is a good problem solver, so I will rest my brain and let him take the lead.

The instructions from the tour company are to find an orange umbrella near the entrance to the Alhambra at the Generalife Gardens, our meeting point, but we need to take a couple of buses to get there.

"We need the bus on that side ... let's go back!" he hollers from the median strip of the calle.

I have already begun scurrying off in the wrong direction and I stop in my tracks, no doubt looking dazed and confused. "Oh, okay, if you are sure." I wait for a car to pass and head back in his direction.

"I can see it on my phone. It must be over here." He seems surprised that I am confused. My internal compass is still set for Malaga.

After a short walk we find the bus that will take us in the right direction, then get off to switch to the next one that will take us up the hill to the starting point of the tour. Johnny has taken charge of directions on his phone, and I remind myself again that I can relax. Although I am the one who has done weeks of preparation and research, he is young and strong and has an excellent brain – not least for the latest navigational aid on his much newer phone. It makes sense to let him take the reins a bit and try to keep any concerns I may have to myself.

Nevertheless, when we step off the first bus, it is not clear where we should meet the next. We are obviously newcomers, and we attract the attention of what we later realize is a homeless or at least jobless man who steps up and waves for us to follow him. He knows where we are going and has seen this act before. Unprepared as we are, and confused as we are, we follow him across the street and after a two-minute walk we find ourselves at a bus stop where, he motions, we can catch the bus to take us up the hill – and up the hill is where we want to go. The man pauses expectantly, and I realize he is waiting for us to pay him. Of course he is. I hand him a two-euro coin for his trouble.

When we had started out, I had enough change in my coin purse for our bus tickets, which cost €1.40 euros each, but I have used it for the first bus and the donation to our local helper. Johnny doesn't have any change at all. The tickets for the tour actually include passes for the bus, but we don't have this paperwork yet – we'll be given it at the start of the tour – and only have the confirmation vouchers. I hope to get access to nine promised bus passes once we have met our guide.

Finally, we board the bus that will take us up to the Alhambra gates. Fortunately, the driver on this second bus just waves off my tour ticket paper when I show him the first bus pass, which seemingly is not transferable to his bus. Here is a man who is used to foreigners and happy to have them as passengers. Later in the day, I will wish for the same luck.

We don't get seats on this second bus either, but that is okay. Standing, we can easily turn our heads in any direction and see what there is to see. My focus has been so much on Malaga, it is a bit strange to see a completely different landscape around us as the bus begins to climb up the hill. The streets are narrow, but we can peek past the nearby structures to see the city and the valley beyond in the distance.

With the various mix-ups that have happened, and my accompanying sense of urgency, our day has begun to feel like a more pleasant version of the TV show, *The Amazing Race*, but without the knots in my stomach that watching the program used to cause me. But we have almost made it to our destination, so I assure myself all is well.

Our last challenge is to meet our guide at the orange umbrella near the entrance to the Generalife, which is the name for the garden area of the Alhambra complex, and the bus drops us off just outside the gardens in good time for the start of the 12:00 pm tour.

I notice gratefully there is a *baño* nearby, but the orange umbrella is a priority. I had been expecting a large umbrella, perhaps shading a table, and possibly a sign saying 'GetYourGuide', the name of the company I'd purchased the tickets from a few weeks ago. But there is nothing of the sort. I narrow down my focus there she is, a young woman with long straight black hair, clipped short around the sides, in a pink hoodie with a clipboard, standing behind a small, faded – although decidedly orange – umbrella, of the exact same size one would use if it started to rain. What a relief. Later, I cannot believe I did not take a picture of her with it, considering the space this object occupied in my mind for several hours.

We approach her and find we are the first to arrive. I ask about the timing and she gives me a decidedly blank look. I try to explain about the confusing phone call and Johnny nudges me.

"Just forget it, ma. It isn't important. She has our names right there."

"Sure, okay, well that is a relief anyway. I suppose I will never know what that call was all about." Johnny smiles as he spans the scene around us. This is a popular spot, with lots of people milling around.

We are here, and we are fifteen minutes early. All is well. Perhaps the call had been some kind of weird spam – although I don't know how they got my phone number. It's a mystery that will never be solved, but it's time to let it go.

I head for the *baño* and find that the 'Senoras' line is a mile long while there is no line at all for the 'Senors', but we ladies move along quite quickly and soon I am back near the orange umbrella where Johnny and I find a bench to sit down on while we wait for the rest of the group to arrive.

Johnny sits down beside me. "Well, here we are. This should be interesting. It's nice to be outside and somewhere completely new."

"Yes, indeed. Although I know next to nothing about this place except for reading a few historical novels recently about both the Alhambra and Malaga's Alcazaba. But I don't think much stuck. I probably couldn't name three facts about this place. Maybe I will need to read those books again after we get home."

"It looks like more of our group has arrived." From our perch on the bench, we watch as people show up, right up to the last moment at noon, and then we join the group.

When all ten of us have assembled, we are given a fresh pair of disposable earbuds and a device to wear around our necks.

Our guide explains they are mandatory for groups of six or more, and since she will be talking to us for three hours, I am happy for her that she won't need to yell. And, as we will be mingling with other groups along the way, I am also happy that we will easily be able to hear the narrative above any external noise.

Johnny and I glance at each other. We are excited. Our much-anticipated tour is about to begin.

Ears, Eyes, and Feet, No Hands

We are about to spend three hours exploring this Alhambra UNESCO World Heritage site. The *GetYourGuide* description reads: *First, visit the Alhambra with your expert guide and learn all about its history. Discover all areas of the complex including the Generalife, Alcazaba, Palace de Carlos V, and the Nasrid Palaces, the most famous area of this complex.*

There is a long list of other attractions that we can visit over the next 48 hours – as well as the nine bus passes to get around – included with the City Pass portion of our ticket – but we won't be around to see or use them. Because I had booked so near the desired date, this was the only means to get the tour that included the Nasrid Palaces, the attraction that is in the most demand. The tour will feature three parts, each lasting for approximately an hour. During the first hour we will explore the Generalife gardens and the relatively modest summer palace around which the gardens were built. The second hour will feature the palace of King Carlos the V, plus various towers and surrounds. The last hour will feature the three Nasrid Palaces, the most impressive architecture of all.

Equipped with earpieces and radios, the whole group follows the young woman in the pink hoodie. Just inside the gate, our guide pleads with us to stay together when we inevitably start mingling with the crowds further along. After testing that all our headsets are working, she tells us to follow her closely as there will be many other groups with headsets following their tour guides and many options for where to go next. We could get lost if we don't pay attention. Her conspicuous pink hoodie will be a significant help in this matter.

She tests the instruction-following capacity of our group by giving the direction via our headsets to gather around a three-sided pillar, each side displaying a sample of the different-textured finishes. With a little extra nudging to the Norwegian couple who are already distracted, we comply. We will see these finishes on various structures throughout the day. One is molded plaster, another wood, and the last is tile. These samples are for us to feel if we wish, so we won't be tempted to touch the actual walls that feature them when we see them.

Through the headset I pick up on the words: "Seven thousand people go through this site every day in peak season."

I wonder to myself: *How many times a day are these samples caressed? Have people already shrugged off the pandemic-inspired caution against touching common surfaces so thoroughly? Now we are encouraged to touch the same surface that hundreds or thousands of others may have done in the past day or so?* Stepping back to give this some thought, it is for me a notable and startling turnaround to the restrictions Spain had in place just a couple of years ago.

So far, I've maintained my health through airports, airplanes, trains and markets by being careful with hygiene, sometimes even balancing my way down steps while trying to avoid the handrail. I decide not to tempt fate here. Just looking is enough. Still, the point is made; don't touch, just look. Fair enough. I don't want, nor had I been tempted, to touch any of it.

It Started with Malaga

As we follow the pink hoodie into the Generalife gardens, the breeze is light and the air perfectly clear. It is a relief to be walking among the trees and flowers. I am so glad we started in the garden area. It is the perfect natural buildup and nature's equal match for the architectural wonders that await. It is a glorious day for this ramble through history.

I can smell the roses without even having to bend close to them, although I do anyway. Their scent is the most fragrant I have ever experienced from a rose or any other flower. We are told that these roses have been here for an exceptionally long time, their roots are directly descended from those originating hundreds of years ago.

Although I can't possibly know this, it is possible – and I would like to think likely – that Queen Isabella herself bent for the scent of the predecessor to these same roses. But for someone who has come so far and at not little expense to be here, I am shockingly devoid of the history of the gardens until weeks later when the trip is over and I have a chance to read more of what a huge part Granada and the Alhambra played in Spain's past – not least the state of Christianity in the world at the time and Queen Isabella's role in it all.

The gardens were first built by the Moorish rulers of Spain, in particular Muhammad II (1273–1302), second sultan of the Nasrid dynasty, who commissioned the estate as a summer palace, and his successor Muhammad III (1302_1309) who enlarged them. It was occupied by the Muslim dynasty until 1492, when Queen Isabella and King Ferdinand overcame the complex as part of their 'Reconquista'.

As we wander through the peaceful manicured gardens and past the plentiful water features, I feel a sense of being welcomed. It might be the oldest garden in which I have ever walked, and I wonder to myself how much it resembles the original garden and how much has changed.

It's a magical way to grasp history, by stepping through it

with your own feet, and later to be able to connect what you saw with what you are reading. I already want to go back and look at it all with new eyes, but for today, I can just absorb and enjoy. I am grateful that I am here in April and not in August, for the temperature today is simply ideal.

There is little to no discussion among the group members, four men and six women, as we are each listening to the non-stop narrative in our earpieces. I am among the eldest and there is just one young woman who is obviously younger than Johnny. The Norwegian couple wanders off and Johnny alerts the guide that her flock is breaking up, so she reins us all in and gives Johnny the unofficial title of assistant guide. We all speak English, but we are the only Americans, and aside from the Norwegians, the rest are from England. Now and then we exchange a smile or pause to let another group member go ahead as we navigate some narrow spaces.

Johnny speaks at one point, "Hey ma, can you get a picture of me here with this archway as a background? I never seem to get enough pictures with me in them."

"Of course!" I am happy to oblige. He has been diligent about getting pictures of me, particularly in my blue jacket, as he has this idea that I might actually write that book someday and he thinks my blue jacket should be on the cover somewhere.

As the tour progresses, we see remnants of the Arab, Jewish, and Christian influences that characterize this part of Spain. From time to time, our guide strives to tell us where one leaves off and the other begins.

"If you see water features, fountains or waterfalls that make noise, those were introduced by the Christians. The Nasrid rulers did not commission noisy features. Also, where you see people and animals, that was added later by the Christians." The narrative is non-stop through our headsets, as there is much to tell.

As we pass a water feature, she tells us that lots of frogs

It Started with Malaga

usually hang out on the lily pads that float on the surface, and I think to myself that it was Mother Nature herself who introduced these – not the Christians or the Muslims that have influenced everything else around here. The sun is too bright to see the lily pads clearly, but I adjust my camera to portrait mode and take a shot of a lily pad-covered pond anyway, with hopes of capturing something. When I review my photo to post for sharing, I suddenly see it – one plump green frog, staring straight at me!

We wander along, weaving in and out of beautifully manicured garden paths. We can see a tidy looking orchard off in the distance, and across that the towers of the Alhambra fortress. Soon we meet up with more groups and it takes a while to funnel into the relatively modest summer palace around which the gardens have been developed. Inside, we soon reach a courtyard featuring a long stream of water, flanked on each side by neatly trimmed boxwood and plenty of spring blooming flowers. Water arcs in dozens of mini fountains, one overlapping into the next into the narrow stream down the length of the courtyard. The effect is as if hundreds of diamonds cascade endlessly.

🌸 🌸 🌸

I find that just when I think this part of the tour is nearly over – and maybe my feet are ready for it to be – there is something new and curious just around the next corner, so I continue to drum up the requisite energy to take it all in. Unfortunately, all the walking I've done during the week – almost 70 miles – is already starting to take its toll on my body, and this impacts my ability to soak in all the information, and I learn later that Johnny's sore shoulder is working against his day, too.

"Johnny, over here …" This is a good spot for another photo and I wave for him to stand looking out a picturesque doorway under a red brick arch and take a shot with him looking out and then another looking back in.

Down to my left I see a gardener near a tall fountain, and he is doing something with a long metal rod in a concrete lined hole the ground, a metal lid tipped to one side. Perhaps he is adjusting the height of how far up the water streams, which looks to be at least 15 feet. This place must require non-stop maintenance. The lone man in work clothing is surrounded by trimmed boxwood, an abundance of pink roses in all shades, and you can see the city of Granada beyond him in the distance.

The grounds are interspersed with an impressive variety of columns and arches that lend appeal to the surrounding gardens, and many of the walls sport intricate Islamic designs. I capture several more pictures of Johnny in this area plus a smiling selfie of the two of us, my hair flying everywhere as usual.

I love the yellow roses that climb aside an ancient wall and get enough shots of this to choose one for a frame at home. This section of my photo collection is full of picturesque architecture, tile rooftops, walls, columns, and arches, blended with abundant greenery, much of it blooming. This beauty is what will stick in my mind later, not so much what came through the headsets, though the narrative is non-stop, louder when I am near the guide and softer when she gets further ahead of me.

It seems like this part of the tour will go on forever and I catch a photo of my two feet against the red of the tile floor to remind myself later I was really here. Finally, when we walk the path between an avenue of tall cedars, we move on to the next section of the tour.

This section also has plenty of Oleander trees, pink, white, and almost red, just like in southern California, and we are told that all parts of the tree is poisonous. Well, I knew this already, but it made an impression on Johnny as he related to me later. I don't see it at the time, but he took a selfie with the trees in the background so he wouldn't forget they were poisonous. He also captured a photo of me in my blue jacket, under an archway of roses and another selfie of the two of us.

Eventually though, he rescinds his request for me to take pictures of him against the architecture, as I might have gone a little overboard stopping him a little too often for yet another picturesque opportunity.

In spite of my aching feet, it has been a glorious and pleasant morning so far. I do not regret at all that I had to buy a two-day pass. This was the day trip Johnny had chosen, after all, and at that late point in time, we were lucky to get any ticket at all.

I think that, someday, I would love to come back here on my own and just wander to my heart's content. I mentally add this to my list of reasons why I need to start planning my next trip.

As we leave the Generalife behind, we enter a world of even more impressive architecture. Next, we wander through the remains of a royal city we can see by the impressive brick foundations, the above ground portions long since destroyed and disassembled. Some of the foundation rises slightly above ground and other walls are only revealed where the soil has been excavated. You can see the outline of what might have been the site of structures such as houses, public baths, artisan workshops, and I read later, even a tannery.

As we wander down the red brick road between the foundations of the royal city that once was, I try to imagine what it might have looked like years ago when the original structures were still standing. The history books tell us that in 1812 French soldiers who served under Napoleon in the Peninsular War used any wood they could find, including furnishings, to build fires, this being one reason only the foundations are left.

I look it up later and see that during this war, Spain, Portugal, and the United Kingdom joined forces against the First French Empire during the Napoleonic Wars. Napolean Bonaparte forced the abdications of Spanish King Ferdinand VII and his father Charles IV and put his brother Joseph Bonaparte on the Spanish Throne. The Spanish didn't go for that and ousted Napolean in the Sixth Coalition in 1814. But I don't know all of this at the time. Just that the guide is not impressed that the French had a hand in the destruction of parts of this site.

A little further along she grumps that when Queen Isabella conquered the Alhambra she destroyed a lot of what was here hundreds of years ago as well, including what had been advanced plumbing for the times, which could be accessed right inside the houses that were once built here.

"The technology of the Queen's time and culture was far behind what she destroyed. How could anyone do that?" she asks. I note to myself, if the guide is any indication, the youth of Spain is not necessarily fans of the former kings and queens that helped make the country what it is today.

Before the tour is done, our guide has also expressed that it is inappropriate to use the word 'Reconquista', because you can't reclaim what was never yours to start with. Added to this, we are advised not to use the term 'Moors' to describe the Muslim inhabitants of long ago, as this word (in her mind at least) has become one that is discriminatory. Hmmm ... None of the other tour guides to date have advised in this theme, but then, all my other tours were in Malaga, and this is Granada.

As a visitor to Spain, this is confusing, as these terms are widely used in literature about Spain. I am just here to see the sights, but yes, I am also interested in the long and complicated history. I certainly don't want to offend anyone. This guide has chosen not to hide her opinions. I wonder if this is a common attitude in those of her age group or if it is a Granada attitude, or if it is just her style.

History's Unstoppable Echo

*R*esearch can tell us who commissioned the various parts of this complex, but I cannot find a word about who actually built all of this in the beginning. Was it slaves? At the time, I never think to ask. Surely, these grand palaces and surrounding gardens have been built by a multitude of hands.

History is full of destruction, rebuilding, and repurposing by conquerors, is it not? And is not what we see today a living proof that quite a lot was left to stand for time immemorial?

I cringe to be trying to recount history correctly here, because although we do listen to three hours of it, there is much I forget. Additionally, it is difficult for me to separate *what* we see from the *history* of what we see, thus the challenge for me now is to record what exactly it is that I have seen with any degree of accuracy.

From here we walk along a cobblestone road and our guide tells us that there are known to be ruins below, although it would disrupt too much valuable history to get to them. It would also require the destruction of the Parador de Granada, which is a kind of hotel built and maintained by the government of Spain. This particular Parador is the one that is most in demand in all the country, so it would be counter-productive to destroy it in order to dig up more ruins.

I can imagine there are a lot more ruins beneath our feet, but for the moment it is all I can do to take in the part above the ground.

By 1:13 pm we are gazing at the impressive Renaissance structure that is the palace of Charles V (Carlos I of Spain 1516–1566), who commissioned the build. Construction began in 1527 in the middle of the Alhambra on top of this hill. Through our earpieces we hear that construction dragged on throughout the centuries and was eventually completed in 1923. Apparently, in fact, it has never been home to a monarch and did not even have any kind of roof until 1967. Why was it commissioned when neither he nor any other Spanish monarch has ever lived here? Was it to symbolize the triumph of Christianity over Islam, as achieved by his grandparents? Before today I had not realized that Charles V, or Carlos 1 of Spain, was actually Queen Isabella I of Spain's grandson, never mind make a judgement about what he or anyone else did on this land hundreds of years ago.

The palace is so immense that I can only get a small part of it in my camera view. I would need to wander a long way from the group to take in the whole building, so I settle for close ups. We are invited to come back and explore the inside of the palace later, but sadly, for Johnny and me, the constraints of time do not allow this. Later, looking online, I am amazed at the circular open-roofed interior, and I wish we could have seen it.

That we travelers of the 21st century can walk in the footsteps of beings that created, inhabited, conquered, lost, built, and rebuilt the legacy that we behold today, is nothing short of breathtaking. I consider it the most precious kind of learning opportunity. This place, like so many others that I have experienced this week, is simply drenched in history.

You can feel the vibe if you stand still for a moment. With just a bit of imagination, I can tune in to the sights, smells and sounds of history's unstoppable echo. Even the passing years cannot strip this presence away. Quite simply, too much happened at this place for me to take it all in. The historical atoms bouncing off these skeletons of a lost time are giving me goosebumps where they collide with my bare skin.

The guide reminds us that we must stay as a group. There is a good reason for this. The keepers of the Alhambra complex are very careful that whoever is allowed inside these walls are who they say they are and are accounted for. I find this quite understandable. I am sure it takes a small but friendly army to manage the site and keep it safe for current and future generations. At the start of the tour we had to show our passports and our coordinating tickets, and we have to show them two more times before the three-hour tour is done.

I've already taken plenty of photos of the architecture, and meanwhile, as we move from one wonder of the Medieval and Renaissance world to the next, I also take some close-up shots of the walls and pathways that many hands made centuries ago. Alongside the magnificent structures they, too, have their tale.

Soon we arrive at an area that yields up a tall and impressively large tower. Through our headsets we hear, "You have fifteen minutes to spend here. I will be waiting on this bench. You might want to climb this tower up 55 steps to the top or you can access the viewpoint on the same level just around that corner. Please be sure to meet back at this exact spot in fifteen minutes."

I look at Johnny who says, "I'm going up there! You don't have to go if you don't want. It is a long way up. I'll take pictures for you."

"No way, I am coming too." Of course I will make the climb with him. This is my Spanish equivalent of climbing the tower of Pisa back in 2019, and I will not let this opportunity pass me by – particularly since Johnny turns to head in that direction and I want to share this experience with him.

"I'm not going to miss this. Are you kidding?" Maybe I am kidding myself? My right knee clicked for six months after I climbed Pisa's leaning tower.

"Okay, let's go." We head toward the access to take us up the tower.

One significant difference between this tower and the Leaning Tower of Pisa is that the steps at Pisa seem to have been made for normal-sized legs – perhaps it was not built to thwart enemy approach. Here at Alhambra, the first few steps of this tower are as high as my knees.

"Good grief; look at the size of these steps!" I compulsively begin to count them as I pull my leg up as far as I can to hoist myself up to the first step.

Johnny reaches back to help me get started. "One, two, three …" I start to count out loud and then I save my breath.

The steps get a little shorter in the rise as we ascend. When we get to the top we are rewarded with a vast and impressive view of the city of Granada and the Sierra Nevada in the distance. It has been worth the climb. After all, in a few days I will be home and I won't have to move much for two weeks at least, except for the short trip to take the garbage down to the road.

Walking around the perimeter, I take a picture of a slab with what I think is the name of the tower at the top, so I won't forget it. The engraved writing is, quite naturally, written in Spanish so I can't make out much except the dates. I check the photo later using Google Translate and it reads: 'In 1840 the bell tower was moved from the north corner of the Tower to the site it occupies today, and in 1841 the bell tower was destroyed by lightning and rebuilt on the same site.' So, it isn't the name of the tower at all, but it is interesting, nonetheless.

Weeks later, as I am reading an intensive history of Queen Isabella I and King Ferdinand, I come across the chapter where they finally conquer by siege the Granada and Alhambra. The story recounts how, in January 1492, after the city of Granada was surrendered, they took their standards up to the top of a grand tower, the Torre de La Vela (meaning Watchtower). I rush to my sources and sure enough, it is the same tower we climbed on that April day. The bell described on the engraving was used to communicate with the farmers about when they could water, and to warn the people of Granada if there was danger coming.

From our high viewpoint, we see that the guide is resting below us on a bench near the arch leading to the next part of our tour. We linger a while, continuing our walk around the tower perimeter, taking in the spectacle of the city below us. Although there are marvels yet to behold, for me, standing on top of the tower with Johnny is the emotional and physical pinnacle of our visit to the Alhambra. We both get some memorable photos of the city below, which as usual, cannot compete with actually being there.

I breathe in the fresh air and gaze down onto the foundations of the former inner fortress below, reminiscent of a Spanish Machu Picchu. Over to the west I see 'The Ravelin', a bastion built in front of the fortress. Again, I do not know at the time what I am looking at, but research tells me later. Right now, I'm happy just to be mesmerized by its historical beauty.

Johnny and I take a selfie before we head down under the stone arched roof that has been built over the top of the stairway. I wonder to myself if it's the same stairway that has existed all these hundreds of years. I'm not sure what makes me wonder this, maybe some small architectural tell, but I also read later that, indeed, the covered stairs, although old, are not original after all.

We descend carefully, as it would be disaster to fall, and I wouldn't want to add my blood to the stain that has certainly been washed from these stones over time. There is no doubt there has been plenty.

Back on safe ground, we walk for another five minutes as a

group and are then set free for a *baño* break as we await the start of the tour of the Nasrid Palaces that is set for 2:00 pm. Johnny heads in one direction and me in the other. It has been two hours of unforgettable sights and what is yet to come is even more spectacular in its own way.

By now, even though we are only two thirds of the way through our tour, I have reached 10 on the *sensoload* scale. The better part of two hours of non-stop dialog is a lot to take in and by now I am feeling a little lost. I remind myself that the 14 hectares of the Alhambra covers several centuries of history, and that Thomas has mentioned in his book that a visitor might easily feel this way, so I forgive myself.

🍇 🍇 🍇

Our group heads toward the final stage of the three-hour Alhambra tour, by now 'shipwrecked on our own mental islands' – an expression that, having lived in the USA until age ten and subjected to the classics that made everyone go out and buy their first TV – will forever bring to mind the show Gilligan's Island, when the passengers were shipwrecked on a three-hour tour.

For the third and last time this day, we show our passports which are matched to our tickets, and we are then permitted to enter the Nasrid Palaces area. Up until now we have been taking pictures left, right and center. Now, the guide instructs, we will want to take pictures 'straight up' because the ceilings are works of art, and although they cannot really be given justice with a phone camera, we will try. She advises us to, instead of leaning back and pointing our phones upwards, hold them in the palm of our hands with our camera set to capture to the back, just as we do for selfies.

This is fabulous way to capture great pictures of the areas above us, without putting oneself in an awkward position. Through the headsets we hear it is also a less space-consuming

It Started with Malaga

method, which is beneficial because the three palaces we have to see are all going to be busy and space will be tight. I appreciate the advice because I certainly don't need to trip over myself or anyone else, noting to myself I can safely use this camera strategy in a lot of future tours.

The three Nasrid Palaces, residences of former Moorish kings of Granada, are the front and center gem of this crown that is Alhambra – the Palace of Mexaur, the Palace of Comares, and the Palace of Leones, which includes the famous Courtyard of the Lions.

While the palace exteriors are rugged and imposing to discourage any enemy, the interiors are soft and delicate, with arches and intricate workings that invited peace and comfort to the daily lives of the kings of old.

As we weave through these impressive structures, I see for myself the details discussed in the video James and I had watched the last night before I left: the lattice-like wall coverings that let in the breeze but shade out the sun, the painted ceilings, the abundant plaster cast ornamentation glued to the ceilings and walls, one piece at a time, and the colorful tiles. A square of floor is roped off here and there to protect footprints made in antiquity.

Each time I take a picture of one of the beautiful symmetrically designed reflection ponds, present in the courtyards of several of the palaces, I am aware that I can never quite put my feet in the exact same place as the architect may have intended for maximum appreciation of his work. Therefore, all my photos are a bit off, never quite capturing the designer's vision of symmetry.

I decide that for me, the passage of time and the limitations of history filtered through story tellers of the centuries cannot reveal the fullness of historical truth to this newcomer. I know that my 21st century perspectives cannot help but be just bit off too, no matter how hard I try to absorb the complicated history where my feet wander today, just like my slightly crooked photos.

By the time we reach the Court of the Lions, which tirelessly spew water from their twelve marble mouths around a central marble fountain, I am, quite frankly, overdosed on the interior beauty of the palaces. I have seen about all I can appreciate. This is timely, because the guide announces that the tour is over and we are instructed to turn in our small radios that have been hanging around our necks for the last three hours. I happily remove the disposable earbuds.

"I might get some of these photos enlarged someday." Silence from Johnny. "Hey kiddo, did you like the tour?"

He removes his earbuds too. Then, "I'm sorry, my shoulder is killing me. Did you bring any Ibuprofen?"

"Sure, I have three in a baggie here. Let's get some water. Did you think our guide has been quite biased against the Christians?"

"She was, and well, I just think she talked too much. I'm ready for food. I hope we can find a pharmacy, too." I think to myself, but that is what we paid for? For her to talk? But I am not surprised. I think Johnny likes more space between mental inputs than what we experienced today, and I too have been somewhat overwhelmed with all the information. It has been a long week for both of us.

"Sure, we have time. But I need to find the *baño* again first, okay?"

"Sure, and near that is the store and I saw some toy swords out front. I really want to go back and get one for middle son. Let's ask the guide if she has a recommendation for lunch, too."

"That sounds like a plan."

One More Important Stop

Johnny is not the only one that is dreaming of a sit-down and some refreshment. He asks the guide about a place to eat and then we thank her, turn in our disposable headsets and wander toward the *baño* and the souvenir shop.

Johnny finds the wooden sword for his son, and I find a silk fan in an appropriate design and colors representing the Alhambra to add to my fan collection begun in Japan thirty years ago. We don't really need mementos to remind us of this day, but we are here, so we pay our economic respects to the little shop and wander out to what we hope is the correct exit.

As it turns out, there is more than one way out and we can't find the exit point where we entered, but there is a small group of people waiting for a bus to take down the hill to the city center, so we head for the bus stop and wait with them.

The bus arrives shortly and we are the first to board – bad planning, as we soon discover. We did not have our official admission tickets for this 48-hour pass including the Alhambra until we met the guide at the orange umbrella, which seems like an age ago now. Only then did she provide us with our official pass for all the attractions we could see in Granada for the next 48 hours, and not least the paperwork to convert our temporary ticket to a bus pass. But we can't actually convert our ticket to use on the bus until we get down the hill to the main road and a machine at a larger bus stop. As I had not thought far enough forward to cover the costs of this €1.4 each for the ride, I am now short of change.

I try to explain our situation to the bus driver, but he is not so accommodating as the tourist-friendly driver of the bus that brought us here. As I try to negotiate with him, a queue is building up behind us.

Suddenly, I hear a shout above the din. "How much do you need?" I am thus rescued by a female tourist at the back of the line – although I can't actually see who it is, who forwards through the group my required €0.40 shortfall. I want to thank her, but once everyone is aboard nobody seems keen to catch my eye. The bus is standing room only, so it is impossible to discover which person sent the funds forward. I call out a thank you to the crowd of heads and hope she hears me. I would have done the same, but you can only hope for random kindness when it is you in the lurch.

After paying twice for the tour and then for an extra 48 hours of admissions to further attractions that I cannot use, it has still been worthwhile. However, I am chagrined that in the end I am short and have had to rely on the generosity of a stranger for the ride back. Oh well, sometimes a person just needs to accept help with good grace and move on. I reflect that the tour information could have explained the bus piece better and I decide to include this in my review. *(I leave a nice review, and although I see it once, later it does not show up, so I am not able to copy it here. I do notice in another review that someone else has mentioned the guide's bias toward one religion over another on an otherwise great tour.)*

Back at the city center, the bus drops us off and we seek out

It Started with Malaga

the recommended restaurant, *The Riviera*. In retrospect, we could probably have found something more authentically Spanish, but nevertheless I have good memories of the experience. There is a statue of an armor-clad knight standing by the bar that reminds me of my favorite hockey team's jersey, and I swear the Las Vegas Golden Knights borrowed their logo from this iconic figure.

As we eat, Johnny declares the food to be ho-hum. He decides that our guide must have recommended the place for reasons other than the food. Looking back at the pictures I took, I tend to agree, but it wasn't too bad, and I didn't leave hungry. The portions were generous, and the accompanying glass of wine made up for a lot.

※ ※ ※

After our late lunch, we manage to find one more place we had set our hearts on seeing – the Royal Chapel of Granada. In fact, once in the area, we cannot miss it as it is such an impressive structure featuring plenty of arches, columns, ornate figures and an intricate design in what I learn later is Isabelline Gothic style. Here is where Queen Isabella I and her King Ferdinand II, Spain's famous Catholic monarchs, are laid to rest. King Ferdinand began the build in 1505, and it was finished after his death in 1516 by their grandson, King Charles V, in 1517. Joanna of Castile, their daughter, and Philip I of Castile, are also buried here.

We step out of the sunlight through a large set of wooden doors and find a spot to sit at the back of the pews to take it all in and give our legs a rest. We are soothed by the quiet peace and tranquility. I sit there next to my son in this improbable place, feeling the intensity of the history surrounding me. It is mind-bending to know that Queen Isabella and her King Ferdinand's tombs are just ahead of us, in the same large and ornate room.

After a bit, I get up and move toward the front of the chapel and into the nave to see what is there and Johnny follows me. There is a fence all around the tombs, which are raised high off the floor, so it is hard to get a good view. The tombs of Philip I and Joanna catch my attention. The massive marble tombs are topped by marble likenesses made, as I later found out in my research, by a Spanish Renaissance sculptor, Bartolome Ordonez around 1519. Isabella and Ferdinand's massive tombs are also here, lying side by side in repose and each topped with a sculpture bearing their likenesses. I see a small stairway leading to a passage under the floor, with an arrow pointing down, then notice another with an arrow pointing up, presumably so visitors don't meet face to face. I am embarrassed to say, I assume that this must be where the *baño* are, and I wonder how those entombed above would feel about that.

I follow the downwards arrow and step down into the passage.

At the bottom and in the center, there is an opening with glass on one side. Through this window, one can see the actual lead coffins of Isabella and Ferdinand, fresh flowers placed between them, then on one side their daughter Joanna I and on the other side their grandson Miguel da Paz, Prince of Asturias. I breathe in sharply, as I feel the intimacy of these grand monarchs so close by, as if I am intruding. This is no *baño*. What was I thinking? It is a testament to my *sensoload* in that moment. I'm overdone! This is probably the most profound moment of the entire trip for me.

King Ferdinand wanted his Queen to be remembered. I remember that our guide had explained that is why he built this site down in the city, so more people could visit her grave, rather than having to climb to her burial site up on the hill where *she* originally hoped to rest for all time. She died before her King did, so I suppose he had it his way.

We are nearing the end of our time in Granada, and nearly

the end of the battery on my phone. I have taken no photographs here at the chapel. On the way to the exit, I remember that I wanted to buy a rosary for Desiree, so I stop in at the small gift shop and choose a pearl rosary that made me think of her when I saw it. *I left it the way it was carefully wrapped at the little shop, and when I was able to give it to her two-and-a-half weeks later, I took a picture as she opened it so I could remember what it looked like.*

🌸 🌸 🌸

As we head for the bus that will take us back to Granada Station, I spot a shop selling miscellaneous items and I consider buying a pretty skirt I see hanging out front. Maybe if I start with a skirt I can break through to a breezy dress.

"What do you think of this, Johnny?"

"Um," … pause… "Pretty color, but is that your size? It looks more like something that would fit eldest daughter?"

"You think?" I ask Johnny to hold my blue jacket while I examine the garment. Indeed, what I took for a waistband is a gathered bodice, and the garment has been made for a much slimmer person than me.

"Do you think she would like it?" The swirls of turquoise-blue patterns had reached out and grabbed me.

"Well, when she started her new school she didn't want to stand out in any way. But now, four years later, she's learned to enjoy the ways she can be different and stand out from the crowd," Johnny says thoughtfully. "So she'll either love it or hate it. Hard to tell, but it is a pretty color and nobody else living near the Idaho border is likely to have anything like it."

The item now looks more like a pair of baggy pants, and I am beyond determining if it is a skirt, trousers, or a dress. I tell myself that I can always make it into something else. For €12 euros, I decide to take the chance.

Johnny tries to barter with the proprietor for some Spanish-looking coasters, although we really don't know if they have been made here or in China, as they do look as if they have been mass produced. I wonder how much of these wares come in on those large container ships. Indeed, it's possible that everything in this shop came out of one of those containers. The proprietor won't budge. Johnny decides to let it go.

Before we board the bus, Johnny and I are finally able to convert our papers to bus passes at a fancy street-side machine next to this major stop. We each get nine bus trips on a card that is disbursed immediately after we scan our transit codes from our City Pass. As we settle in for the ride back to the station, Johnny admits to me that his shoulder and collarbone area has been aching all day, and that this has made him quieter than he would have been. This is an old injury that has been made worse by the travel from Marbella early this morning with his luggage, and the fact that he carried it some of the time instead of rolling it on its fiddly little wheels.

Unfortunately, the last three Ibuprofen tablets I'd brought with me are now gone, so we decide to search out a pharmacy close to the station. Luckily, we find a small shop that is not far out of the way. We manage to communicate what we need and make the purchase, but by the time we get to the station, I realize that Johnny is *really* suffering, and he has been keeping it to himself so as not to put a cloud on our day.

This gives me a chance for a mom moment. I still have the empty Ziplock that contained the now depleted supply of Ibuprofen, so I wonder if I can score some ice. There is a coffee shop at the small train station, so I look up, "Please may I buy some ice?" in my translation app and bravely try it with the patient attendant behind the counter. It works. I am presented with a cupful of those huge ice cubes I now know are standard size for Spain, and they provide some comfort for Johnny's shoulder. My nurturing mom beast awakened; I wish I could do

It Started with Malaga

more. Soon we are on the train, and he is asleep again. It has been a long day.

I, too, am glad of the opportunity just to sit and catch my breath as the train speeds us back to Malaga, where we will arrive at 8:00 pm. I reflect that tomorrow will be our last day to make Malaga memories before we have to get ourselves, locals style, to our flight to Dublin.

From the window of the train, I see the Spanish Sierra Nevada off in the distance, billowing clouds hugging their peaks for the entire span. I remember that when I lived in California, where we had a vast view of the California Sierra Nevada mountains, whenever we saw that kind of cloud hugging the mountain tops, it meant there was wind on the way. I wonder if it is the same here in Spain. After a while I doze off, too, hypnotized by the miles of olive trees.

It is only appropriate that in a sort of Spanish Tourist Pay It Forward gesture, Johnny had passed his Granada city bus card with remaining trips on it to a young man arriving at Granada Station. I hadn't thought fast enough to do the same, so I offer mine to a young woman who is boarding the train for Granada back in Malaga. She tells me she doesn't need it as she is going by train, not the bus, but I insist, and she finally understands and accepts my unused card so she can use it in Granada for the local bus after she arrives.

I like this 'pass it forward' system. I am the type of person who often lets the shopper with only a few purchases go ahead of me in line at the grocery store, and I am always grateful when someone does the same for me. This time, it feels like I'm somehow returning the favor of the 40 or so cents paid by the unknown lady on the bus down the hill from the Alhambra.

Sangria with a View

Back in Malaga, after disembarking from the bus, we take a breather at the apartment to freshen up before heading out again for our last evening. We take a few steps out of our way and pay tribute to Casa Mira, Malaga's finest ice cream shop, by getting ourselves a couple of medium sized cardboard cups of Malaga ice cream. It tastes like honey and raisins. Johnny says something about wine.

My foggy brain replies, "No, I don't think it has wine in it."

He says, "Oh, I thought it did."

Later I realize that, of course, he was right. What was I thinking? Malaga flavored ice cream does have Malaga sweet wine in it, along with raisins from Malaga Province. To this day, I have not corrected my error with him. I do recognize, though not always at the time, that sometimes my brain gets overloaded and I make mistakes. I feel bad for nixing his bit of Malaga research. It was important to him at the time, the one tidbit he managed to squeeze into everything else, even with the shoulder pain, and I nipped it in the bud. To be fair there is no flavor apparent of any wine I have ever tasted, but it is a flavor rather more like honey.

Carrying on from the ice cream shop, I share with Johnny my secret alleyway and we stroll past the Michelin star restaurant. He thinks it is cool, too. For the second night in a row, I gaze through the windows at those people eating fine food, me outside with my cup of ice cream. This time I also notice the bigger window, behind which there is much 'cocina' (kitchen) action going on as chefs prepare food. We feel like we have had a peek into a secret world.

We are both tired, and we don't want to be out too late, but there is still one thing I want to do with Johnny, and it must be done tonight because we will be at the airport tomorrow by the time it's dark.

I wanted to enjoy the view of the lit-up Alcazaba and Roman Theater from the Alcazaba Rooftop Bar and had scoped out how to access it the day before. An accompanying refreshment wouldn't be bad either.

Waving at the top of the building just past the cinema, I said, "See those people up there? That's a rooftop bar. Would you like to go up for a nightcap? For our last night here?" Here's Mom, trying to cram one more event into our day.

"Sure, but how would we get up there?" The tall building looks intimidating, like a party that is private, where only cast members with a secret password are allowed to go.

"The entrance is just past the corner of that building. I checked it out yesterday, in case we had time. The fellow at the door said if we're just going up for a drink, we don't need reservations." I am a tiny bit smug that I can show my son that I have been preparing for this cool adventure in advance.

At the door, there is a velvet rope. On the left side of the rope is the queue for the restaurant, but you won't get in if you don't have a reservation. I know this because yesterday I tried to reserve a table with a view for this evening, but was told there were no spots available. Fortunately, we are not hungry enough for a meal now anyway. When I did my advance research, the

It Started with Malaga

fellow at the door informed me that if we want to go to the rooftop bar, just enter via the right side of the rope, and just walk through to the elevator. He said we don't need to ask or wait for anything, so this is what we do.

The modern elevator has glass walls, which makes for an interesting ride. It is a contemporary surprise amidst all this ancient history. When it stops, we are at the very top of the building and exit to an area that is buzzing with people. To our right there is the outdoor rooftop bar, and this is where we want to be. We look around and see pretty much shoulder-to-shoulder happy people.

The bartender helps us look for a table, but sadly there are no empty seats. I am disappointed, but on the other side there is another lounge filled with large white sofas, so we check that out. It is noisy here, as this area is partly enclosed, and I don't know how anyone can hear anyone else speak, though they are all trying. This side isn't going to work for us either.

We make our way back to the elevator, and just as we are having one last hopeful look around, we see that there are a couple of people just leaving. The spot they are leaving is the outside corner facing the Alcazaba and is directly over the Roman Theater. It is exactly the prize spot I had in mind. Our timing was exactly right, and I am delighted to get these seats.

The waiter is busy, so Johnny goes up to the bar to order two glasses of Sangria.

This spot is an amazing piece of real estate, and I am happy we persisted. We are looking out over the calle I have worn with my own feet these past several days and it looks dramatic to see it from above. The lights of the Alcazaba are like magic, and we can also look straight across at the top floor of Antonio Banderas's property.

The only thing out of place is the Burger King joint at street level, and I wonder how that ever came to be. Maybe the Spanish really like Burger King, otherwise how would it be profitable in such a setting? But who am I to say? I might be starting to *feel* like a local, but I sure am not one – just a greenhorn to the scene.

After about fifteen minutes of gazing at our surroundings in the cool spring air, we speculate that the waiter has forgotten our Sangria. Johnny goes to ask about it and they tell us it comes from the bar next door, the one near all those large white sofas. Finally, we are served two large icy glasses of sangria, and it is delicious. I remember all the work that went into making it at the cooking class. I wonder if we have made a faux pas and ordered it at the wrong time of day? Surely not, as this perfect April evening, with a light sea breeze and just the right temperature, seems the nicest time to have one.

We will never know. It is Johnny who takes a picture of the two glasses, as my dead phone is back at the apartment charging. Malaga's Alcazaba is lit up in the background, and we are peering down from this height with a perspective the ancient residents could never have achieved, and it is just right.

It is April 19, a day I always associate with my beloved Grandpa Joe who was born in 1905 a child of Irish immigrants. I always think of him on this date. Now I will add to this special date the memory of this amazing day where we took a day trip from Malaga to Granada, lured by the mystery and history of the Alhambra, and then stood by the graves of Isabella and Ferdinand. It is something that will stay with me forever.

Back at the apartment, a search on my phone for pictures taken April 19, 2024, reveals I took 298 photos before my phone battery gave up.

My Fitbit app tells me I have walked 16,856 steps, just seven miles recorded before that battery dies too. I am ready to sleep.

30

Our Last Day

Both Johnny and I sleep longer than planned on this last morning, but that's okay – we have a long journey ahead of us. I don't want to get up out of the bed I have found so comfortable. I find myself wishing we had one more day, although by the time we get home I have revised this opinion and come to the conclusion that for this particular trip, it was exactly the right amount of time. I have a hunch about what our marathon journey over the next 48 hours might hold, but I don't know the half of it.

Meanwhile, there is packing to do followed by one last look around my dear Malaga. It takes us longer to get moving than I might have expected. Thomas knows what I have seen already and has sent me a long email outlining some of the places and things I have missed, but even he knows we cannot do it all, even in a perfect world. Malaga is a remarkably interesting place, and no matter how many days you spend there you will find much to fill them. In our case, there is so much that will have to wait until next time.

I reflect on how thankful I am to have had this opportunity to travel and spend time with Johnny, and I think he too is grateful that I was able to come along. If I hadn't come with him, he would have just flown in and out and made his way to and from Marbella, so this has been an experience for both of us, albeit one that has gone too fast.

We finish our packing, stashing a few clothes and other necessities in our carry-on packs for our Dublin Dash layover. I'm a little stressed about that leg of the journey. There are things we're not sure about – for example, are they going to check our luggage all the way through to Spokane? Are we going to be able to get out of Dublin airport easily for our planned dash and breakfast downtown?

We discuss our concerns as we pack, and by the time I make it to the coffee stand to grab us something for breakfast, it is 9:56 am. At 11:04 am, we download a map of Dublin airport to help us navigate it. At 11:10 am I am sentimentally taking pictures of our apartment – the sewing machine, the fake lemons in the jar in the kitchen next to the keys, the closets, my packed but still open suitcase on the bed, and even my bathroom shower.

We have paid extra for a late check-out at 2:00 pm, and at 1:00 pm I am carrying out the one task for our last day that has been requested of us by the property management people – taking out the trash. I get all the way down to the main floor and remember I didn't take a picture of the instructions about the trash from the back of the door. I know there are bins across the plaza, but I can't imagine they would ask us to go that far, so I dash back upstairs, happy to have one last glance at our little temporary home and take a picture of the instructions. I have had all week to sort this piece of information but, of course, I have left it to the last minute. Oh, well. A quick map search shows the bins are right next to the building on a side street, so off I go.

Johnny stands with our suitcases on the sidewalk, while I deposit the small amount of trash we have collected during our

It Started with Malaga

stay. These are not trash bins as we know them. They are giant steel receptacles with lids that remind me of the top of my barbeque back home. When you open one, you can see that, far below the chute, there is a huge bin waiting to catch what must be a *lot* of trash in a day. There are four of them, possibly one for general rubbish, one for paper, one for plastic, and one for glass but I cannot make out the writing on each lid. I make my best guess and take a picture to interpret later. I sincerely hope that I deposited our trash in the correct chutes. It really is fascinating how different countries solve domestic needs in such a variety of methods.

It is 1:05 pm when the taxi we have hailed from the ever-present line up on the calle next to the Plaza takes us through the tunnel I have been gazing at from the apartment window for a week. This tunnel goes under the hillside that the Alcazaba rests on. It must have been quite the engineering project at the time to dig it out. At the other end of the tunnel is the property management office where we will leave our luggage for the afternoon. It is a short taxi ride, but since the tunnel is unfinished for pedestrians, it saves us from dragging our belongings the long way around on the cobblestone and marble footpaths. We're going to have enough of dragging stuff around in the very near future.

I am hoping to see the helpful Cynthia of my last visit, but it is Saturday and someone else is on duty. I give her my last unopened package of Spokandy mints, because I am not going to take these back to Spokane. I hope she enjoys them. It might even help her remember me, and this is important – but that will come much later.

After depositing our luggage, we are footloose and fancy free for the rest of the afternoon, so we head to the calle that runs alongside the port to catch the C1 bus. The final thing I want Johnny to experience in Malaga is the market. We are pros with using the Malaga bus pass now, and I have plenty of trips planned to take us through the day. By 1:44 pm we are exploring the market, and I take pictures of all the produce on display including spices, walnuts, almonds, fruits of all kinds, vegetables of all kinds, drinks of all kinds, a multitude of various seafood and so much more. I am an old hand at the market by now, this being my third time there.

Leaving the market, we stroll around *Centro Historico* area, and in an as yet unexplored section of streets, we find a good spot for a very late breakfast. It is a family-run restaurant named *Sabor Con Encanto*, and the menu purports to feature 'Brunch and Healthy Eating'. This turns out to be true and we enjoy a tasty breakfast and a delicious cup of coffee. The *baño* is huge and very modern and clean. This place is a find, and I tell myself to remember it for next time. The plaza outside boasts a playground for kids and also hides an underground parking area, making it a popular spot, and by the time we leave it is filling up with happy-looking people.

I have another ticket that I had originally planned to use on Monday but hadn't because we had met with Lori. It is for the Hop-On-Hop-Off bus to get up to Malaga's Gibralfaro Castle at the top of the hill behind our apartment.

Johnny manages to get his ticket via phone and an app, so we head in the direction where we hope to catch the festive-looking red double-decker bus. We head down the pedestrian walkway Calle Larios to the main street, which fortunately turns out to be the closest stop. At some points in Malaga, your Hop-On destination is more than a Hop-Off away because so much of the historical district is pedestrianized – but that's okay with me.

We hop on and each break open our package of disposable earbuds which we plug in and choose English so we can hear about what we are seeing along the way. I wonder to myself if these earbuds and their plugs work across all touristy-type

It Started with Malaga

devices. For example, could we have re-used those from the Granada tour here on this bus? Otherwise, I guess that tens of thousands of these gadgets get thrown away every day across the tour-taking world. Such a waste.

But back to the moment. When my hoped-for return to Malaga becomes a reality, I plan to take full advantage of the three Hop-On-Hop-Off tour routes on offer, but this time I am happy just to do this route – and it's all we have time for, anyway.

We drive past the beaches, where I have spent no time at all, and stop momentarily at the Automobile Museum. I did have a look at this online in my weeks of advance research, but there is no time for a visit today. Eventually, we arrive in the area close to where I had taken the Civil War tour, and the bus winds its way up a steep hill to the top. We hop off here.

We wander around for a while and take pictures of the double stone walls, which are so thick you can easily walk on them. On a nearby hill, I can almost see the castle where I posed for a picture and deadheaded a geranium a few days prior. It is a beautiful day, and we are atop the crown of Malaga. It is the perfect view to capture on one's last day in the city. At 5:00 pm I take a photo from the top. Time is ticking and we remind each other we need to keep moving.

Since we don't know when the bus will come back, we decide to go by foot down the steep path, its stones worn smooth by thousands of visitors. I wouldn't want to do this when it is wet. I hold onto Johnny's good arm at the steepest grades, as a fall right now would be catastrophic. It takes around twenty minutes, but we finally emerge next to Calle Victoria. We have descended all the way back to our apartment and ended up on the same road where we started the day, where I disposed of the garbage below the steel lids.

I take a picture of the seldom-seen back view of my

apartment building, along with its inevitable graffiti. Nowhere in Spain seems to be safe from this crazy painting and tagging. I suppose it would be an endless and futile task to keep cleaning it up, but it is incongruous with everything else I have seen. It is one puzzle that this visitor will just shake her head at.

We are happy to be back here, because this is where we will have our last dinner, at yet another Plaza de la Merced Cafe. There is no place I would rather be to say goodbye to Malaga, and it won't be too far back to the property management office where we need to collect our bags.

※ ※ ※

Mentally taking stock of my gifts for home, I tick off the small pottery items I've bought for Jane and Faye, and the crazy dress for Johnny's eldest girl, and belatedly realize I have been remiss. Unfortunately, I am travelling too light to bring home gifts for all the kids, but I do need to buy something for Johnny's other kids, middle boy and littlest girl. I need something for James, too. Where did the time go?

I must make one more stop at the souvenir store just a few steps off the plaza. A quick detour finds us out front, and to my delight there is a Spanish soccer ball that will be perfect for middle boy. I go inside to pay, and I choose a small, colorful bull for James from a variety of options. It can join his favorite small elephant on the mantel in the bedroom at home. I think he will love it. Next to the register there is a small red bell that reads 'Ring for xxx.' The imp inside me thinks this will make hubby laugh, so I buy it too. As I hand it to the little man behind the register, I see a wave of something like discomfort cross his face. Well? If you don't want to sell it, why have it here? My weariness and the oddness of it all threatens to make me hysterical. I laugh out loud.

Johnny hears me chuckle and says, "What's up?

I say, "Oh, you don't want to know." Awkward pause ... which in the moment I find even funnier, and my laugh turns wicked.

He gets out of the store in a hurry ahead of me. "Don't show me! I don't need to know."

What on earth does he think I have just purchased? I laugh out loud for most of the next block.

※ ※ ※

We still have the tickets to Picasso's birthplace, Casa Natal Picasso, so we stop in and spend about a half an hour being educated on this historical figure. At around $4 a person, it is definitely worthwhile, especially since the proximity to Picasso's birthplace was a key point that attracted me to stay at Calle Victoria in the first place. I am so happy we have tucked this last visit into our day. I know Johnny would have enjoyed the glass museum, too, and if it had rained, we might have made it to more of these special indoor places, but the weather has been perfect for us, and time has run out.

All that is left is our last dinner on the Plaza – garlic shrimp and wine, of course, for me and a hearty-looking meat pizza and Malaga's Victoria beer for Johnny. I try to express my gratitude to my son that he brought me along on this trip, but before I can finish what I want to say I get choked up and feel my eyes welling up with tears. Johnny smiles at me and says, "Mom, it has been great. I'm so glad this trip made you happy." He pauses and looks to connect with my eyes. "Don't cry, okay? Ah, you are going to cry." He glances at the people at the surrounding tables and smiles at me.

I hold myself in check. "You cannot know the half of it, kiddo. Thanks for letting me tag along." For a minute or two, I don't try to speak, and Johnny is quiet too.

At 7:07 pm I turn and take my last picture of the apartment

building in the distance, and we make our way to the property management office to collect our bags from their free storage for the day. The attendant had told us she would be there until 8:30 pm, but we don't want her to have to wait any longer than necessary, so we arrive around 8:00. There had been plenty of bags there earlier in the day, but ours now sit by themselves, the last to be retrieved. It is easy to stuff my latest purchases into the new extra bag I'd purchased for souvenirs by just unzipping one end and slipping the items in.

We thank the attendant, say our goodbyes and drag our luggage – mine a pack and now two suitcases, and Johnny his zombie apocalypse bungee-wrapped bag and a pack – out into the street. We know where we can catch the C1 bus to the station because we did it once already today on the way to the market, so we head in that direction. I feel sad to be leaving what has become my familiar stomping ground for the past week.

The bus ride is good, even though we have to stand for part of it with our luggage close by. There are padded boards for leaning against when you can't get a seat, and these are quite comfortable and help you keep your balance. For about fifteen minutes, we wind our way back through the streets of Malaga, craning our heads for one last view.

At one stop, an advertisement for a new film titled *Civil War* catches my eye. The details are hard to make out, but Johnny enlightens me. "That's not about Spain. It's a Black Hawk helicopter."

Ah, so they've made a film about Civil War in America, I think to myself. Hmmm ... And it's not the one that's already in the history books. Something to do with an upcoming election... Interesting. I snap a blurry picture through the glass so I won't forget this curiosity, and the bus moves on.

Soon we are at the train station, and we move forward to buy our tickets for the train to the airport, just as if we knew what we are doing. We have a new purpose, and that is to get there on time get through security, and find the Aer Lingus check-in. We still have a few unanswered questions about the logistics of it, and this distracts me from feeling the full impact of the finality of our Malaga City departure.

But really, I don't know what more I could have squeezed in. It has been epic.

The Dublin Dash

Our trip to the airport has cost us under US$5, a fraction of what it cost to get to our apartment by cab on the first day. This is useful information should I ever come back, I tell myself. I'm still trying to nail down an indisputable reason for a return trip.

In spite of our fears, airport security is a breeze. It is late on a Saturday evening, which means there are not many flights leaving and, therefore, not that many travelers. We have barely a wait and then we are through. The Departures section of the airport looks completely different to what we'd seen when we arrived. It is more than a short walk to find the Aer Lingus check-in.

It will be all too easy to get our boarding passes – or so we think. We make our way to the baggage check in, and at the last minute realize that just as in the start of the trip, we have not been issued the upgraded next to each other. I have the seat that was reserved with the extra $50 fee weeks ago, while Johnny's ticket is still for his original seat at the back of the plane. Argh! We should have remembered earlier, because this same issue was easily remedied last time when we'd spotted it immediately. It's too late now, unfortunately.

We are distracted from our disappointing discovery when we take our place in the Aer Lingus lineup with, not surprisingly, a lot of chatty Irish people. Very quickly, the discussion turns to whiskey. It turns out that both the people in front of us and the people behind are all experts in this beverage, and one is an agent who sells it.

Well, this is fun. In the few minutes we get to know these folks, who all live in Dublin and who are sharing our plane, we are all but asked to come for a visit. Johnny is smiling a lot, which is a good thing. His shoulder has calmed down a bit and, despite the mix-up with the tickets, I am fairly calm, too.

I am worried about my bags' weight, so I roll them one at a time over to a weighing machine. Our new friends stop me. "Just take it up to the counter and weigh it there." No one is there and it seems no one will mind. This is what I do with the remaining bag before the attendant arrives and I thus assure myself my luggage weights are within limits.

I am thinking this whole time that my bag full of souvenirs will need to be checked and that this might cost me a penny or two. But when the attendant arrives and it is my turn, the helpful and friendly Irish woman says, no, that is 10kg or less so you can check it as a second bag free. Perfect.

We also explain to her about the issue with our tickets and, somehow, she manages to make some corrections in the system. Johnny and I have new seat assignments which, although not exactly what I had paid for weeks ago, are side by side and in the same general area. All is well.

The gate for the Dublin flight is a long way away and we must take a shuttle, which reminds both Johnny and I of our stops at Heathrow. I don't mind though. We must do what we have to do. My pack is lighter now because this time I put the

It Started with Malaga

Surface Pro in a checked bag. Lucky me, now there is plenty of room for last-minute purchases at the duty free in Dublin.

Because everything has gone faster than we thought it would and we still have at least an hour before we board, we find a comfy spot on one of the plentiful lounges and plug in our devices. I put my feet up for a bit. Already, it feels like we are a million miles away from Malaga.

🌸 🌸 🌸

Somewhere near midnight, the wheels leave the ground, and Johnny and I are on our way to Dublin, side by side, one with a window and one with an aisle seat, just the same way we arrived.

But inside, I am not the same as when I arrived. I can't believe that just two months ago, I had never even heard of a city named Malaga – and Spain, the country, was most certainly not on my radar. Now, it has crawled right under my skin. *Suerte para mi.*

As we fly into the night I lean back in my seat, close my eyes and look back in wonder at the last, adventure-packed week. I love that I have been able to enjoy Spain, and Malaga in particular, in 2024 – the people, the food, the culture, the history, the gleaming white structures, the hosed-down tiled streets ... they have all grabbed my heart. Three years ago, the worldwide pandemic would have made all of this impossible.

Phew, close call. I feel like a train roared by and just missed me.

I am fascinated, too, by Spain's long and complicated history. If I have discovered anything, it is that Spain cannot be judged in terms of right or wrong, black or white, try as I might to put this down in black ink on a white page. I have no intention of judging. I just want to have my eyes and ears open, and to learn. Maybe in traveling we come to realize that we are more alike our fellow humans than not. I know this is not a perfect world, but I hope for my part to contribute more to the good than the alternative.

Thank you, Spain, for bringing me out of a post-pandemic, post-retirement funk into a light-filled place where I can live my best life. I've been waiting my whole lifetime to knock on your door. I am as in love with Malaga as I have ever been with a city, but it is not so much that I am in love with Spain –it is more that I am in love with the exploring, learning, inquisitive *me* I became while I was there. And all that, in just six weeks of preparation and seven days in the Malaga sun.

Although the Malaga part of the adventure has come to an end for now, you might have guessed that, for me, Malaga is also just the beginning.

🌸 🌸 🌸

Our plan is to sleep as much as we can on the flight to Dublin, because we know we won't have much time to sleep when we arrive. Luckily, we both sleep well, perhaps not surprisingly. This past week has taken all my available energy, and the pace had not slowed down right to the end. We had paid extra to be seated toward the front of the plane, so we can be among the first off the plane. Time is of the essence. We arrive at Dublin airport just three and a bit hours after leaving Malaga at midnight, but because we have gained an hour, it is around 2:00 am Dublin time.

We exit the plane and walk up the connector that takes us from the plane to solid ground, then weave through a few otherwise empty cordoned-off passageways that guide us to where we need to go. After a while we turn into another section of the building and the path makes a hard left through a double set of double doors. What I see stuns me.

"What? You've got to be kidding me. Really?" I blurt, and then I laugh out loud to no one in particular in the middle of the

It Started with Malaga

night. It seems that we are now required to walk up three flights of stairs, as the escalator is not working and is roped off at the bottom step.

I march up the steps ahead of Johnny, consoling myself that my backpack is, after all, the weight of a Surface Pro lighter than last time we landed in Dublin. Johnny, who has been trailing a few meters behind, hears me, but tells me later he thinks I was crying. Nope, it was laughing, I insist. But really, who knows what sort of animal noise I made? At least our main luggage is checked through to Spokane.

Some unknowns are about to present themselves, and all we can do is hope for the best. We are headed toward the exit and hope to find a shuttle to The Clayton Airport Hotel, which although conveniently located is still too far to walk.

We are hoping to get a few hours' sleep before Dublin wakes up and we can find a place for breakfast, so I really hope the hotel still has our room. At the time of booking, I'd sent a note that we would be arriving after 2:00 am, but I didn't get a reply, and a late email to them earlier this evening has also not resulted in a reply. We had also tried to call them from Malaga, with no luck. Even worse, by the time I saw the 'check in' link when we landed in Dublin, the app said it was too late to check ourselves in and we now needed to check-in at the desk.

I am consoled because we have paid for the room in advance through Expedia. Surely everything will be okay! Now, oh joy, Johnny gets through to them on his phone – a local call now, of course –asks about a shuttle and is able to confirm that, YES, our room is waiting.

There is another walk from where we exit the airport to the meeting point for the shuttle, and who should be there but our whiskey friends from the Aer Lingus lineup. It is the middle of the night, but the atmosphere is convivial. A bus arrives, but it is for the hotel across the street from the Clayton, then five minutes later our bus pulls up.

A few minutes later it drops us at our lovely looking hotel. We don't have to wait long at the counter to get our door keys, then we head up to the third floor in the elevator, my Fitbit, as usual, recording every step.

Our room is lovely. There is a king-sized bed and a single. I take the single, since I could sleep anywhere right now, and it is very comfortable. Johnny decides to have a shower. Easy for him, no hair to dry. I decide to wait until later in the morning. We set our alarms for 7:30 am and in two seconds flat I am asleep.

※ ※ ※

I wake up just a few minutes before the alarm goes off and I do not want to get up. But I remind myself this is the big day we have looked forward to, and I need to have a shower. The shower really helps to wake me up. I glance out of the window. The sun is shining outside. Dublin awaits!

Our original plan had been to have a full Irish breakfast in the Temple Bar area, but on the evening before our Granada day trip, Johnny's wife, Jane, had sent him a tentative itinerary for our time here. While we had been charging our devices at Malaga Airport, and based on her suggestions, Johnny had gone ahead and booked us a tour at both the Guinness Storehouse and the Jameson Distillery. Good planning, Johnny. I can't help thinking that the apple hasn't fallen that far from the tree. He is optimistic about our timeline and ability to get back into the airport, through security and even through pre-clearance in time to catch our flight home.

What the USA calls 'pre-clearance' is when passengers go through Customs and Immigration (CBP) at the Departure airport, rather than the Arrival airport. There are currently 15 airports worldwide who have this system, and both the international airports in Ireland, including Dublin, use this method. We decide it is worth the risk. What's the worst that can happen? That we may need to come back on a later flight? It is an adventure, after all. All we can do is hope for the best.

Johnny calls an Uber ride, and we head for the city for breakfast. The trip into Dublin is a bit of a wonder. Around seven miles of it is underground in a tunnel! Our driver says it saves time and has also saved lives as it is very safe. There is a speed limit, and every fifty meters or so there is a camera, so you cannot speed without getting a ticket. Our driver is chatty and helpful once he finds out this is our first time in Dublin. He tells us speeding in the tunnel is rare and that the result is fewer accidents. For me as a nervous passenger, I really like to hear this.

When we pop up out of the ground, we are all of a sudden in the city, and our driver starts pointing out famous landmarks, the Samuel Beckett Bridge, built with 31 cables shaped like a harp, the post office where the Easter Uprising took place, Dublin Castle, and more. Soon we are at the Copper Alley Bistro, where Johnny has decided we will have breakfast. It is early, and not everything is open yet. As much as I like to plan, at this moment I am grateful he has done all of this, and I just sit back and go along for the ride.

We are seated at a window seat, which has stained glass windows above it, and order breakfast. I snap a shot of the menu. Later, I realize that for €10.50 we receive a full Irish breakfast for the same price as our French omelet in the 'British' café with Lori in Malaga. Thomas was right. Although we had enjoyed our French omelet, it was definitely pricier than most of the other restaurants in Malaga. We didn't think too much of it at the time because it was still a lot cheaper than we would have paid back in the USA. Great food for less is a bonus that many travelers from USA or Canada might not consider ahead of a trip abroad. It seems everything is less expensive in Europe. I now live in Washington State, and before that California, where now the minimum wage is approximately US$20 an hour and people still cannot live on it. It's complicated, but I am happy to have moved back to the state where I was born. But I digress.

We devour our hearty breakfast – and a couple of large cups of coffee for me –before I visit the historically appropriate facilities on the way out and we set off to walk the streets of Dublin.

First, Beer ...

We leave the bistro and stroll down the street, pointing our steps through the gates of Dublin Castle. I had thought I might need a light jacket, but the sky is blue with nary a cloud and the temperature is incredibly mild – so unlike the usual April day in Dublin. I take a beautifully framed picture of Dublin Castle with a display of green trees and cheerful spring flowers in the foreground and the bright blue sky above. We could not have asked for a more perfect setting in which to see Dublin for the first time.

My mom has been developing an ancestry tree for over two-and-a-half decades, and there are plenty of our family's grands, greats and great-greats who have lived in Dublin over the years. They surely must have walked these same streets at some point, maybe on a sunny Sunday morning in April. I want to reach back and talk with them, find out what their challenges were and how they lived. In the memorial section of Dubh Linn Gardens, it is not hard to find a stone with an O'Connor, named Declan, with the identifying numbers of 21517A, but I don't know the significance. It's another item for research later.

"Johnny, this looks like a great place for a picture. Will you stand over here?"

"Sure, and I will get one of you, too." We take photos in the stone doorway between the memorial section and the rest.

"Look over there, Johnny. Look at what that large window has painted on it …"

He checks the direction I am waving in and sees the words 'Gift of a Lifetime', written large on the glass wall of windows over the door to the Chester Beatty Library.

"That's what this trip is to me, Johnny." He just smiles. If he says anything, I might start crying again. Well, at the moment, I simply could not be happier.

After a pause, "The Guinness Storehouse isn't far. Do you think you can make it? Do we really need a cab?" The enthusiasm of youth.

There's me, looking forward to an easy ride to St. James Gate, site of the Storehouse and nearby Guinness Open Gate Brewery. I mentally adjust and take stock of my physical state, from my muscles to the soles of my feet, and the tips of my toes that have finally stopped rubbing. Yep, the shoes are finally broken in as we experience our last day.

I give Johnny's question some thought as, after all I have accomplished this past week, I do not wish to be seen as a wimp – and it is such a beautiful morning in Dublin.

"Well, it depends. If it's less than two kilometers or not much over a mile and we don't have to walk too fast, I can do it. More than that, and I need a ride. I'm more spent than you know, kiddo. I'm trying to fight back old age, but this last week has taken a chunk out of me. I'm at the end of pushing it."

Johnny searches for St. James Gate on his mobile map. "It is just around a mile. Let's go for it. We'll see more that way."

And we do. We pass by several churches: St. Catherine's Church of Ireland, St. Nicholas's, and then St. Audoen's Catholic Church. Not far from a police station we observe plenty of

Dublin cultural color including some paintings along a wall in mural format depicting how at least one street artist represents various personalities in the history of the world – from Mickey Mouse, Batman, Marilyn Monroe, an Astronaut, ET, Christopher Columbus, Cleopatra, Elvis, Jesus, to Wonder Woman, and even a particular light-haired US past-president, who is sandwiched in between Mother Teresa and a rock star in an army jacket holding his guitar. James would know who that last figure was if I asked him.

At first, it seems we are the only people out walking this early Sunday morning, as if we gained admission to the theme park ahead of the crowds, but as we get closer to the Guinness Storehouse, I notice other couples and groups heading in the same direction. We are not the only ones headed for this famous three-century-old landmark. Gradually the street changes to cobblestone, and we are there. Johnny spots a horse and buggy outside, ready for rent.

"Let's check out the price in case we can use this for transit to our next tour at the Jameson Distillery."

"We will see. It would be cool if it works out." I've gone by horse and buggy twice in Malta and once in Florence, Italy, and it is always fun, adding a taste of the travel means of by gone days.

Meanwhile, Johnny fiddles to get our tickets downloaded onto his phone since the 10:15 am tour is entering the building, and we think ours is next. But he can't get connectivity, so I log into his account on my device. When we finally are able to check out our tickets we find our tour is, in fact, the 10:15 one, not 10:30, so we are immediately escorted inside.

"That fifteen minutes might be significant by the time we get back to the airport, kiddo."

"Don't worry. It isn't the end of the world for me if I have to stay in Dublin another day. We'll be fine, either way."

"Okay, then." I tell myself not to worry. He's right. Right

now, we are on this big dash together. It is very special time with each other.

This is a self-guided experience, with mini optional guided tours along the way. Before we start, on the ground floor there is a shop selling Guinness memorabilia, and I promise myself that at the end of the tour I will buy a trinket or two for the family and something for JO's Place.

Guinness has done a spectacular job of displaying and explaining the different stages in the making of their beers. Beer has been brewed in this building for over 250 years. The tour experience spans seven floors which begins with introducing the grains that are used and ends on the top floor with The Gravity Bar, where we can taste a full glass of beer by presenting our tickets.

We ride an escalator up to the first exhibition floor where the ingredients are featured and the brewing process is explained, very realistic wheat fields are simulated – and we can even smell the wheat. Then, the pure water pumped in from the Wicklow mountains, which is used in Guinness beers, is displayed in falls and fountains that spell out the word 'Guinness' and form liquid outlines of beer mugs. Barley plants grow in containers on the walls. The lights are dim, so the features all are beautifully showcased, the wheat golden and the water blue.

Next, Arthur Guinness's life is portrayed in frames and photos on a brick wall as we stroll along, and we see historic equipment such as a Ganz Mill, a Copper Lid used in 1936, a walk-in display simulating the 300 million bubbles that are in every pint, and the technology, including pipes and fittings, that is used in the brewing process. The official Guinness Clock shows us that every hour is tasting time.

The next floor features the Cooperage, where we learn how barrels are made and look at pictures of giant pyramids made of stockpiled beer barrels from days of old. A small diesel-electric Engine 47 used on the narrow-gauge Guinness Railway that was used in the transport of Guinness at this very site is preserved, and next to it sits a very different Engine 17.

The third floor holds the Guinness Academy, where we are shown how to pour the perfect pint and could sit for additional refreshment if we had time, but we pass on this and trudge up the next staircase.

The fourth floor showcases various Guinness advertising props from the history of the brand. We take some pictures of each other here alongside famous icons, the green turtle, a kangaroo, and a seal balancing a pint on its nose.

"Here is a mini tour, Johnny. Do we have time?" Checking his watch, "Sure, the sign says the tour starts every five minutes. Let's go with it."

"You won't get an argument from me. I think we are on track for time." We line up at the very start of a queue, having just missed the last group. For a few minutes I am compelled to stare at the countdown clock, which shows in red dots when the door to the sampling room will open and we can enter.

Finally, it is our turn. Inside the initial tasting room, there are four stations, each featuring the aromas and flavors that beer connoisseurs know create distinct types of beer experiences. One station is for hops, another for barley, another for yeast, and the fourth for malt. I love that I finally understand what these ingredients offer, but ten minutes later I'm not so sure I could differentiate the flavors if I were tested. Oh well. At least I have more to go on than I did before the tour. Since I don't drink much beer, I wonder if I will experience my next beer with greater appreciation.

Floors six and seven form one large restaurant and store, and at the very top level sits the 360-degree bar from which you can see all of Dublin.

It's thirsty work and I must admit if I had known in advance that we would have to climb seven flights of stairs to the top where the free beer is served at the end of the tour, I would surely have opted for an Uber to take us there. But it is too late now, and I am not going to give up. Of course, one *can* take the elevator between floors, if one chooses. but I don't want to be separated from Johnny, so I opt for the stairs each time. At least, my pack isn't heavy, although Johnny offers to carry it for me anyway. Good thing I left my souvenir shopping for the end. It was a very wise decision.

Seventy miles of walking this week; what's another seven fascinating flights of stairs to reach the pinnacle of the exhibit. I am squeezing the last out of the year of being 68 after all. I'll never again be this young.

The very top floor is a large room surrounded by glass windows through which we can gaze over the city of Dublin. There is a round bar near the middle where we can cash in the drink ticket that is included with the tour. Amazingly, we find two places to sit at a tall table. It is 11:07 am when the bartender pours us both a large glass of dark, foamy Guinness – just enough time to drink it before we have to head off to the next tour.

"This Guinness is really good! It is a lot lighter than what I remember." Normally, I avoid the dark beer.

"I think so too. Maybe it is a special blend. I wish we could get this kind at home. Or maybe we can." Later we find out it was, indeed, a special blend.

"Can you believe where we are?" Once again, I take in the moment with my son, grateful for being able to have this experience with him. "I am so glad Jane scoped this out ahead of time and paved the way for us to be here."

Sipping our drinks appreciatively, we linger for as long as we feel we can afford, gazing through the glass at the city and the countryside in the distance.

"Can you believe we aren't looking out over a dark, cloudy day?" All around us, people are marveling that it is 70°F. "We must have brought Malaga weather with us."

"I would have loved more time here, but maybe we will come back some day. It's a place I could easily visit twice. I'd like to get some things at the gift shop on the ground floor, so let's take the elevator down." We give up our seats to a grateful couple with a baby and head in the direction of the elevator.

A couple of minutes later we are back where we started. At the merchandise store we quickly pick up a few Guinness-branded T-shirts, and I wonder if I will wish they were a larger size once I get home. *(I did, and when will I learn? No time soon it seems.)* I also snag some Guinness-flavored chocolate bars at the checkout that I know will be a huge hit with James. But for my worries that the chocolate might melt along the way, I would have bought more.

Outside, we skip the buggy ride and opt for the more convenient Uber that has just discharged another couple coming for the tour. Without a minute wasted, or another step taken, we are on to the Jameson Whiskey Distillery – the second target of our Daring Dublin Dash.

...Then Whiskey

The Jameson Whiskey Tour begins at 11:45 am and is scheduled to take 45 minutes. We arrive at the distillery, an old brick building on Bow St in the Smithfield part of town where Jameson Whiskey was founded over 200 years ago. As with the Guinness tour, we log into the ticket on my phone but use Johnny's account as he was the one who booked it. It is 11:37 am and the tour starts in eight minutes. So far, we are on track, and we just hope that the tour really does end at 12:30 pm in time to catch an Uber back to the airport for our 3:20 pm departure. Lightheaded from the large glass of Guinness consumed before noon, I'm not feeling too anxious. We're either going to make it, or we are not.

"Hey kiddo, it feels like we're back on *The Amazing Race* again," I say to Johnny "Maybe we should apply for the show for real?" Two seconds later, I think again. "Well, you know, you and your brother Jay would make a great team."

Johnny chuckles at the thought. "Do you really think so? Ya, that would be fun, but hmm ... might be stressful."

As with the Guinness tour, this tour begins by telling the story of the founder, John Jameson, a Scotsman who came to

Dublin in the late 1770s and established the distillery in 1780. The operation was taken over by his son, John Jamieson, in 1805 followed by his grandson and great grandson, also both Johns, who ran the business until 1905.

Unlike the Guinness tour, this is very much a guided tour. At the start, we are led into a large, carpeted room and instructed to gather around stations stocked with all sorts of whiskey-discovering props. We stand no more than three around a station, where we sniff and taste the important flavors used in the creation of this famous beverage.

The guide asks if anyone needs a chair and, silly me, I do not speak up. The lights are then dimmed and we turn toward the lengthy side wall where creative graphics, one by one, are illuminated to accompany the guide's narrative. We are presented with the complete processes involved in making whiskey. A few minutes in, I sit down on the carpeted floor, making sure to keep my feet tucked under myself so I won't trip anyone in the dark.

I have to say the whole experience is top notch.

After this, we move in a line through the corridors and past the ladies' *baño*. I take note of where this is so I can circle back to it later. We are shown to seats in a lovely room that is prepared with at least five generous samplings of whiskey and some water for cleansing the palate in between. As I am not the whiskey connoisseur that Johnny is, although I do taste the samples – and they are all very enjoyable – I save some of mine each time and slide it over to Johnny, only leaving enough for a swallow for the group toast at the end. Later, he says I am a good person to be with on a whiskey tour, as I shared so much of mine with him.

At an opportune moment in the starting presentation, which is displayed on a flat screen TV, I whisper to Johnny, "I'll be right back."

I make it back in time for the end of the recorded portion of the tour and the start of the important part. The guide instructs us in proper tasting techniques and explains the differences between

It Started with Malaga

several types of Jameson whiskey. All but one of our samples, which is only available on site, we have back at JO's. I forget most of what our guide said, but I do remember that all the Jameson whiskey is made in Middleton, no matter where in the world it is sold. This will be significant to my wallet before the day is done.

Even without the full allowable dose, I'm feeling the effects of all this alcohol when it is barely noon. Although I remind myself that I do need to stay upright to get back to the airport, pretty soon I stop even thinking about the flight and whether or not we'll be on time. Well, almost. The last bit of drink has been saved for a final toast by the group all together. With the swirl, sniff, and swoosh with air in the mouth mastered, now we can be whiskey snobs!

We collectively raise our glasses for the final 'Slainte', pronounced 'Slaan-cha' and then we are done. Johnny looks quite relaxed.

Then, it is time to go to the bar and order our choice of whiskey for which, again, we have a ticket included with our tour. I order a Jameson Caskmates IPA with tonic and lemon. It is delicious and I don't share this one. I take a picture of the menu so we can try to duplicate some of these back at JO's Place. Later, I wish I had taken more pictures of the whole experience, and I think to myself that when Johnny sends me his by Air Drop, I will have more to add to the website I plan to build for pictures of this trip.

We finish our complementary drinks and have just a couple of minutes to make it to the gift shop. I'm aware that shopping right now is really pushing it, but I go for it, anyway. The people ahead of me have a snag with their purchase and I try to just breathe and not be impatient as their order takes enough time for three or four orders to be processed. Eventually it is my turn. As I reach the cashier I grab another chocolate bar, this time Jameson-flavored, plus a long street sign with the factory's address on Bow Street in Irish for JO's Place from the items placed near the till for those of us prone to impulse shopping. We know that all of these items are available at the airport, but at this point we don't know how much time we'll have to spare there or even if we will be able to access that part of the airport ahead of pre-clearance.

Johnny is the one waiting patiently this time.

I take a picture of the main floor outside the gift shop. It is 12:45 pm and we really need to get moving. We exit the building and, magically, just as before, an Uber is just letting some passengers out, so in we get.

I glance at Johhny, "Can you believe our luck? We couldn't have asked for better timing."

"We do seem to be having good luck for sure. We will make it. Don't worry."

As our driver winds expertly through the traffic – he clearly has an intimate knowledge of how to get to the airport as quickly as possible – he tells us we are lucky it is a Sunday, as during the week it could easily take an extra hour to make the same trip. I make a mental note for next time if there is one.

Along the route I take some last photos of Dublin. We don't go back through the tunnel, which makes me wonder if it is just one-way. Apparently not, but it seems it is not such a direct route to the Departures side of the airport and was built to be convenient for arrivals. Thank you, Dublin City Planning for our extra time this morning.

We breathe a sigh of relief when we arrive at the International Terminal, and I make sure to tip our driver appropriately for getting us there in plenty of time. Back inside the airport, we are lucky because security is also amazingly fast. We find ourselves launched back into the Terminal 2 shops area, *exactly* next to the little shop where Johnny sampled some whiskey on the shorter layover on the way over. The Irish seem to know how to plan this.

It Started with Malaga

Johnny buys three bottles of whiskey that we cannot easily get at home. This stirs something in me and I think sentimentally of 'lovie', a pet name James and I sometimes use for each other. By now I am – well, not drunk, exactly, but let's say, very happy. Things are moving along reassuringly well. I have a t-shirt that might not fit, the little bull and the bell, but this seems so small compared to the gift he gave me by supporting my trip. After all, the little bell is just for show, right?

I can do better. Inspired by another customer who buys an expensive bottle of Midleton 'Very Rare' Whiskey, in a moment not unlike when I splurged on my platter, I shake off my reservations and I decide to buy my husband the same. He deserves it. After all, I'm about to arrive home bursting with tales to tell. The whiskey will help.

At 1:37 pm I take a picture of the smiling clerk with James's fancy bottle, and I thank my lucky stars that my backpack now has room to stuff it inside. One last purchase, an Irish-themed bright green T-shirt for red-haired littlest, and I am all set.

Later, when I round up all my receipts, I discover this trip has cost just $100 over my original budget, if you don't count the platter and the shipping at the end, or this nice bottle of whiskey. I think I've done very well.

Homeward Bound

The moment I take the photo of the smiling sales assistant with the whiskey translates to 6:32 am Pacific-time in the USA though it is 1:32 pm here. Our plane leaves at 3:20 pm Dublin time and we now only need to pass through USCBP the preclearance, and then get to our gate.

Then ... words I am not entirely happy to hear.

"I have one more stop at the VAT."

VAT is short for Value Added Tax. The USA does not have this kind of tax, so travellers visiting countries that have one can get a refund on certain items, but we have been told we must fill out a form and present it at the VAT counter just prior to leaving for the USA at the last point of departure.

Gulp. I keep silent, but a small red flag waves in my mind. I had thought we were almost home free. I hope there isn't a big line at the VAT counter. Everything I have read says people often don't allow enough time at the airport for the paperwork, so most people just skip it, relinquishing a few dollars here and there.

Another startling article reported that in one day up to 1000 people missed their flights out of Dublin just a year ago, due to long queues. We cannot yet know what awaits us at the CBP or if there is a shuttle to wait for afterward for the gate. There are many unknowns before we are safely on time. As much as I enjoy an adventure with my son, I really don't want to become one of the missed flight statistics for Dublin airport.

Johnny had tried to collect on his VAT receipts for gifts he bought in Dublin's Terminal 2 when we came through on arrival, but the clerk had told us we can do it only on our way back to the USA. Reimbursements are tricky. If you do not get a special receipt at the time of purchase, you can't claim the tax refund. Later, I read that you can't get VAT reimbursements for food and rooms, anyway – and why would you? You only get the tax back on products you take home. I look at my receipt for my platter, which is being shipped, and there is no sign of any tax at all, so I am not worried about it personally. But Johnny has purchased the whiskey and some other things at the airport, and he does have special receipts for some of these.

A two-minute walk finds us at the VAT counter, and happily, there is just one person ahead of us. Johnny presents his receipts. The assistant processes them and tells him the credits will show up on his credit card in a month or two. (I will have to ask him if they ever did.)

Relieved, we head in the direction of the US preclearance. There is no line at all, and we show our passports and boarding passes and are directed down the escalators to a lower floor. Once there, we follow the cordoned lanes, around and through a doorway. Beyond are more lanes winding back and forth, clearly able to accommodate hundreds of people in line.

There is absolutely nobody ahead of us.

We make our way up to one of the staffed immigration portals and walk right up. Johnny has chosen a different lane to me, and he goes straight through after answering a question or two and showing his documentation as instructed. I get up to my officer, same thing, one or two basic questions – I can't even

It Started with Malaga

remember what they were – a look at my passport and a stamp in it, and I am through. All that is left is to go to our gate.

I catch up with Johnny and he says, "Wow, would we have felt stupid if we had missed out on our Dublin Dash for this?"

I agree that this time, we would have been sorrier to be so safe, when usually we are trying to be more safe than sorry.

Of course, this was on a Sunday. On a weekday, things could have been different. We don't know. We just know that this time, here and now, our Dublin Dash has been a complete success. If this really were a leg of *The Amazing Race*, most certainly we would have been the first to arrive.

However, our run of smooth sailing doesn't last. Once we have boarded the plane, there is a fiasco in getting us seated.

Well, here we go. We haven't had any big mess ups the whole time in Spain and here we are at the last and of course things are going to fall apart. We have used up all our luck!

Remember the bit about the nice lady changing our seats so we can sit together? I had paid $50 each for us to upgrade to two side-by-side window/aisle seats, and. she had actually written our new seat assignments on our tickets. But as they scan our tickets to board, the names do not line up with the information they have. It seems the changes did not make it to the computerized system for this flight like they did for the flight from Malaga to Dublin. Johnny is still stuck back in Row 33. I had originally been in Row 13, but am supposed to be in Row 16, as is Johnny, so we could sit together.

We are sent through to the plane to see if the seats really are messed up – and they are. I am directed down the near aisle and Johnny the far one. My original seat in Row 13 is occupied – as I would have expected as this was changed when I upgraded the seats before we even left home, so I put my bag in an empty seat at Row 16, in my newly assigned spot according to the Aer Lingus gate attendant in Malaga. I try without success to get Johnny's attention across the heads of dozens of other passengers, because there are two seats next to mine that are empty.

Johnny goes to his mis-assigned seat in row 33. At least Johnny has an aisle seat. He plans to see if anyone sitting next to him might want to trade forward to my seat, as he doesn't yet know I have one empty near me, but when he gets to it, his seat has a child's drink in it. There is a lone three-year-old in the seat next to him, her daddy off using the restroom. The little girl takes one look at Johnny and bursts into tears. She then points at the screen on the seat in front of her and complains that the TV is broken. She's not crying because she's scared of a stranger; she thinks she has found someone who can fix her technology issue. Poor Johnny. He gets that a lot.

For a few minutes things get worse for me, too. It turns out there are three other people booked into the seats in Row 16 that Johnny and I had supposedly been switched to in Malaga. So now, I don't have any seat at all. Both my original seat in Row 13 and my new seat in Row 16 are occupied.

I am told there is a single seat available back in Row 38, so I struggle up the aisle against the traffic. As I head back, I duck into a passageway just near the heads to collect myself.

A flight attendant comes to see if she can help me as, clearly, I am confused. When I explain what has happened another steward appears on the scene. Apologies are made and then I ask about a refund on my two upgrades. There is discussion among the attendants, and something appears to be in the works, so I wait hopefully.

Suddenly, a miracle happens. In some kind of seat-scheduling vortex, it seems there are three empty seats just one row ahead of where Johnny and I *should* have been seated. A lone passenger, a man, is sitting in the middle. I can hear the flight attendant offering him an alternate seat and he agrees because it has a window.

If I were to make a movie about this adventure, I would let

It Started with Malaga

my imagination fly. For weeks, I have had ready support from my friend Thomas, who I only know through his book and via email. I'll never meet him, as he lives in England in another world from mine and, aside from his love of Malaga, I know nothing about him. I would end the movie by revealing to the viewers that the man who gave up his seat for us was Thomas, and that none of us ever knew – that we just passed like the proverbial ships in the night, having come this close to meeting face to face.

I never do get the chance to tell Thomas about my movie idea, because after the trip ends and I am safely home, I never hear from him again. I do hope he is okay and didn't have some sort of mishap. As I write this months later, I still don't know why our communication ended. It has added an element of mystery to my wonderful Spanish experience.

But back to the present. Johnny and I are seated next to each other after all, and only three rows ahead of where the nice Aer Lingus lady tried to put us when we checked in at Malaga. By now there is no room above us in the carry-on storage areas, but I don't need it, anyway. The seat next to me is empty and the young woman on the other side of it and I agree to share it. She has already placed her book, *Atomic Habits*, by James Clear on it. A gold sticker brags, 'Over Four Million Copies Sold'. Ironically, a picture of this book was my last photo taken during this entire trip to Europe.

Once we are all settled, I breathe a sigh of relief. All is well. The Dublin Dash was, ultimately, a success. I vow that next time (if there is a next time – I'm still trying to justify another trip in my mind, and constantly plotting how to make it happen) I will be sure to book the tickets for myself and my companion at the same time, so our seats together are locked in from the start.

We sleep quite well on the nine-hour flight, perhaps not surprisingly after all the running around. Aer Lingus feeds us twice, a meal near the start, and a hot snack a while before we land. I accept the small bottle of Tempranillo when it is offered as it was on the trip over, but the print is still too small for me to read if it was from Spain.

🍇 🍇 🍇

When we get to Seattle, we exit the plane immediately next to where we will catch our connecting flight. There is no need to go through Customs and Immigration, as we have already done so in Dublin. This is convenient, but now we have four hours to wait for our one-hour flight to Spokane. We could have driven home in that time.

Possibly out of boredom rather than hunger, we seek out a light meal and a drink while we wait. We are shocked to see the meals are all at least US$22 each for what now appears substandard to what we have been used to in Spain for half that price. Johnny is disgusted. I have always liked Seattle airport, and I do not recall ever having had a complaint about it in the past, but today, it seems dirty and the people less friendly. We are clearly not in 'the most hospitable city' any longer.

Heading back to the gate area, Johnny says, "Look Ma, there's a flight leaving for Dublin. Do you want to catch it?"

My heart leaps and I, only half-jokingly, say "Yes."

"Really? Not me right now. I can't wait to get home." Well, it's different for Johnny. He is assured of travel for work. His sales group meets somewhere across the globe each spring, and the day-to-day business often takes him to Arizona and California to see clients. In fact, he has a trip to San Francisco coming up within the week.

Our flight to Spokane is scheduled to board in another three hours and we are supposed to land in Spokane in another four-and-a-half hours, making it twenty-one-and-a-half hours since we rolled out of bed at the Clayton Dublin Airport Hotel and

It Started with Malaga

thirty-eight-and-a-half hours since we got up in our apartment in Malaga.

We are almost home, but in the way that the journey home is never quite as much fun as the trip away, there is an issue with the gate apparatus for our flight out and it is delayed for another hour. When we finally land in Spokane we are delayed for twenty minutes on the tarmac. We finally disembark at 10:00 pm, a full hour past the scheduled time. Poor James has been parked in the cell phone lot all this time waiting for us to call and say we are ready with our luggage at the departures area. None of my texts to let him know we would be delayed had made it to his phone. I'm so glad I have the special whiskey.

Thirty minutes later, we are home. Johnny collects his truck from our place and is gone in a jiffy, as he has another 20-minute drive. I am sure Jane and the grandkids are waiting.

When I walk into my kitchen, I am truly glad to be home. I declare I am not going to unpack anything tonight because I am simply too tired.

And then I do.

The contents of the souvenir bag and my backpack explode. James always makes the house tidy for when I return, but in an instant, it is a mess. We stay up for another two hours just getting started with the sharing of the story.

I am not sorry at all, because life is just too short not to enjoy it. Not only did we sample a variety of meats, cheeses, olives, and chocolates from Malaga but, just as I had imagined, James cracked open the fancy bottle of whiskey and had a taste. It really *is* delicious, all of it.

What I do not open is my special bottle of Malaga wine. I want to save this for when the whole family is here and can taste it with us. If I remember correctly, the name of it means something like, 'To save from sadness'. I am happy to be home. But I am sad that this trip is behind me. I need to find a reason to go back, not in years, but months. I'm turning 69 in two days. I don't have any time to waste.

Epilogue

It is Cinqo de Mayo, Sunday May 5, but it is also Bloomsday here in Spokane, Washington. Spokane's Bloomsday celebrations began in 1977, a run, originating in the downtown area of the city with around 1000 participants. Forty-seven races and several decades later, over 30,000 participants will cross the finish line, some walking, some running, and some at every speed in between. Last year, I even jogged my own virtual Bloomsday, which has been a thing ever since Covid, and earned myself a Virtual Bloomsday t-shirt.

For the record, Spokane's Bloomsday must not be confused with Dublin's Bloomsday, observed annually in the form of a variety of cultural activities, not least pub crawls and marathon readings of his book, to celebrate the life of Irish writer James Joyce. I did not know this before I looked up the Spokane version to get the latest count on participants.

But back to today…

Johnny's family, all four but the littlest, are registered to run/walk this year's Spokane Bloomsday, the 7.5-mile Spokane signature trek through the city. I have been home for two weeks and I've been under the weather, not the 'C' word or anything – I did two tests to make sure – but a nasty enough cold to keep me away from other people, and I've been mostly back in my PJs, just like in my pre-Malaga days.

I don't mind too much, as I have wanted to hunker down and get my Malaga story on paper before I forget anything. Johnny has asked me to hang out with littlest granddaughter today, and I jump at the chance.

She was going to come to my place but Johnny texts me at seven in the morning that she is not feeling great. I dash out of bed and drive over to their place instead, my flamenco dancers' music blaring in my car CD player.

It is the first time I have seen Johnny since the Sunday night we returned. Finally, I can share with the kids the little souvenirs I brought back. Jane assures me the small piece of pottery I bought for her is just what she needed. All are pleased with my small gifts.

Mom, Dad and the older kids spend some time pinning their race numbers onto their T-shirts and eventually manage to get out the door.

I have brought my pillow, more as a hopeful extension of my sleep from which I had barely awakened, and if the littlest is still under the weather, I can at least cozy up and read on my iPad. But she is up, bouncing around the room, seemingly glad I am there. Maybe she just didn't want to go out that morning. We snuggle with the pillow on the couch, her head a perpetual tangle of red hair, reminding me of a modern-day Pippi Longstocking. Not to be left out, Finnigan the dog puts his head on my bare feet on the floor. We three have literally been left to my own devices.

I now have a captive audience to hear all about my trip, something that has evaded me for weeks.

"Grandma, will you read some of your story to me?"

Okay, I will always bite when someone shows an interest in my new passion that is Malaga, and the fact that she is just six

It Started with Malaga

years old matters not. I launch the Travel Diaries app where I have recorded the beginning notes for this memoir on my iPad.

"It was a dark blue sky by the time we exited the airport, and the air was warm and humid, with a slight taste of the sea."

I keep reading with a break here and there. All of a sudden, a sweet voice interrupts: "My very first experience this first morning in Malaga is hearing the birds chirping outside."

What? SHE has started reading off the page herself! I hadn't realized that at only six years old, she was such a good reader. From that point on, I let her read out bits and pieces. I tell her that a lot of people are reading this story now.

She replies, "My nana would like this story."

"Really, do you think so?" What a great idea. I had been thinking of sending Juanita the link, because littlest's nana, Jane's mother, had been born in Spain, although her family moved back to Ireland and then to Pennsylvania within her first year and she has never been back.

"Sure." I text Juanita the link. I know she likes to read, so why not my Malaga story?

10:57, Sunday morning. Me to Juanita:

> Juanita, I hope you are well. I'm hanging out with the Littlest this morning while the rest of the family run Bloomsday. I have been thinking of you and wondering if you might like to read the story I am writing about my preparations and time in Malaga. It's just in first draft and not finished yet, but I'm going to spruce it up and then I hope to publish it on Amazon. I've been reading it to the Littlest, and she thinks you would like it. Here is the link. Just let me know if you do.

10:58.

> Sounds totally awesome! I'm opening the link now.

10:59.

> I know you like to read.

Sharing the link has been on my mind and her comment has put me over the top.

11:51.

> Not only do I like to read, but as I was born in Spain, I cannot think of a better topic! I used to adore hearing my parents talk about their adventures and watching my dad's slide shows with comments from both Mom and Dad! I'm flying through the reading so far and loving it!

We all know Juanita was born in Spain. It is one of the many stories she likes to tell us all whenever we meet, as if it were the first time, every time. We all know people like this. Heck, people probably think I am like this now, when I talk about Spain.

11: 52.

> Thank you for saying so.

11:52.

> I'm serious! I'm truly enjoying this! I need to see if I can find Dad's slides and get them digitized. He had some extraordinary photos of Spain.

12:00.

> Oh, there is an app I discovered the other day that digitizes negatives and slides. I'm reading everything I can about the Civil War days, too. New books even since I got home.

12:05.

> I'll need to develop them myself. I so wish I'd been able to tape my mum. She was a history teacher (as well as English), but her accent and storytelling style just made those mini-histories she'd recount spellbinding!

There is a thirty-five-minute pause and then …
1:40.

> This is so fun for me! Reminds me of the stories I heard growing up. They were in Castelldefels, just outside of Barcelona, but the culture, cathedrals, people, and places are so reminiscent of those stories.

1:44 **at exactly the same time** …
Me:

> I should go back and take you and we can start where you were born and then take the train to Malaga.

Juanita:

> Me too!! Honestly, we need to travel together someday!!

Me:

> Two Grandmas' minds thinking alike …

❀ ❀ ❀

And just like that, my second book, *Two Grandmas in Spain*, is born. It's now two days since our text chat and already the wheels are in motion for our trip late September and into

October 2024. We have four days in Castelldefels, Juanita's birthplace, four days in Madrid, two days in Cordoba, and seven days booked back in Malaga at Calle Victoria. Plus, amazingly, we will stay at Lori's for five days at the end of the adventure. She has sent me some pictures of her beautiful place and is looking forward to our visit. This is a Big Wow.

James sighs. "You'd better get onto those Spanish lessons again."

Tienes razon. That is precisely what I was thinking.

Afterword

It is 5:08 am and as I work on my memoir, I have been home an entire week. I am awakened by a weather alert on my phone that indicates it is going to rain in Malaga around 2:12 pm CEST, continuing off and on over the next half hour. As I lie half asleep in the darkness, I think to myself that even my devices won't forget Malaga. I'm so sentimental.

At 5:21 am I am alerted that lightning has struck 13 miles NE of my location, which my phone is programmed to think is still Calle Victoria in Malaga. It's true, a piece of me still is. The alert reads "Tap to see what's coming".

And what is coming for Malaga?

I only know the tiny slice of Malaga history that I have grasped in the span of two months.

But between April 13 and 21, 2024, I "tapped to see what is coming" for Malaga, and to my visitor's eye, it looks quite promising! I sincerely hope I am able to "tap in" again at some future time. Because now I know that living stories of Malaga's tearful past are still walking around this most hospitable city, driving the buses, making the tapas, and even giving the tours. In spite of the recent nearly buried history, the Malaga of today will not be forgotten or set aside. The Malaga of today invites us to listen and to learn, to participate and to enjoy. In short, the thoughtful visitor is more than welcomed.

Having been at her gravesite, I've decided to update my study of Queen Isabella, because what I have mostly just read historical novels and I went to know more about her in this decade of my life, since she was so important to Spain. I'm starting with *Isabella of Spain: The Last Crusader,* by William Thomas Walsh, which was originally published in 1930.

To further my study of Civil War days, I have also watched the documentary, *The Silence of Others*, or in Spanish, *El Silencio de Otros*. I paid US$4.95 to Vimeo to see this well-made program that threatens to make your heart stop for Spain and the undermining of a large sector of her people.

I still have so much to learn.

RECIPES

Spain Food Sherpas has kindly given me permission to include the three recipes, as they have written them, from their cooking class. At home, I ordered a made-in-Spain paella pan online, because my extra bag of souvenirs had been too full to take one home with me!

Seafood Paella
Traditional Sangría
Gazpacho

SEAFOOD PAELLA

INGREDIENTS FOR 2 PEOPLE

<u>Roasted Tomatoes - (Salmorreta)</u>
2 ripe tomatoes
1/2 head of garlic

<u>Fish Stock - (Fumet)</u>
8 prawn heads and their shells
2 tomatoes
1 onion or leek
1 clove of garlic
White wine or manzanilla sherry
1 liter water

<u>The Rest of the Ingredients</u>
160gr Bomba rice
320gr fish stock or fumet
50gr salmorreta
25gr red bell pepper
25gr green bell pepper
50gr cuttlefish
8 peeled prawns
Extra virgin olive oil (EVOO)
Salt
Sweet paprika
Turmeric
Saffron (pinch)
White wine or manzanilla sherry

PREPARATION

- Roast tomatoes and garlic in the oven at 200 degrees Celsius for 1 hour.
- Blend everything with a bit of EVOO and reserve for the salmorreta.
- For the fumet, sauté prawn heads and shells on high heat.
- Add vegetables in mirepoix (onion, garlic, tomatoes).
- Cover with white wine or manzanilla, sauté, reduce to low heat, and cover with water.
- Cook covered for an hour and a half, then blend and strain, reserving the broth.
- For the paella, soak saffron in the broth for at least 30 minutes.
- Heat paella pan with extra virgin olive oil on high, add diced cuttlefish & bell peppers.
- Sauté and add spices (one teaspoon of each).
- Add salmorreta, cook for 5 minutes.
- Add white wine or manzanilla, let the alcohol evaporate.
- Add fish stock, wait for it to boil.
- Add rice evenly and cook on high heat for 4 minutes.
- Reduce to low heat, add prawns, and cook for 15 minutes.
- Cover with a cloth and let rest a few minutes before serving.

TRADITIONAL SANGRÍA

INGREDIENTS FOR 8-10 PEOPLE
- 1 bottle of red wine
- 2 Fanta orange sodas
- 1 bag of ice
- 1 apple
- Can of peaches in syrup
- 2 lemons
- 2 oranges
- 1 cinnamon stick
- Syrup: 60g of sugar and 60ml of water

PREPARATION

- To make the syrup: Mix the sugar and water in a saucepan; cook over medium heat for 10 minutes. Let cool.
- Dice the peaches and slice the citrus fruits.
- Squeeze the orange and lemon and set aside.
- Mix the wine, peaches, peach syrup, sugar syrup and juices in a pitcher.
- Add the cinnamon stick and refrigerate for two hours.
- Add the ice and Fanta before serving.

GAZPACHO
COLD VEGETABLE SOUP

INGREDIENTS

1 kg ripe tomatoes
1 green pepper
1 cucumber
2 cloves of garlic
50 ml extra virgin olive oil (EVOO)
30 ml vinegar
5 gr salt
250 ml water

PREPARATION

Grind the vegetables in a mixer or blender. When it's done, add the vinegar and salt and mix again. Now add the olive oil to the mixture. Pass it through the colander with the help of the cold water. Try it and add more salt or vinegar, if necessary.
The garnish usually consists of finely chopped tomatoes, green pepper, onion and cucumber, but it can be enjoyed as well without it.

A Request

I hope you enjoyed reading the first volume of the Blue Jacket Travels Series. All Amazon ratings and reviews, even those with just a few words, will be gratefully received.

Please feel free to send me an email if you have any questions about this book or the series. I will be happy to hear from you at bluejacketpress@gmail.com.

You can follow along at the accompanying website to see pictures of events described in this memoir and learn more about future books in this series.

What happened next?

If you enjoyed reading Karen's first book, *It Started with Malaga*, you will love Book 2 in the Blue Jacket Travels series – *Two Grandmas in Spain* – where Karen continues her cultural and culinary adventures.
Read on for a tantalizing first taste …

Chapter 1

Failure is Not an Option

I had only been home for two weeks. The plan for Trip Two was born before I even had my last notes for book one recorded in my travel journal. The entire time I had been in Spain, I found myself greedily searching for a convincing excuse to come back a second time. And I didn't want to wait years and 'maybe' go back. I wanted to have a concrete plan in place as soon as possible. Malaga had so much more to offer than I had been able to fit into just seven days!

That Sunday, I found myself at Johnny's place, looking after littlest girl while the family ran Bloomsday, a local 7.5-mile marathon in Spokane, Washington. We were taking turns to read the story of my first trip to Malaga on my laptop when said littlest girl, her tangle of red hair on a pillow in my lap, suggested that her nana (she always called me grandma), would love my story. I decided to send Juanita the link to my online travel journal to see what she thought.

After an initial "Great, I will check it out," there was silence. Then, within 30 minutes, Juanita texted back. She loved what she had read of the story! Having been born in Spain it had brought back a lot of memories for her. She said she had almost cried when she got to the sangria recipe, as she remembered her mom had loved this iconic Spanish drink – and everything about Spain for that matter.

We continued chatting, excitedly texting back and forth, and within two hours, we two grandmas had a mind meld. The plan for Trip Two was born. We decided we were going to Spain together in five months' time, exactly six months after my spring trip, and a lifetime since Juanita had last been there.

※ ※ ※

When I go home later that day, I wait for the right moment to break the news.

James seems to be in a good mood, foot tapping in thin air, earbuds in, reviewing songs from his iPad to play on his guitar. The words 'Failure Is Not An Option' are splayed across his chest on his favorite Navy SEALS T-shirt. Since he had been in the Navy years ago, he lives as if he owns that motto personally.

I pause for a minute, knowing I can't put this genie back in the bottle once I utter the words.

"Lovie, I have something I want to talk with you about. I'm so excited."

Glancing back at his iPad, he reluctantly pokes at the screen to pause his song. The buds are out, but his ears are not yet tuned to receive my voice.

"What?"

Not as in, what are you talking about, but rather, I didn't hear you. He really needs a hearing aid. Damage from two years on an aircraft carrier in the Navy's Sixth Fleet has plagued him his entire life, and it isn't getting any better now that he is living the upside of his '70s. But, of course, he denies it.

"What did you say?"

"I hope this is going to be okay with you. Something has come up."

He looks at me with new attention. "What are you waiting for? Don't make me wait. Just say it." He is hoping this is good news.

Left to our own devices, James and I are generally happy and content. Most of our turmoil comes from without. Indeed, we have a saying between ourselves: *All is well and we feel great. Who ('what a-hole' when from James's lips) is going to come along and spoil it?*

He can see I am full of something I can hardly wait to share, and in turn I can see he is bracing for something he might not like. I can tell. I need to put him out of his misery.

"I want to go back to Spain next fall." I pause to let that sink in. "And somebody wants to go with me. Can you guess who?"

He leans back into the couch as if he has been hit by something invisible as he absorbs my words. Getting his response together will take a long, thoughtful minute. I wait expectantly. He already knows I want to go back sometime – but then, everybody says that when they get home from a trip. I don't know if he really has understood how serious I am about this.

Imagining various possible reactions, I hold my breath, drumming up my defense if I need it.

"Oh, okay, well sure. I'm okay with that if that is what you want to do. Who is it? Tamilika? Sharron?"

"No ... it's Juanita!"

"Are you kidding? Seriously? No... Does that woman ever stop talking? Do you know what you're getting yourself into? Isn't she having medical issues? You don't even really know her."

I knew my choice of travel companion would surprise him, but even after 29 years together James doesn't know everything that goes on inside my soul. Sometimes I turn up a thought that he isn't expecting. And sometimes, he does the same to me. This keeps things interesting.

And I wouldn't be at all surprised if Juanita tells me her husband had a similar response. (What she did later tell me was that his reaction was ecstatic, because after hearing her say for the past fifty years that she wanted to go to Spain, he was now off the hook.)

Girls just like to have fun, I guess?

Continue reading in Book 2 of the Blue Jacket Travels series
TWO GRANDMAS IN SPAIN

About the Author

Karen O'Connor was born in Seattle, Washington, in what is now Discovery Park, the former site of Fort Lawton Army Hospital. She has lived in Washington, Oregon, British Columbia, Japan, California and is now back in Washington.

After 36 years teaching Business Technology and earning a Master's Degree in Education, she is happily retired and lives with her husband, James, on a few acres that keep them busy renovating the interior and managing the landscape. Over the years, they have explored the Western United States, travelling over 50,000 miles on their Honda Goldwing.

Karen loves cooking, walking, reading, gardening, sewing, writing, and playing bass guitar. She has recently become obsessed with Spain and is learning Spanish. With three sons and eight grandchildren, she is a busy grandma.

Contacts and Links

Email: bluejacketpress@gmail.com
Website: www.bluejacketpress.com
Facebook: https://www.facebook.com/bluejackettravels
Instagram: https://www.instagram.com/bluejacketpress

We Love Memoirs

The We Love Memoirs Facebook group claims to be the Friendliest Group on Facebook, and I have experienced their friendliness firsthand. This informative and interactive group offers much that is worth your time for both the reader and the author.

Check it out at:

Acknowledgments

The evolution of My First Book requires a wide scope of thank yous!

I have to start with my youngest son, for letting me hitchhike on his trip. My only question for you is, "Where are we going next year?"

A huge shout out to *all* my tour guides; you did not disappoint, though a few stand out specifically:

Thank you to Lori Saunders, for taking a chance on a couple of strangers and helping our first days in Malaga feel like one great big welcome to Spain.

Thank you to Spain Food Sherpas for the use the recipes. Especially Javi, who did not give up when I was not where I was supposed to be. I look forward to the tapas class next time! www.spainfoodsherpas.com

Much appreciation to Juan Diego for sharing some of his family's story and the very special Civil War walking tour we shared that day in April. I look forward to the second tour and the other perspective! https://voilamalaga.com

And Laura, thanks for being such a good driver and for the excellent history of the area on the road to the pretty vineyard. Now everyone knows why your driving skills meant so much to me. https://www.whitehousetours.com

Thank you to Paco and Gabbi at www.welovemalaga.com and https://www.getyourguide.com Granada version.

To my eldest son I am grateful for setting me up with www.

bluejacketpress.com and my new website, all in the week prior to your fall semester preparation. And your lovely wife for being one of the few who read my original travel journal to the very end.

Thank you to my first readers, Lori, Kelly, Linda, Tammy, Jan, and Mom, whose reactions to my journal helped me believe my story might be interesting to others by prodding me to open the next chapter.

I cannot forget Thomas Martin, author of *Malaga – A Comprehensive Guide to Spain's Most Hospitable City*, for his *relentless* support before and during my travels.

Oh, and littlest girl for suggesting I send a link to Nana… so that I could wear my blue jacket back to Spain and Book Two could be born.

Above all, I am most grateful for this: the transformation from a travel diary to something readable would have never happened if it were not for stumbling accidentally into memoirs as a genre and Victoria Twead, author and owner of Ant Press, who I discovered through her captivating series *Chickens, Mules and Two Old Fools*. I feel I have a new friend just 8000 miles away. All those publishing decisions? Icons, logo, the title. I trusted her! And I was never wrong in doing so.

Victoria also matched me with my editor Anne Lawton. When I read my first email from Anne, her words smiled off the page at me. I had the uncanny sensation I was reading something I had myself written to a student while giving feedback over the decades. What better person for an editor than someone whose words make me believe I am reading my own? I have never felt that before, nor had the concept entered my mind. And we hadn't even started yet.

Because without these two, this book would never have been published.

And thank you to my husband James, for his unfailing

support for my travels and for my writing. His support and encouragement have made all the difference in the world.

This is probably the longest acknowledgement I will ever write, but when I think of how for a blink here and there this story might never have been told, I have so many to thank.

Printed by Amazon Italia Logistica S.r.l.
Torrazza Piemonte (TO), Italy